Directions to Servants
and Miscellaneous Pieces
1733–1742

Frontispiece

JONATHAN SWIFT

DIRECTIONS
TO SERVANTS AND
MISCELLANEOUS PIECES
1733–1742

Edited by
Herbert Davis

XIII

BASIL BLACKWELL · OXFORD

1964

First published 1959
Reprinted 1964

PRINTED IN GREAT BRITAIN
BY THE COMPTON PRINTING WORKS (LONDON) LTD., LONDON, N.I
FOR BASIL BLACKWELL & MOTT LTD.
AND BOUND BY
THE KEMP HALL BINDERY, OXFORD

The CONTENTS

ILLUSTRATIONS

INTRODUCTION

THIS volume contains the last of Swift's prose works, dating from the years 1733 to 1737, and the unfinished *Directions to Servants*, which was printed in 1745, the year of his death. I have put this first because of its greater importance and also because Swift claimed to have had it by him for many years. It is first mentioned in a letter to John Gay, written from Powerscourt on August 28, 1731, in which Swift tells him that he had retired into the country 'for the public good, having two great works in hand'. The first was the *Art of Polite Conversation*—

> the other is of almost equal importance, I may call it the Whole Duty of Servants, in about twenty several stations, from the steward and waiting-woman down to the scullion and pantry-boy.[1]

Again the following summer, in a letter to Pope from Dublin, dated June 12, 1732, he speaks of still requiring a long time to perfect it, though it had been begun, like the *Art of Polite Conversation*, 'above twenty-eight years ago'.[2] But it is not until 1738, when he seems to have thought of finishing it off for publication, that we get a little more definite information about it. For in a note to Faulkner, his Dublin printer, dated August 31, he describes it as 'a treatise, called Advice to Servants, in two volumes':

> The first was lost, but this moment Mrs. Ridgeway brought it to me, having found it in some papers in her room, and truly, when I went to look for the second I could not tell where to find it. If you happen to have it, I shall be glad; if not, the messenger shall go to Mrs. Whiteway.[3]

Nothing seems to have come from this enquiry, for we hear

---

[1] See *The Correspondence of Jonathan Swift, D.D.*, edited by F. Elrington Ball, London, 1910–1914, iv, 258–259; cited hereafter as *Corr.*
[2] *Corr.*, iv, 309.   [3] *Corr.*, vi, 96.

of it once again in another appeal to Faulkner for help, on December 4, 1739:

> I cannot find a manuscript I wrote, called Directions for Servants, which I thought was very useful, as well as humorous. I believe you have both seen and read it. I wish you could give me some intelligence of it, because my memory is quite gone; therefore let me know all you can conjecture about it.[1]

Somehow, with or without Faulkner's help, it was found, for Mrs. Whiteway reports to Pope in a letter of May 16, 1740:

> There is one treatise in his own keeping, called Advice to Servants, very unfinished and incorrect, yet what is done of it, has so much humour, that it may appear as a posthumous work.[2]

This must have been the manuscript included in the list of 'Mss: found in the Dean's Study' and described in the Abbotsford Manuscript as "(A Copy) borrowed by y⁰ Rev: Dʳ. King".[3] It is now in the Forster Collection, in the library of the Victoria and Albert Museum. It is endorsed: 'No. 528—Swift. Directions to Servants, in part. Only the corrections in Swift's handwriting.' It consists of forty-seven foolscap leaves, 12½ by 7¾–7½ inches, written on one side only (except page 15 and page 37, which have additional passages written on the verso), each page containing from thirty to thirty-two full lines, with narrow left-hand margins, so that where the leaves have been trimmed, the marginal notes are mutilated and in the last leaf, which is very worn, the text itself is defective.

Most of it is written by an amanuensis, who was evidently working from an earlier draft and had been instructed to include all annotations and directions, whether they occurred in the middle of the text or in the margins. A section at the beginning of more than two pages and some later insertions are in another hand. This indicates that additions as well as corrections were made at different times in this copy; it also points to the probability that, although the leaves are numbered throughout consecutively, the introductory portion, entitled 'Rules that concern all Servants in general', was composed

[1] *Corr.*, vi, 145.   [2] *Corr.*, vi, 161.
[3] Harold Williams, *Dean Swift's Library*, Cambridge 1932, pp. 32–33.

separately—Swift had spoken of 'two volumes'—and probably later than the chapters of directions to individual servants.

These begin on page 12 with 'Directions to the Butler', the only chapter which is specifically numbered *Cap. 1*, and headed by the general title of the book. But there is no doubt that the 'Instructions to the Cook' beginning in the middle of page 26 were intended to come next, the connection between them being at once stated: 'your part naturally follows the former, because the Butler and you are joined in Interest'. There is one other complete chapter, with the heading simply of 'Footman', a section of six leaves numbered 34 to 39 with the insertion written on the verso of 37. The remaining eight leaves, numbered 40 to 47, have each a separate title—'Nurse', 'Laundress', 'Porter', etc.—with heads or hints only for the contents of each chapter. Thus, under 'Dairy-Maid', we have such notes as 'Fatigue of making butter', 'Keep cream for your sweetheart'; under 'Laundress' some general topics, such as 'About tearing linnen in washing'; under 'Children's Maid', hints such as 'Tell the children Storys of Spirits when they offer to cry, &c.' It seems as though Swift had become bored with his theme and laid it aside. At any rate he never finished these meagre notes, though some of them were full of possibilities, and were intended to be illustrated by examples from life and literature: e.g. 'Ld Peterborough's Steward that pulled down his House, sold the Materials, and charged my Lord for Repairs, or of the Steward of Gil Blas, who sent his Lord his own money.'

The other section, which occupies the first eleven leaves, and forms a sort of general introduction to his theme, was also never completed; as, copied here from an earlier draft, it contains notes for rearrangement or for further expansion: e.g. 'instance them', 'more Expedients', 'This said in other Parts'. As he went over it later, he contented himself, however, with making a very few small verbal changes, as was his custom when reading over his manuscripts, pen in hand. More than this, with his bad memory and his ill health, he was unable to do. And so he kept the manuscript by him, and it was not printed until the year of his death, when it appeared in London and in Dublin.

And then, as we shall see, it was not printed from this corrected manuscript, but from another, which had somehow come into the possession of Faulkner who provided the copy for the London edition. In a letter he wrote to W. Bowyer, the London printer, on October 1, 1745, he speaks of enclosing 'Part of the Advice to Servants' and continues:

> Fix your day of publication, and I will wait until you are ready, that we may both come out the same day. I think the middle of November will do very well, as your city, as well as Dublin, will be full at that time. . . .
> The Advice to Servants was never finished by the Dean, and is consequently very incorrect. I believe you may see some Irishisms in it; if so, pray correct them. . . .
> As you are famous for writing prefaces, pray help me to one for Advice to Servants, for which I have not yet printed the title . . .
> I am whimsical, and send you the beginning of Advice, etc., and the remainder to Mr. Hitch, that you may print it immediately.[1]

The London edition was printed without a preface. The publisher was content to put on the title-page simply a couple of sentences from Swift's letter to Pope, already mentioned. For the Dublin edition Faulkner wrote his own preface,[2] signed G. F., and dated November 8, 1745, in which he claims to have printed it 'in the same Manner as we find it, in the Original, which may be seen in the Printer's Custody'; and he refers also to 'some scattered Papers wherein were given Hints for a Dedication and Preface, and a List of all Degrees of Servants.' His words seem to mean nothing less than that he had some of Swift's drafts of the work in his autograph, and that he was prepared to show these as proofs of the authen-

---

[1] *Corr.*, vi, 223–224.

[2] I cannot believe John Nichols, who says that Bowyer wrote this preface for Faulkner: John Nichols, *Literary Anecdotes of the Eighteenth Century, Comprising Biographical Memoirs of William Bowyer, Printer . . .*, 2nd ed., London, 1812–1816, vol. ii, p. 177. Bowyer would be unlikely to have had the information contained in it, and would surely have used it for his own London edition, if he had written it.

ticity of the work as he had printed it. And later, in his preface
to Volume VIII of the collected *Works* (Dublin 1746) he says:

> The *Directions to Servants* he ordered to be published before his
> last Illness, in the Way of a Pamphlet: This, with *several original*
> Poems he gave the Printer in his Life Time.

Faulkner's claims have been often set aside too lightly.[1] It is
now possible to prove that he had at least some of these
originals, and that they were Swift's autograph drafts of the
Directions to Servants, as far as he had completed it. For a very
precious part of this original draft, corrected throughout
entirely in his own hand, was purchased at the Normanton
Sale at Sotheby's on October 14, 1946 by Lord Rothschild,
who most kindly allowed me to examine its frail leaves in his
library, and generously provided photographs for the facsimiles which are reproduced here. It was found among
the papers of Charles Agar, first Earl of Normanton, who was
born in Dublin in 1736, was made Chaplain to the Lord
Lieutenant in 1763, and became Archbishop of Dublin and
Primate of Ireland in 1801; it is possible that he may himself
have acquired it from Faulkner.

The manuscript consists of seven half-sheets of foolscap
paper, folded to make fourteen quarto leaves of about 8 by $6\frac{8}{10}$
inches, endorsed at the top of the first page: 'Manuscript of
Dean Swift.' It is a draft which Swift had not troubled to
protect by a cover or even by an outer blank sheet; it was not
even securely stitched together, and the outer pages are dirty
and torn. But it does not date from the early years of the
century, when Swift said that he first began to write it.
It appears to be the same paper as that used by Swift when

---

[1] For further evidence of Faulkner's possession of 'originals', see Nichols,
op. cit., vol. iii, pp. 207–208, note, who asked Faulkner in 1774 for material
to be included in the seventeenth volume of Swift's *Works*. Faulkner's reply—
'I have not one original paragraph of Swift that has not appeared in your English
edition'—certainly implies that he still possessed some of Swift's manuscripts.
A more specific statement occurs in a letter from Dr. John Lyon to Deane Swift,
March 8, 1783 (Victoria and Albert Museum, Forster Collection, Swift MSS.,
No. 570): 'Many things did fall in my way as Executor of Mrs. Dingley, besides
what I had saved from the hands of the Auctioneer, when he was put in possession of the Deans Library, for the purpose of making a Catalogue—But Faulkner
very easily got everything that he thought fit to take, without fee or reward.'

writing to Charles Ford between June 1724 and August 1725, the watermark being *Pro Patria* over a lion and the maid of Dort within a palisade, and with the countermark IV.[1] Although it cannot be assigned to a particular date, it reveals the earlier stages of composition, and shows the later process of correction in the three chapters included in the draft, namely, the directions to the Butler, the Cook, and the Footman.

The opening page, reproduced here in facsimile, shows quite clearly that these three chapters were written first and in this order. For here is the original title as Swift had first set it down, when he began:

Directions
To Poor Servants.

As the title is repeated in the very first line, it looks as though, even as he wrote that, he had decided to improve it by deleting the adjective 'Poor'. And the further corrections in the first sentence reveal an important change in attitude and point of view. At first he had evidently intended to assume the character of a butler, for he wrote:

> In my Directions to Servants, I find from my own Observation and Experience, that you Brother Butler, are the principall Party concerned.

Nothing is more characteristic of Swift than this adoption of a specific role, so as to put himself into a particular place, to make his observations always in the same scale and avoid the blurring caused by changing the point of view. This was evidently quite satisfactory so long as he was concerned with the duties of the Butler and the Cook, but when he came to write his 'Directions to the Footman', he found himself slipping into the role of a footman, and perhaps decided that this was a better vantage point for his purpose. It seems to have offered more scope for picturesque details; and therefore he may have decided to leave it so, and to remove the earlier references to

---

[1] See W. A. Churchill, *Watermarks in Paper in the XVII and XVIII Centuries*, Amsterdam 1935, No. 133. Cf. also E. Heawood, *Watermarks*, Hilversum 1950, No. 3696.

Manuscript of Dean Swift

Directions
To ~~the~~ Servants.

Cap. 1.

Directions to the Butler

In my Directions to Servants, I find from my
long ~~and~~ Observation ~~and Experience~~, that ~~you~~ ^angry^ ~~a Butler~~
Butler are the princi~~pall~~ Party concerned. Your
Business be^ing^ of the greatest Variety, and a
requiring the greatest Exactness, I will
as I can recollect, run through the Severall Branches
of your Office, and order my Instructions
accordingly.

In waiting at the Side-board take all possible
Care to save your own Trouble, and your master's
Drink and Glasses. Therefore first, since those who
Dine at the Same Table, are supposed to be Friends,
Let them all drink out of the Same Glass, without
washing; which will save you much Pains & will
as Hazard of breaking them. ~~Then Give to~~ ^give no^ ^Person^
Liquor till he has called for it thrice at least;

~~ty~~

his past experience as a butler. We must not forget when we read *Directions to Servants* what knowledge and experience the author is said to have had:

> I have a true Veneration—he says to the Footman—for your Office, because I had once the honour to be one of your Order, which I foolishly left, by demeaning myself with accepting an employment in the Custom-House. But that you my Brethren may come to better Fortune, I shall here deliver my Instructions, which have been the Fruits of much Thought and Observation, as well as of seven Years Experience.

In this original manuscript the 'Directions to the Butler' occupy the first fourteen pages, breaking off suddenly in the middle of a sentence[1] concerning the advantages to be obtained from the mistress who loves cards:

> ... they will change the cards so often, that the old ones will be a considerable Advantage by selling to Coffee-Houses, or Families who love Play, but cannot afford better than cards at ...

Evidently Swift had inserted one or two leaves between pages 14 and 15, containing the rest of the chapter, because immediately after the sentence in which he promises to enlarge his instructions on the art of bottling (on page 9 of the manuscript), there is a hand drawn in the middle of the text, pointing to a marginal note:

> what follows must
> be writ first and
> compard with the [? form^r]

And the rest of the page is marked with a line in the left-hand margin, at the top of which is Q^{r}X, with this note in brackets, between the lines:

(All this must be compared with P. inserted after P. 14)

This missing section must have contained the paragraphs which are included in the Forster manuscript and appear fitted together and rearranged in the printed text. They describe the process of bottling a hogshead of wine, and seem to have given Swift a great deal of trouble. For in the original and in the copy the topic is dealt with in two different places; probably he wrote down a few sentences at odd times as they

[1] p. 25 below.

came into his head, and intended eventually to combine them at this point. But it must remain doubtful whether the text as finally printed in 1745 had been so fitted together by him, or was afterwards so arranged by the printer. This is what he wrote first:

> (I) The art of bottling being an affair of great importance in your office, I hope you will allow me to enlarge my instructions upon so weighty an article.
>
> When a Hogshead of wine or any other liquor is to be bottled off, wash your bottles immediately before you begin, but be sure not to drain them by which good managem^t your master will save some gallons in every hogshead
>
> In bottling wine, fill your mouth full of corks together with a large plug of tobacco, which will give to the wine the true tast of the weed, so delightfull to all good judges in drinking.
>
> Before you come near the bottom of the hogshead for fear of drawing muddy wine, shake the vessel strongly, and carry your master a glass of it, who will praise your discretion, and give you all the rest as a perquisite of your place. I exhort you to the same expedient when you are ordered to decant a suspicious bottle when a pint is out, give y^r hand a dextrous shake and show in a glass, that it begins to be muddy.
>
> This is the time that in honor to your master you ought to show your kindness to your fellow Servants, and especially to the Cook. What signifyes a few flaggons out of a whole hogshead, but advise them if they get drunk to go to bed, and leave word they are sick, which last caution I would have all the Servants observe, both male and female.

There is a unity here which suggests that this was composed and written down at one time. But the subject is not exhausted and these instructions can clearly be further enlarged upon so weighty an article. Thus later on he takes up the subject again, with some repetitions and additions, copied by the amanuensis from the missing pages which Swift said he had inserted after page 14. They are given here as they appear in the Forster manuscript, which has in the margin a reference back to the section just quoted:

> (II) I come now to a most important part of your Oeconomy, the bottling of a Hogshead of Wine, wherein I recommend three

virtues, Cleanlyness, Frugality and brotherly Love. Let your Corks be of the longest kind you can get; which will save some wine in the neck of every Bottle. As to your Bottles chuse the smallest you can find; which will increase the number of Dozens, and please your Master. For, a Bottle of Wine is always a Bottle of Wine, whether it hold more or less, and if your Master hath his proper Number of Dozens, he cannot complain.

That your Bottles may not leak, [*deleted*]

Every Bottle must be first rinced with Wine for fear of any Moisture left in the Washing; Some out of mistaken thrift will rince a dozen Bottles with the same Wine; but I would advise you, for Qᵣmore Caution to change the Wine at every second Bottle: a *Naggin* will be enough. Have Bottles ready by to save it; and it will be a good Perquisite, either to sell, or drink with the Cook.

Never draw your Hogshead too low; nor tilt it for fear of disturbing the Liquor: When it begins to run slow, and before the Wine grows cloudy, shake the Hogshead and so have done: What is left is your Legal Perquisite: You may tilt the Hogshead the next day, and in a Fortnight get a Dozen or two of good clear Wine to dispose off as you please.

During the Course of your bottling, you are not to refuse any Brother-Servant, as many Glasses of Wine as he desires; but make them be drunk in your Presence, for fear they should be given to other Folks, and so your Master be defrauded.

If your Master finds the Hogshead to fall short of his Expectation; what is plainer, than that the vessel leaked: that the Wine Cooper had not filled it in proper Time: that the Merchant cheated him with a Hogshead below the common Measure?

In the manuscript the word 'Naggin' is underlined and queried in the margin, perhaps by Swift, who may have wondered whether this was after all too small an amount; but he did not change it. In the printed texts, however, it is changed to 'Jill', perhaps because the printer preferred the simpler word. There is no authority for the change, nor for the rearrangement and joining together of the passages. I am inclined to believe that Faulkner, or some friend, must have been responsible for trying to carry out what Swift had clearly intended to do. For the opening sentence of (i) is replaced by the first three paragraphs of (ii), except that in the last of these, the rather abrupt 'and so have done: What is left is your Legal Perquisite' is removed to make room for the more vivid passage from (i):

> and carry a Glass of it to your Master, who will praise you for your Discretion, and give you all the rest as a Perquisite of your Place.

Then the rest of (i) is added, but in a changed order which confuses the details; and finally, as if in fear that nothing should be lost—and therefore more like an editor than Swift himself—the last sentences are botched together in a clumsy patchwork that Swift, with his dislike of repetition, would not have accepted:

> (II) But make them drunk in your Presence, for fear they should be given to other Folks, and so your Master be wronged:
> (I) But advise them, if they get drunk, to go to bed etc.

Swift had written:

> make them [i.e. the Glasses of Wine, referred to in the sentence finally omitted] be drunk . . . for fear they [the Glasses of Wine] should be given to other Folks.

The editor changed it to: 'make them [i.e. the Servants] drunk' and the following 'they' is left suspended and has to be awkwardly connected with the 'flagons' of the previous sentence.

Again, at certain points Swift wrote instructions in the margin for his own guidance. For instance, after the passage directing the Butler to treat badly any humble person at the table, who is little regarded by the master or the company, he noted: 'Find a reason.' The note is repeated in his own hand in the Forster copy; but no reason is given. In the printed text, however, the paragraph ends with the addition of these words: 'and you cannot please your Master better, or at least your Lady.'

At the end of another paragraph there is a marginal note in both manuscripts—'something wanting here'; but no reference was given for the insertion of a misplaced passage, nor was anything added. In the printed text of 1745, however, the missing paragraph has been found and brought into its place here.

Cook

Scrape the bottome of your Pots and Kettles with a Silver Spoon, for fear of giving them a tast of Copper.

When you send up butter for Sauce, be so thrifty as to let it be half water; which is also much wholsomer.

Never make use of a Spoon in any thing that you can do with your hands, for fear of wearing out yr master's plate

When you find that you cannot get dinner ready at the time appointed, box put the Clock back, and then it may be ready to a minute. [mistake. [Footman] X
X Take off a heavy dish of Soup from the table with one hand, to shew your strength; but always do it between two Ladyes, that if it happen to Spill the Liquor may fall upon their cloaths and not daub the floor
X Keep a plate under your arm, or within your wastecoat that you may have both your hands ready upon any occasion: but, when you are forced to cough, take out the plate and hold it before your mouth to shew your good breeding (The whole doctrine of plates marked P... good indo: P. refer to it. X [P.] If the Butler be shut out of the room at dinner and some body wants a glass of liquor; go to the side board; and, to avoyd mistakes first shake the bottle to find whether there be any thing in it; than, tast it to know what the liquor is; and, so round to every bottle till you find the right one: then, for cleanlyness sake, wipe it with the palm of your hand and so fill the glass.
18th cop. nd P 28 [The place to the mark X mistaken.

Other instructions which Swift evidently intended for his own guidance were left for the printer to do what he could with, such as:

> Stet if it be not repeated
> For some other servant
> Sd before
> This after

and sometimes elaborate cross references are given which are properly followed in the final version. But the comment, 'I am in doubt whether it should not be a Man-Cook,' which appears at the head of the 'Instructions to the Cook', is silently ignored by the printer.

Though the work as a whole must be looked upon, as its first publisher reminded us, 'as a rough Draught with several Outlines only drawn,' we can see pretty clearly from a study of this Rothschild manuscript, which contains the three most fully developed chapters, that the scale Swift had in mind would have made a large volume, if his design had been completed. There is a certain formality in the introductory remarks, promising an orderliness which is never achieved, particularly in his address to the Cook, where the voice of the Dean himself seems to be heard most plainly:

> And, now Mrs. Cook, I proceed to give you my Instructions, which I desire you will get some fellow servant in the family to read to you constantly one night in every week, upon your going to bed, whether you serve in Town or Country; for, my lessons shall be fitted to both.

It is clear that he intended to add further instructions, for he left off writing in the middle of page 23, but evidently thought that not sufficient to complete the chapter, and therefore left the next page also blank. There is one particularly good example in this chapter which shows how difficult it sometimes was for Swift himself to piece together the details and scraps that he had often inserted carelessly in the draft, and how impossible he has left it for an editor to be certain what order to follow. The passage, as written in the manuscript, also proves that he was composing it as he wrote it down, and

B

shows further why the copyist got into trouble when trying
to transcribe it. It begins at the bottom of page 22:

> If you have a Silver Sauce-pan for the kitchin use, let me advise
> you to batter it well, and keep it always black: This will be for
> your masters honor, *for* [*deleted*] because it shows there hath been
> constant good housekeeping: And

in

and is continued on the top of page 23:

> in the same manner, if you are allowed a large *kitch* [*deleted*]
> Silver Spoon for the kitchen, *let* [*deleted*] have the bole of it be
> worn out with continuall scraping and stirring, and often say
> merrily, this Spoon *has done* [*deleted*] owes my Master no Service.[1]

Some time later Swift added in a very cramped hand at the
bottom of page 22: 'Make room for the sauce pan by wriggle
[*sic*] it on the coals &c.', which was probably intended as a
hint for another point. The printer then tacked this on—
including the '&c.'—to the first half of Swift's sentence, and
made a separate section of the second part, beginning 'In the
same Manner, . . . ' Ultimately in the 1751 edition the two
halves of this same sentence are further separated by inserting
between them two lost paragraphs which had been written
on a separate sheet. The two paragraphs do not occur in
either of the remaining manuscripts, but they were first
printed by Faulkner in the first Dublin edition, 1745, at the
end of the book on page 79 as a 'Postscript', with this note:
'The following paragraphs belong to the Cook, but were left
out by mistake.' He did not indicate where they were intended
to be placed, because he did not know. The London printer
took the trouble to fit them in as well as he could with reference
to the topic handled; but there is no indication in the manuscripts warranting insertions at either of the places he has
chosen. Faulkner in his next edition in 1746 printed them

---

[1] The deletion of 'let' seems to have been a later correction, for we find the
copyists responsible for two versions:
(1) 'let the bole of it be worn out' (Forster copy).
(2) 'let half the bole of it be worn out' (copy used by Faulkner).
Thus one copyist dropped the 'have'; the other misread it as 'half'; and Swift
himself kept 'have' and deleted the 'let'.

Footman y De misake P. 28

Your employment being of a mixt nature extends to a
great variety of business; and you stand in a fair way of
being the favorite of your Master or Mistress, or of the young
master and Misses. You are the fine gentleman of the family
with whom all the maids are in love. You are sometimes a
pattern of dress to your Master, and sometimes he is so to You.
You wait at table in all companies, and consequently have
the opportunity to see and know the world and to understand men and manners, & confess your
perils are but few, unless you are sent with a present, or
attend the tea in the Country: you But you are called
mister Mr in the neighbourhood, and sometimes pick up a fortune;
perhaps your Master's Daughter; and I have known many some
of your brits to have good commands in the army. In Town you
have a seat reserved for you in the Play-house, where you
have an opportunity of becoming Witts and Criticks. You
have no professed enemy except the rabble, and my Lady's waiting woman who are
sometimes apt to call you Skip-Kennells. I have a true
veneration for your office; because I had once the honour
to be one of your order which I foolishly left by
demeaning my self with accepting an employmt in the
Custom-house. But that you my brethren may come to
better fortune, I shall here deliver my instructions, which
have been the fruits of much thought and observation as well
as of seven years experience.

In

as the last two paragraphs of the chapter. This was less dangerous than trying to find a place to insert them, but almost certainly not what Swift intended.

The chapter addressed to the Footman has in its final shape a completeness and variety not wholly fitting into the general framework of the book; but we should perhaps be prepared for this, remembering the author's claim that he had a special understanding of the duties of this office as a result of his own long experience. Nevertheless, even here, his instructions have been written down at different times, and without much consideration of order. For instance, after the formal introduction which occupies the whole of the first page, Swift sets down a number of short items, now concerning behaviour at meals, now when attending his master or mistress in the street, interspersed with general comments on his chance for advancement in the world, and then returns to the duties of waiting at meals. In copying this from Swift's draft, the amanuensis has increased the confusion by inserting three items, which Swift had entered under the Cook by mistake. Finally, the additions which completed this chapter must have been made on at least three different occasions: first, a sentence or two, not in the hand of the copyist, but in a less formal script—perhaps dictated to a friend; second, the instructions on good behaviour when going to be hanged—the last section to be added by the copyist; and third, the paragraph on the theme 'Be not proud in Prosperity'—a passage which is not included in either manuscript, but may have been taken from the 'scattered papers' which are likely to have contained scraps or afterthoughts. This piecemeal manner of composition accounts for the perplexing change of tone which marks these 'Directions to the Footman'. At first, they are in accord with the rest of the book, taking the simplest form of irony which is used throughout, e.g.:

> In Winter time light the dining-room fire but two Minutes before dinner is served up: that your Master may see how saving you are of his Coals.

But the later additions were written in an entirely different mood and fall into a different style. The catalogue of minute

particulars—what to do and what not to do, and the explana-
tions and excuses gravely supplied with such ingenuity and so
abundantly set forth—now gives place to passages of eloquence
in which the ways of this wicked world are exposed, and one
who knows it well allows himself to utter warnings and advise
his brethren how to meet its vicissitudes:

> Be not proud in Prosperity: You have heard that Fortune turns
> on a Wheel; and if you have a good Place, you are at the Top of
> the Wheel. Then remember how often you have been stripped,
> and kicked out of Doors, . . . Remember how soon you grew
> shabby, threadbare, and out at Heels; . . . I say, remember all
> this now in your flourishing Condition.

Or he uses the occasion to make fun of the world and those
who have great places of honour and profit in it:

> To grow old in the office of a Footman, is the highest of all
> Indignities: Therefore when you find years coming on, without
> Hopes of a Place at Court, a Command in the Army, a succession
> to the Stewardship, an Employment in the Revenue (which last
> two you cannot obtain without reading and writing) . . . I
> advise you to go upon the Road.

Or he gives instances of other possibilities which have sometimes come as a reward to those who know how to win the
favour of their mistress, like Tom, who married an Earl's
sister, 'but unfortunately taught her to drink brandy, of which
she died'; or like Boucher, the Duke of Buckingham's steward,
who succeeded in winning fifty thousand pounds, and then
proceeded to dun his former master for arrears of wages.
And finally, he brings his hero to a tragic end, and forgetting
the simple duties of the kitchen and the servants' hall, offers
him advice on how to behave before an admiring public
when on his way to be hanged.

It may be worth suggesting that the reference to the famous
gamester 'Boucher', or Richard Bourchier,[1] who died in 1702—

[1] An account of his life and exploits appeared, it is true, in 1714. See Theophilus Lucas, *Memoirs of the Lives, Intrigues and Comical Adventures of the Most
Famous Gamesters and Celebrated Sharpers* . . . , London, Printed for Jonas Brown
without Temple-bar and Ferdinando Burleigh in Amen Corner, 1714, pp. 142 f.
A modern edition of this work was edited by Cyril Hughes Hartmann, *Games
and Gamesters of the Restoration*, London, 1930, where the account of Bourchier
is to be found on pp. 195 f.

whose fantastic exploits are likely to have come to Swift's ears as a matter of common gossip at that time—may be taken to indicate that the first sketch of this chapter belongs to a period before 1704, when Swift said he first planned this work. I can find no further indications in the manuscripts of the dates at which he began or resumed the task. For, although the paper seems to have been part of a supply which he was using first in 1724–1725, and the handwriting has all the characteristics of his later years, this Rothschild autograph is evidently not a first draft, but a fair copy, written in a large clear hand, with new material added from time to time as well as corrections. It is very likely therefore that this is the manuscript which he was working at in the country in the summer of 1731, when we first hear of this book. The foolscap sheets used for the Forster copy have a different watermark, with the inscription *Pro patria ejusque Libertate*, encircling a crowned lion on a pediment inscribed VRYHEIT, with the countermark J. Honig & Zoonen, of which Del Marmol gives an example only after 1732.[1] As this transcript in its uncorrected form was the source of the copy from which Faulkner printed his first edition, it probably dates from about 1738 or 1739, when Faulkner is said to have seen it. But then it must have come back to Swift, because he later on corrected it from his own copy. After Swift's death we hear that it had been borrowed by the Rev. Dr. King, and in this way had presumably come to England. It seems probable that it afterwards came into the possession of Deane Swift and was among the papers belonging to his son Theophilus Swift, which are now a part of the Forster collection.

This Forster copy, *after* Swift had corrected it, cannot have been in Faulkner's possession or even seen by him; it cannot have been part of the papers which he claimed to have had in his custody in November 1745, for he uses the phrase 'in the Original', and speaks of part of the manuscripts as

---

[1] See Ferdinand Del Marmol, *Dictionnaire des filigranes classés en groupes alpha-bétiques et chronologiques*, Namur 1900, pp. 75–76. But a great variety of similar marks were common about the middle of the century. See E. Heawood, *op. cit.*, nos. 3148 ff.

'scattered Papers' containing hints, which were also presumably jottings by Swift himself; nor can it have been the copy which Faulkner may have been referring to in his preface of January 1746, when he says that Swift had given it to him with several original poems in his lifetime.

For when we examine the text of the first edition, which appeared as a separate volume in Dublin in November 1745, at the same time as Dodsley's edition in London, we discover that Faulkner has printed from a copy which is more complete than either of the extant manuscripts, since he is able to give us four additional chapters, containing 'Directions to the Groom, the Chamber-maid, the Waiting-maid, and the House-maid'—but a copy that is less correct, as far as we can now check it, because it contains all the errors introduced by the Forster copyist, and none of Swift's latest changes and corrections. Thus the texts of Faulkner's editions of 1745 and 1746, as also (with minor changes) the text of Dodsley's edition of 1745, reprinted in the collected *Miscellanies*, published in London in 1746, were printed from a copy, which is identical with the Forster manuscript copy, *before it had been corrected by Swift*. These last corrections consist in part of restoring the original readings of his own manuscript, where the copyist had introduced errors, and in part of further improvements involving verbal changes or modifications of the punctuation. For example, the copyist had changed 'scurvily' to 'saucily'; 'party' to 'person'; 'scum' to 'stir'; 'scraps' to 'scrapes', etc., or more carelessly had corrupted a whole phrase, by changing 'the great Extravagance of late Years among the Gentry upon the Article' into 'of late Years the great Extravagancy among the Gentry upon the Articles.' It is curious that some of these literal errors in transcription have been remedied by the copyist himself, but evidently not until they had already got into Faulkner's copy-text. Of the later corrections made by Swift, some occur only in the Forster copy; and some, more important and more numerous, only in the Rothschild autograph manuscript. And it is very important that these two sets of corrections be observed carefully and kept distinct. For we find that those very few variants in the Forster copy alone never appear in any later printed version; but on the other hand most of the later changes which occur in Swift's autograph draft alone are, astonishingly, to be found incorporated in the text which Faulkner reprinted in 1751 for a new edition of Volume VIII of the collected *Works*. I can give here only one significant example from the third page of 'Directions to the Butler'. Swift had originally written, his amanuensis had copied, and the printer had printed in 1745 and 1746:

> There is likewise a Perquisite full as honest by which you have a Chance of getting every day the best Part of a Bottle of wine for your self; for you are to suppose that Gentlefolks will not care for the Remainder of a Bottle.

In the Forster copy, 'for' in the second line is changed to 'to' and the final negative is altered and then restored; but in Swift's autograph, the sentence finally shakes itself free of all repetition and awkwardness and reads:

> There is likewise an honest Perquisite by which you have a Chance of getting every day the best Part of a Bottle of Wine to your self; for you are not to suppose that Gentlefolks will value the Remainder of a Bottle:

And this is what Faulkner prints—with the addition of two commas and an extra capital letter—in his edition of 1751. Other final corrections, which had been made by Swift *only* in his autograph manuscript, are first printed then, in this third Dublin edition. Someone had compared the text which was to be reprinted with Swift's manuscript, and had made these corrections; but, as we should expect, some corrections are still overlooked, fresh errors are introduced and modifications in spelling, punctuation and capitalization occur without any consideration of Swift's own usage in these matters. Nevertheless, it is necessary to scrutinize very carefully all important variants in this edition, which are to be found in those sections of the book for which we have no manuscript authority; for it is evident that they may likewise be corrections from the 'Originals' in Faulkner's hands.

* * *

The shorter pieces that occupy the rest of this volume are concerned with matters which Swift had often discussed before, such as the woollen manufacture, the coinage and agriculture; or they were written as a result of his participation in Parliamentary affairs and in Dublin politics, from 1733 until the end of 1737.

The first is only an election broadside. On January 30, Francis Stoyte, Recorder of the City of Dublin died, and in the *Dublin Journal* for February 3, it was reported that several gentlemen had set up as candidates to succeed him. The chief of these were Mr. Forbes, an alderman's son, and Mr. Stannard, a Member of the House of Commons and a zealous patriot. On February 10 Faulkner printed some verses in recommendation of Stannard, and probably about the same time the half-sheet was published in which Swift set down *Some Considerations in the Choice of a Recorder*, in which, though he mentions none of the candidates, he emphasizes the importance of this post and its influence on the well-being of the dealers and shop-keepers of the city, and says plainly that it is not enough to be the son of an alderman. So when on Thursday, February 15, the election came on at the Tholsel, the Petition sent on behalf of Forbes from the Right Hon. the Lord Mayor and Alderman was rejected by the Common Council, and on February 19 Eaton Stannard was elected in accordance with Swift's recommendations. He was afterwards appointed by Swift one of the executors of his will. Commenting on this appointment in an answer to a letter Swift had written to him that very day, Lord Carteret says:

> I know by experience how much that city thinks itself under your protection, and how strictly they used to obey all orders fulminated from the sovereignty of St. Patrick's. I never doubted their compliance with you in so trivial a point as a Recorder.[1]

In the following summer Swift was again active in the parliamentary election, caused by the death on July 8 of Samuel Burton, one of the representatives of the City of Dublin. At first, the two most important candidates were the Mayor of

[1] *Corr.*, iv, 406–7.

Dublin, Humphrey French, and Alderman John Macarell, who held a post under the government as Registrar of Barracks. Swift immediately began to use his influence in support of the Lord Mayor. In a letter of August 6, 1733, Swift's old friend Barber, then Lord Mayor of London, writes:

> They say you are making interest for my brother of Dublin to be member of Parliament; pray come over, and do the same for me, and have the credit of both. My brother behaves himself well I hear; if it is proper, my service to him.[1]

On August 4, Macarell had been given the freedom of the Corporations of Smiths, Goldsmiths and Weavers, and two days later the Lord Mayor had been made free of an even larger number of Corporations.[2]   Probably at this time, when the rival parties were most active in Dublin, Swift thought it necessary to let it be clearly known why he was supporting the Lord Mayor. He printed a short paper, entitled *Advice to the Freemen of the City of Dublin, in the choice of a member to represent them in Parliament*, in which he concentrates on the point that an office-holder cannot be expected ever to vote against those who have the power over that office; he therefore supports the Mayor, who has no employment under the Crown, and is not likely to seek any, and has shown his quality and firmness of character during his year's term of office. This paper doubtless gave Swift the further satisfaction of indicating once more his distrust of the representatives of the Crown in Ireland. The Lord Lieutenant, the Duke of Dorset, returned to Dublin in the latter part of September, and shortly afterwards there were rumours that Swift's paper had been suppressed. Whereupon Faulkner issued an advertisement denying this and 'assuring the public that the said paper is sold by most of the Booksellers in this City, where Gentlemen may be supplyed with any number they want.'[3]

Meanwhile the contest for the election had changed its character. When it became clear that the government's candidate would be defeated, another attempt was made to oppose

---

[1] *Corr.*, v, 25.   [2] See *Dublin Journal*, Aug. 4 and 11, 1733.
[3] See *Dublin Journal*, Sept. 29, 1733.

Humphrey French, who had just been succeeded in the
mayoralty by the Rt. Hon. Thomas How, who was sworn in
as the new Mayor on October 5. Shortly after this he was
put forward as a candidate, but when the voting was going
against him, he withdrew on October 29, and Alderman French
'was Carried amid the acclamations of many thousands of
people to the Parliament House.'[1]   The Drapier and his
supporters had again won; and apparently their candidate
justified his election to Parliament. At least Swift continued
to think highly of French, and after his death made some
efforts to gather particulars of his public activities, in order
to write an account of him. Though he does not appear to
have carried out this intention, his attitude to French is very
warmly expressed in a letter to George Faulkner, written on
January 6, 1737–8:[2]

> I take him to be a hero in his kind, and that he ought to be
> imitated by all his successors, as far as their genius can reach.
> I desire you therefore to enquire among all his friends whom you
> are acquainted with, to press them to give you particulars of
> what they can remember, not only during the general conduct of
> his life, wherever he had any power or authority in the city,
> but particularly from Mr. Maple, who was his intimate friend,
> who knew him best, and could give the most just character of
> himself and his actions. When I shall have got a sufficient
> information of all these particulars, I will, although I am
> oppressed with age and infirmities, stir up all the little spirit I
> can raise, to give the public an account of that great patriot,
> and propose him as an example to all future magistrates, in order
> to recommend his virtues to this miserable kingdom.

One of the things which Swift admired in French during his
term as Mayor was his courage in taking action against dishonest traders. And it may well have been these exposures
that led to an open attack upon certain shopkeepers in Dublin,
who are mentioned by name as importers of foreign cloth
to the detriment of the Irish woollen manufacture, in a paper
entitled *The Case of the Woollen Manufacturers of Dublin*. It was
printed on a half-sheet, without name of author or publisher,

[1] *Corr.*, v, 45.   [2] *Corr.*, vi, 58–9.

in November, 1733, addressed in a style reminiscent of the Drapier, to 'the Nobility and Gentlemen, and other well-wishers to the Happiness and Prosperity of this Kingdom;' accusing seven of the merchants of Dublin, who are named, for importing within four months, according to the Custom House entries, woollen commodities and foreign silks to the value of £4,000. They are charged further with having attempted to get this foreign stuff sealed with the Seal of Ireland, and also with selling inferior imported stuff as superfine Irish cloth to the damage of the local trade.

Early in December an advertisement appeared in the *Dublin Journal*, signed James Lombard, one of the merchants who had been represented as an enemy to his country, protesting that he was not justly chargeable with any of those things imputed to him. He claims that he would be glad to sell Irish goods, as there is a greater profit in them; but he cannot persuade the makers to prepare the kind of goods which are in fashion, and is therefore obliged to import them. For 'an indolent spirit prevails.' It must have been about this time that Swift set down his *Observations occasioned by reading a paper entitled The Case of the Woollen Manufacturers of Dublin etc.* which seem to have been intended for publication, though unlike his usual practice he writes here without disguise, openly as the Dean of St. Patrick's, who has had eighteen years experience in his dealings with the handicraftsmen and shopkeepers of Dublin. I have found no copy printed then; and it appears to have been first published by Nichols in *Miscellaneous Pieces in Prose and Verse . . . not inserted in Mr. Sheridan's edition of the Dean's Works*, 1789.

Although his first observation is that the censure of these 'seven vile citizens . . . is an hundred times gentler than enemies to their country deserve,' Swift does not concern himself here so much with the sins of the shopkeepers who sell these goods, as with the unreliable craftsmanship of the makers of Irish cloth. For as he looks back over his long experience, during which 'it hath never been once my good fortune to employ one single workman who did not cheat me at all times to the utmost of his powers in the materials, the work and the price',

he is forced to believe that the failure of the attempt to encourage the local woollen manufacture is due mainly to the
clothiers themselves, who *are defective both in the quality and
quantity of their goods*. The remedy he proposes is the same as
he had constantly suggested, namely, a pledge from the
shopkeepers promising to improve the 'Cloaths and stuffs
of the Nation and a guarantee from the more substantial of
them to provide only reliable goods at reasonable prices to
establish credit'—but none of them would listen; 'the spirit
of fraud had gotten too deep and universal a possession to be
driven out by any arguments from interest, reason or conscience.' And he claims to have had more opportunity to
observe the facts than usually fall in the way of men who are
not of the trade. For often the master and wardens of the
company had been to the Deanery to desire his advice, and
often also ten or a dozen of the workmen had gone to him
with their complaints. And he had several times proposed his
scheme to the corporation, and had also proposed it to some
Dublin shopkeepers, but 'always in vain'.

Even those who might have benefited by Swift's recommendations were unable to use the opportunity. John Barber,
the woollen draper, whose wife was recommended by Swift
to his English friends to get subscriptions for the volume of her
Poems to which he contributed a prefatory note,[1] showed up
no better than the rest. For when at Lady Betty Germain's
suggestion he was asked to provide for the Lord Lieutenant's
liveries, 'the first thing he did was to ask a greater price than
anybody else, and then he found he had not cloth near enough
in his shop, and found they would not be ready against he
came over.'[2]

This was a recent experience which may have been in
Swift's mind when writing these *Observations*, and the mood
in which he writes shows that even at the height of his influence
and power in Dublin, in this matter that lay nearest his heart, he
could only confess that he had been defeated. Nevertheless
he continued to be regarded as the patriot, the champion of
the people of Dublin, and when he was threatened by those he

<hr />

[1] See below, p. 71.   [2] *Corr.*, iv, 262–3.

had satirized like Sergeant Bettesworth and the Honourable Richard Tighe, the inhabitants of the Liberty of St. Patrick's banded together to defend him; and when a false rumour got abroad in February, 1733-4, that the Dean of St. Patrick's was dead, there was great perturbation followed by relief and general rejoicing as soon as it was known that he was, in fact, in good health. Again, a few months' later, the following report in the *Dublin Journal*, June 11, 1734, shows that at least Swift had not lost his influence even upon those craftsmen in whom he had little confidence:

> Several Weavers having lately assembled in great bodies to search for foreign Manufactures, accidentally met with that worthy Patriot, the Rev. Dr. Swift, D.S.P.D., who exhorted them to be quiet, and not to do things in a rash manner, but to make Application in a peacable way, and he did not make the least Doubt, but proper Means would be found out to make them all easy &c. whereupon they immediately dispersed to their several Homes, crying out, Long live Dean Swift, and Prosperity to the Drapier, and returned him Thanks for his good Advice, which they said they would follow.

Swift must have had a wry satisfaction in the Act passed at this time to encourage home consumption of wool, by burying in woollen only:

> 'it is enacted that from and after the first day of August, 1734, no Corps shall be buried in Linen or in any thing but what is made of Sheep or Lambs Wool only, or be put into any Coffin lined or faced with any Cloth or Stuff but what is made of such materials upon Pain of forfeiting £5 etc.'

But another piece of legislation, which had been first brought up in the Irish House of Commons in December, 1733, for the further Improvement of the Flaxen and Hempen Manufactures contained a clause which seemed to lay such an unfair burden upon the lower clergy that Swift drew up and signed a petition which was presented on December 24, and counsel were heard on it on December 29.[1] As a result of this, certain modifications were made in the clause relating to the tythe of Hemp and Flax, and the Bill finally passed on a third reading,

[1] See J.H.C. of I, iv, 110.

April 20, 1734. In connection with this matter Swift had drawn up a statement of the claims of the clergy which was printed by Faulkner in January, 1734, together with a list of 'Some further Reasons against the Bill', which had been submitted to him, and which he appended 'in the author's own words.'

He begins with a compliment to the present House of Commons, who had just defeated the attempt which had been made to repeal the Sacramental Test by their vote of December 11, 1733,[1] and expresses the confidence this had aroused in the clergy, and their grief that now a Bill should be hurried through containing a clause which would deprive the Church of two-thirds of its tythes in flax and hemp. He is careful not to object to the Bill as far as its object is to improve the linen manufacture, but submits that the clergy, already defrauded of a large part of their tythes, cannot justly be subjected to a burden, which 'neither the Nobility, nor Gentry, nor Tradesmen, nor Farmers, will touch with one of their Fingers.' And he is indelicate enough to express surprise that the 'Court Party' in their own interest have not shown the least zeal against the proposals, since the value of the King's patronage in the disposal of vacant sees or deaneries would be considerably lessened and there would be fewer good preferments for the dependants of the Viceroy. To judge from the *Advertisement* when it was reprinted in 1751,[2] he seems to have been content to accept the points that had been submitted to him, probably by his friend, Alexander McAulay,[3] and to have added a sort of preamble to stress the obvious injustice of placing these burdens on the clergy alone. The protest was so far successful that some amendments were made in the clauses concerning tythes.[4]

In the spring of 1734 Swift received an appeal to interest himself in another matter for the good of Ireland, namely, to encourage his countrymen to engage in the white-herring

[1] See Vol. XII of this edition, p. xlvi.
[2] See *Works*, Dublin, Vol. VIII, p. 128.
[3] See below, p. 105.   [4] See J.H.C. of I, IV, 120, 147.

and cod fishing. The proposal came in a letter from Francis Grant, who describes himself as 'a merchant in London', who had carried out large investigations for several years and had acquired a thorough knowledge of the whole matter, which he and other gentlemen were endeavouring to bring to the attention of the Parliament in England. And he sends Swift a copy of the shilling pamphlet he had just published in London, entitled *The British Fishery Recommended to Parliament. Shewing the great Importance of it, to the Trade and Navigation of this Kingdom. . . . With an Exact Map of the Coasts of Great-Britain; in which, all the Fishing Stations, and those Ports where the Dutch Fleets fish for Herrings, are described.* Swift replied at once in an admirable letter, in which he speaks of having discussed the matter at once with various members of the Irish Parliament, but has little hope that the proposal would come to anything, although in fact a Bill was enacted during that session concerned with the encouragement of the fisheries. Fifteen years later, in 1749, the matter was brought up again in England and a number of pamphlets appeared, including another appeal by Francis Grant, with more specific proposals, entitled *A Letter to a Member of Parliament, Concerning the Free British Fisheries, with Draughts of a Herring-Buss and Nets, and the Harbour and Town of Peterhead.* There can be no doubt that it is by the author of the letter to Swift; he shows the same thorough knowledge of his subject, has similar practical proposals, and even the same ten lines from Thomson quoted on the title-page:

> With adventurous Oar,
> How to dash wide the Billow; nor look on,
> Shamefully passive, while Batavian Fleets
> Defraud us of the glittering finny Swarms,
> That heave our Friths, and croud upon our Shores;
> How all-enlivening Trade to rouse, and wing
> The prosperous Sail from every growing Port,
> Uninjur'd, round the sea-encircled Globe;
> And thus, in Soul united as in Name,
> Bid BRITAIN reign the Mistress of the Deep.

But more than that he includes in this later pamphlet Swift's reply, which had never been printed, introducing it thus:

> The Reasons why such Encouragements have not hitherto been obtained might possibly be best past over in Silence, especially as it is greatly hoped they shall no longer prevail. But as they happen to be touched upon by a late eminent Writer, in an original Letter which he wrote to a Gentleman who was concerned in the last mentioned Attempt, and who being discouraged by the little Regard shewn here at that Time to a Matter of such National Consequence, had wrote to that eminent Person, moving him to espouse the like Project in *Ireland*, I cannot help troubling you with a Transcript of it. I dare say I need make no Apology for rescuing any Piece from Obscurity that claims no less a Person for its Author than the late Dean *Swift*, were it less apposite to the Subject; I shall therefore give it you without the least Alteration, though in some Particulars I think he goes too great Lengths.

This is certainly the first printing of Swift's letter; it was reprinted in the *Gentleman's Magazine* for 1762, as 'A genuine copy of a letter from the late Dean Swift to ——, Esq., a Scots gentleman.' It was then included in Swift's *Works*, 1762, Vol. X, by Faulkner, with the following misleading note:

> Edward Vernon Esq; the brave English Admiral, who, with six Ships only, took the Town, Citadel and Port of *Portobello* in *America*, in the Year 1739, from the *Spaniards*; having the *British* Fishery much at heart, in Opposition to the *Dutch*, wrote a Letter to Dr. Swift, D.S.P.D. on that Occasion, to which the following is an Answer.

Faulkner's mistake was probably due to his confusing Grant's pamphlet which appeared in December 1749 and contained Swift's letter, with another pamphlet on the Fisheries, printed in 1749, which is generally attributed to Admiral Vernon. It was entitled *Considerations upon the White Herring and Cod Fisheries: in which the Design of carrying on and improving them, in the Manner proposed by a Society trading with a Joint Stock, is fully explained, and freed from all Obligations*. It was published with an Abstract of the Bill for the encouragement of the Fisheries, and was mainly concerned with answering objections

against the proposal to set up a joint stock company. It shows
no detailed knowledge of the actual conditions of the fisheries
around the coasts, such as is shown in the writings of Francis
Grant.

The letter was published again by Deane Swift in the London
edition of Swift's *Works*, 1763,[1] under the title *Letter to Francis
Grant Esq. Merchant in London*, with the following note:

> Francis Grant Esq. of London, Merchant, younger son of
> Sir Francis Grant of Cullen, Baronet, having an high opinion
> of the herring and other fisheries in the British Seas, writ and
> published a pamphlet, in the year 1733, on that subject; principally
> with a view to excite the encouragement of the public, to such of
> the mercantile people as might engage in a project so extremely
> beneficial. The pamphlet was much esteemed; but the ministry
> of England in those days, fearing to offend the Dutch, were not
> inclined to favour it. Whereupon, Mr. Grant writ a letter to the
> Reverend Doctor Jonathan Swift, Dean of St. Patrick's Dublin,
> who was then very eminent in Ireland, to try if the patriot party
> there would espouse the design, and reap benefit to their country
> from what was thus rejected in England: To which letter the
> Dean writ the following Answer, which greatly shews the man,
> as well as the general opinion he had of those times.

He had, indeed, given several instances of excellent schemes,
which had been ruined by the laziness and knavishness of the
'vulgar folks of Ireland.' 'Oppressed beggars are always
knaves, and, I believe, there are hardly any other among us.'
And he concludes: 'I have always loved good projects, but
have always found them to miscarry.'[2]

During this year, 1734, Swift was also occupied in looking
over the proofs of the edition of his collected works which
was being printed by George Faulkner. After considerable
delay the first three volumes were ready for subscribers on
November 27, 1734, and the fourth volume was promised for
January 6, 1735.[3]

In preparing the text for this edition, I have found no

---

[1] See Vol. VIII, pt. ii, p. 266.   [2] See below, p. 113.
[3] See *Dublin Journal*, Nov. 23–6, 1734.

C

evidence against the assumption with which I began that Swift himself took a good deal of interest in the printing of these first four volumes of the Dublin edition, and possibly a little also in the two following volumes, which Faulkner published in 1738. I have reprinted here in the Appendix the Advertisements to Vols. I, II and IV[1] because I believe that the impersonal tone of these advertisements, the use of such phrases as the 'supposed author', 'those Gentlemen in this Kingdom, who seem to know the Author best' indicate that the *Publisher's Prefaces* were at least designed by Swift and carried out under his careful supervision—if not actually written by him. We know from his letters that Swift took considerable trouble in preparing the text of *Gulliver's Travels* for Vol. III, correcting errors and removing interpolations. Is it not then almost certain that he must himself have penned these words in the Preface to the *Works*, Vol. I, which refer to the advantage the Dublin Publisher had of 'consulting the supposed Author's Friends, who were pleased to correct many gross Errors, and strike out some very injudicious Interpolations, particularly in the Voyages of Captain *Gulliver*?'

After Swift's death Faulkner usually introduced the volumes with a *Publisher's Preface*, unmistakably his own work, such as that prefixed to his edition of *Directions to Servants*, which is signed G. F. and dated November 8, 1745. And again in 1758, when he published Swift's *History of the Peace of Utrecht*, he signs and dates his Preface to the Reader, and speaks openly of the authenticity of the text. Doubtless Faulkner in 1734 would have perferred to issue his Prospectus of the Dean's *Works* with similar statements claiming directly that the author had approved the text. But this was not Swift's way. He would not even allow his name to be put on the title-pages, which as a result assume some strange shapes. Vol. I is unmistakable enough with its initial letters—THE WORKS OF *J.S.* D.D. D.S.P.D.—but after that we have Vol. II (III) (IV) OF THE AUTHOR'S WORKS. And the farthest he would

---

[1] For the Advertisement to *Gulliver's Travels* in Vol. III, see Vol. XI of this edition.

go in acknowledging the things contained in these volumes was to allow it to be said

> that the supposed Author was prevailed on to suffer some Friends to review and correct the Sheets after they were printed; and sometimes he condescended, as we have heard, to give them his own Opinion.[1]

And before the last paragraph which contains an apology for the delay, owing to the edition having swelled to many more pages than at first expected, there is, I think, a pleasant hint as to who was really responsible for these advertisements, when the Publisher is made to say:

> This is all we have been allowed to prefix as a general Preface; but before each of the three ensuing Volumes, there may perhaps be a short Advertisement.

There is further evidence I think of Swift's responsibility to be found in the very long delay that took place before the volumes finally appeared. After the volumes had been announced for many months in the *Dublin Journal*, a notice appeared on Saturday, December 29, 1733, that the fourth volume was in the press and would be finished by the middle of the next February. But that spring Faulkner went to England to arrange for subscriptions, provided with letters from Swift to the Earl of Oxford, Bolingbroke and others, returning to Dublin on May 17, 1734. A month later he issued another advertisement allowing subscribers until the end of June; and even then the volumes were still not ready. When Oxford, writing to Swift on August 8, asks what has prevented Faulkner from sending over the books, which he had promised for the end of May, Swift admits that he himself had caused the delay:

> I have put the man under some difficulties by ordering certain things to be struck out after they were printed, which some friends had given him. This hath delayed his work, and, as I hear, given him much trouble and difficulty to adjust. Farther I know not, for the whole affair is a great vexation to me.[2]

In spite of Swift's attempt to dissociate himself from Faulkner's doings, except by interfering in such a way as to

---

[1] See below, Appendix D, p. 182.   [2] *Corr.*, v, 85.

cause this very considerable delay, his admission is enough to show that he was not willing to leave it to his friends to decide what should finally be included. If he had ordered some things to be removed, he must also have allowed more to be added, because Faulkner, in apologizing to his subscribers for the delay, claims that it was caused by 'several new Pieces which came late to our Hands; we have inserted them without additional charge.' And in another advertisement he says the four volumes will contain 500 more pages than first reckoned.

The first three volumes were eventually ready on November 30, 1734, and the fourth on January 7, 1734–5. When it was completed, the publisher was not prevented from stating that

> In this Edition are great Alterations and Additions and like-wise many Pieces in each Volume, never before published . . . so that it may be truly said a genuine and correct Edition of this Author's Works was never published till this Time.

Nevertheless, though it must have given him some satisfaction to see his *Works* printed in Dublin in this quite elegant edition, Swift does not seem to have been over-much concerned with what might happen to many of his writings still not included in these volumes. He seems to have been more concerned with plans to provide another kind of memorial in Dublin. For he had been occupied in drawing up his will and choosing executors to carry out his project of leaving all he had to found a hospital for lunatics. On January 17, 1734–5, he presented a Memorial to the Mayor and Council of the City for a grant of a piece of ground in Oxmantown Green suitable for the hospital.[1] This was duly granted to him at the Quarter Assembly Day in the summer, July 17, 1735. The Dublin papers did not lose the opportunity of publishing various squibs on the announcement of Swift's intentions, e.g.

> The Dean must dye?—Our idiots to maintain?
> Perish, ye Idiots!—And long live the Dean!

Meanwhile another old problem, which had not been solved by the triumph of the Drapier in keeping out Wood's copper coinage, was causing fresh difficulties. It is rather odd to find

---

[1] See *Dublin Journal*, Jan. 21, 1734–5.

Faulkner complaining of the difficulty of finding change for
the purchasers of the sets of Swift's *Works*, and putting a notice
in his paper appealing to subscribers 'to send small money
for their books as it was impossible for him to get change for
so much Gold.' The gold coins themselves, French, Spanish
and Portuguese fluctuated in value, and there was a shortage
of all other currency. In 1733 it had been rumoured in the
newspapers that eleven thousand pounds worth of copper
coin was being coined at the Mint in London, for use in
Ireland. Now the shortage of silver had the effect of lowering
the value of the English gold guinea, and the premium on
silver led to its increased export and the danger of further
devaluation. In these circumstances it was proposed by the
government to fix the rate, recognizing the value of the English
guinea at £1 2s. 9d. (it had been fixed at £1 4s. in 1687) and also
to import some copper coinage. This produced protests from
the merchants and traders of Dublin, and on April 24, 1736,
Swift supported their petition, going with them to the Tholsel,
and making a speech against lowering the gold.[1] This speech
was at once printed as part of a small tract, entitled *Reasons why
we should not lower the Coins now current in this Kingdom*. For Swift
the issue was clear. Any devaluation, and consequent fall in
the price of commodities, would benefit only the office holders
under the government and the Absentees, whom he regarded
as the greatest enemies to Ireland—

> Can there be a greater folly than to pave a bridge of gold
> at your own expense, to support them in their luxury and vanity
> abroad, while hundreds of thousands are starving at home for
> want of employment.

There seems to have been no immediate occasion for the
paper which Swift began on May 24, 1736, *Concerning that
Universal Hatred which prevails against the Clergy*. It was left
as a fragment in manuscript, and was first printed by Deane
Swift in 1765. It was evidently his intention to try and discover
the causes of that disgust which had lately manifested itself
against the clergy both in England and Ireland, and had

[1] See *Corr.*, v, 324 and *Pue's Occurences*, 24–27 April, 1736.

brought about various attempts in Parliament to interfere with their rights and privileges. But having allowed himself to be reminded of 'the detestable tyranny of Henry VIII' in his plundering of the Church, he is diverted into violent abuse of that 'infernal beast', and then into a comment on 'the impieties of the Reformation which in England was brought in upon the same principle of robbing the church'—and there in the middle of a sentence he breaks off, and the paper remained unfinished. But the subject was much in his mind, and is referred to in his letters to Sheridan of May 15 and May 22:

> We are the happiest people in the universe; we have a year and a half before the Club will meet to be revenged farther on the clergy, who never offended them, and in England their Parliament are following our steps, only with two or three steps for our one.[1]

But these things did not prevent him from trying to use his influence to obtain preferment for his young protégé, William Dunkin, 'a gentleman of great learning and wit, true religion, and excellent morals.'[2]

There remained yet the project which Swift had had in mind for more than ten years, for the better ordering of the poor and needy in the city of Dublin, which appeared in a small sixpenny pamphlet published by T. Cooper in London, entitled *A Proposal for giving Badges to the Beggars in all the Parishes of Dublin* by the Dean of St. Patrick's. It was dated April 22, 1737, and that was presumably the time when Swift finished writing it. It works out more fully an idea which he had jotted down earlier on a paper, dated Deanery House, September 26, 1726.[3] There he had proposed that the Archbishop of Dublin should call the clergy together and renew the attempt to enforce on beggars the wearing of badges to show what parish they belonged to, and to prevent them begging elsewhere. A workhouse had been set up in Dublin in 1704 for the relief of the poor of the city. In 1728 a new corporation was created and an act passed by which certain

---

[1] *Corr.*, v, 331; see also pp. 335 f.   [2] See Appendix, p. 188.
[3] See Appendix C.

funds were set aside to enable them 'to receive common beggars and children of all denominations above six years old'[1] while children under six were supposed to be cared for by the families to which they belonged. But since in this way many children perished, a new act was passed that after March 25, 1730, the governors of the workhouse should receive all exposed children of whatever age or sex. Thus the poorhouse had become a hospital for foundlings, and as Swift complains, the streets of Dublin were infested with 'strollers, foreigners and sturdy beggars.' To remedy this he had applied for some years to the Mayor and the Archbishop of Dublin, who appeared to favour his proposal to confine beggars to their own parishes, by providing severe penalties if they did not wear badges which showed where they belonged; for there was no justification for beggars to put us to the charge 'of giving them victuals, and the carriage too.'

It is an admirable pamphlet, written in Swift's most direct and forthright style, and gives a delightful glimpse of the proud Dean, who was 'personally acquainted with a great number of stout beggars' roused to anger by these miserable wretches who were 'too proud to be seen with a badge, as many of them have confessed to me.' And he tells us that this 'absurd insolence' has so affected him that for some years past he has not disposed of a single farthing to a stout beggar.

In July, 1737, Mr. Stannard, one of the members of Parliament for a borough of Cork, was entrusted with a silver box, containing the freedom of the city, to be presented to Swift. To this he replied in a very characteristic letter, dated August 15, thanking them for the honour they intended him; but he returned the parchment and the box with the request that they would assign their reasons for making choice of him, and suggested that his name might have been inscribed on the box, together with a statement that it was a present to him from the city.[2]

When, in spite of the protests which had been made, a proclamation was issued in September, 1737, regulating the value of the gold coin, Swift caused a black flag to be hoisted

[1] See W. Harris, *History of Dublin*, p. 439.   [2] See Appendix, p. 190.

at St. Patrick's and ordered a muffled peal to be rung. He may well have been responsible for the following item, which appeared in Faulkner's *Dublin Journal* for December 6.

> Great Quantities of new coined Raps, in imitation of the new Halfpence, are very current about the Town; but it is hoped that proper Care will be taken to prevent their Currency.

These public activities during his seventieth year were evidently not unappreciated, if we may judge by the verses which were written in his honour, sometimes apt enough, like *A PUN on Dr. Swift, D.S.P.D., Proving him Immortal*:

> If DEATH denotes to be at rest
> Of SWIFT he'll never be Possess'd;
> As Sure as Water's in the Ocean
> While SWIFT is SWIFT, he is in motion;
> Then while in motion 'tis confess'd;
> That SWIFT will never be at rest:
> What's SWIFT is QUICK, then on this head,
> SWIFT can't at once, be QUICK and DEAD.[1]

And his seventieth birthday was celebrated 'with the utmost Expressions of Joy and Gratitude, by all the People in and about the Liberty of St. Patrick's, and in many Parts of the City and Suburbs. The Bells rang as usual on the most solemn Occasions, nineteen Petararoes were fired several Rounds, four large Bonfires were upon the Steeple, and the Windows illuminated: Such extraordinary Rejoicings have not been practised on that Occasion these several Years past, by which it appears, that the People are now more sensible than ever of the many Obligations they lye under to so great a Lover of his Country.'[2]

On December 13, 1737, he wrote a short prefatory note, recommending Alexander McAulay's *Thoughts on the Tillage of Ireland*, and sent it to Faulkner, with a private letter, desiring him to print it 'in a fair letter and a good paper'. The author is a loyal and virtuous gentleman, but one who 'cannot be blind or unconcerned at the mistaken conduct of his country in a point of the highest importance to its welfare.' And he

[1] See *Dublin Journal*, Nov. 26, 1737.
[2] Ibid., Dec. 3, 1737.

notes that it seems very timely, since several resolutions of the last sessions show that the House of Commons seem to be of the same sentiment—'although the increase of tillage may be of advantage to the clergy'. But 'by the great providence of God, it is so ordered, that if the clergy be fairly dealt with, whatever increases their maintenance will more largely increase the estates of the landed men, and the profits of the farmers.'[1]

In the following year, 1738, Swift's letters are full of complaints of the increasing burdens of age—giddiness, deafness, loss of memory—of being good for nothing and very much out of favour with those in power.[2] He was concerned about the publication of his *History of the Last Four Years of Queen Anne* and may have looked at the proofs of the Dublin edition of his *Compleat Collection of genteel and ingenious Conversation*, which was published by Faulkner on March 21, 1738.[3]

Faulkner later stated that all the sheets of Volumes V and VI of the *Works*, which appeared in early August of this year, had been submitted to Swift in proof, and he was allowed to put in the Publisher's Preface to Vol. VI, that he had been assisted in the Correcting by the 'supposed Author's Friends'. Whatever this may mean there is enough evidence in the contents of these volumes to indicate that Swift approved what should and should not be included. Even if he was having difficulty in getting his *History* published, he could at least reprint here the most important of his political writings during those years when he was in the service of the Ministry before the death of the Queen. In the fifth volume then he put the *Examiners* he had written and the *Conduct of the Allies*; in the sixth, which it must be admitted is a very untidy ill-ordered collection, the other pamphlets written at that time, together with some of the products of the last few years, including *Polite Conversation*, a few poems, and a few letters reprinted from 'the first volume of Pope's Literary Correspondence, lately published by himself'.

I submit that there can be little doubt that the prefatory advertisements, or 'Publisher's Prefaces' to such pieces as

---

[1] *Corr.*, vi, 55–6.   [2] *Corr.*, vi, 63, 77, etc.
[3] See Vol. IV of this edition.

Advice to Members of the October Club, The Public Spirit of the Whigs, Considerations upon Two Bills, were written by Swift himself. What 'Intimate of the Supposed Author' was there in Dublin in 1738, who could have provided the 'piece of Intelligence' contained in the Preface to the first of the above pieces, except Swift himself? And I am indeed inclined to think that some of the smaller changes in the text of the later pieces, such as *Considerations upon Two Bills,* 1731, were made by Swift in proof. For instance, to reduce the inferior clergy to beggary, a living of £500 a year is divided into *ten* not *two* parts; and it hath *too often* rather than *sometimes* happened that the Bishops soon forget the condition of the middling rate of clergymen, who were their old companions 'before their great Promotion.'[1]

He was also occupied with the business of investing his money in lands for the endowment of his hospital, and on July 13, 1738, sent an advertisement[2] to Faulkner to be printed, at the same time complaining to him:

> I believe no man had ever more difficulty, or less encouragement, to bestow his whole fortune for a charitable use.[3]

I have already had occasion to quote from the letter Swift wrote to Faulkner on August 31, enquiring whether he had the second volume of the unfinished manuscript of *Advice to Servants.*[4] This seems to me to indicate very clearly the degree of confidence with which Faulkner was treated at this time. It shows further that Swift was still interested in those unfinished pieces which he had by him, and may well have continued to make from time to time some corrections and additions to prepare them for publication.

There was little more that he could do, except occasionally to alleviate the sufferings of the poor, whose miseries—said Mrs. Whiteway—'have shortened his days and sunk him even below the wishes of his enemies.' So on September 15, he 'distributed a handsome sum of money to upwards of forty

---

[1] See Vol. XII, 193, 198; 342–3.   [2] See Appendix.
[3] *Corr.,* vi, 85–6.   [4] See above, p. vii.

decayed housekeepers to buy coals and other necessaries for the ensuing winter.'[1]   And he still interested himself in the welfare of his young friends. He exerted all his efforts to obtain for William Dunkin, of Trinity College, the living of Coleraine, with the same zeal as he had shown three years before in applying on his behalf to the Provost and Fellows.[2]

In the spring of 1740, he made the final arrangements to carry out the plan which he had had in mind ten years before to give

> the little Wealth he had
> To build a House for Fools and Mad:

making a will and appointing trustees, with directions for the purchase of land and the provision of funds for St. Patrick's Hospital. There exist some fragments of an earlier draft and a codicil, dated April 1737,[3] but the last will was dated May 3, with a codicil, dated May 5, 1740. It is a remarkable document, and it is not surprising that immediately after Swift's death it was printed, first in a shortened form 'As far as it concerns the public to know it' and then in full; and this was at once reprinted in London, and afterwards included in all the editions of his Works. It shows, as Faulkner said in his Preface, his 'Love of the Publick Good'; and it shows also his care to plan for all contingencies, including the possibility that another form of Christian religion might become the Established Faith in Ireland, and to remember in his private bequests the needs and idiosyncrasies of his friends, and sometimes to leave a record of his unsuccessful attempts to secure for them what he had felt was their due.

He continued to keep an Account of the Cathedral and Charity Money until April 18, 1742,[4] but the last of his writings is a document drawn up and signed with his own hand as the Dean of St. Patrick's and addressed to the Sub-Dean and Prebendaries on a matter concerning the behaviour of the Vicars Choral and affecting the dignity of the Cathedral. It was dated January 28, 1741–2. For the last time he is roused to anger at the insolence and insubordination of some members

---

[1] *Corr.*, vi, 97.   [2] See Appendix, p. 189.
[3] See Appendix I, pp. 198–200 and *Corr.*, vi, 48.   [4] *Corr.*, vi, 219.

of the Choir, and at the thought that the honour and dignity
of the Chapter should suffer by reason of his infirmities.

> My resolution is to preserve the dignity of my station, and the
> honour of my Chapter; and, Gentlemen, it is incumbent upon
> you to aid me, and to show who and what the Dean and Chapter
> of Saint Patrick's are.[1]

Meanwhile Faulkner continued to publish further volumes
of Swift's works and correspondence, adding Vols. VII and
VIII to the collected edition in 1741 and 1742. And the third
Dublin edition of *A Tale of a Tub* appeared separately. At the
same time in London, the *Miscellanies in Four Volumes*, by
Dr. Swift, Dr. Arbuthnot, Mr. Pope, and Mr. Gay, were
reprinted, and in the next four years were extended to 11
volumes. Immediately after Swift's death, Faulkner reprinted
the *Works* in 8 volumes with a Dedication dated January 27,
1745–6, to the Earl of Chesterfield, then Lord Lieutenant of
Ireland, and a compliment to the Countess for her 'noble
Example . . . in wearing and recommending the Use of Irish
Manufactures to the Ladies of this Kingdom, at a Time
when Trade was at a Stand, and the poor Tradesmen starving
for want of Employment: This is a Work, which although our
great Author had very much at Heart, he never could accom-
plish.' In 1763, Faulkner in reply to the attacks made on his
edition by the London editors of 1755, added a long address
To the Reader, giving an account of his relations with the
author, and their partnership in this Dublin edition of his
Works. As the text of this edition is so largely based on the
assumption that Faulkner's claims were true, I have thought it
fitting to print his statement at the end of this volume.[2]

[1] See Appendix, p. 197.   [2] See Appendix, p. 201.

Directions to Servants

DIRECTIONS

TO

SERVANTS.

By the Revd. Dr. SWIFT, D.S.P.D.

DUBLIN:

Printed by GEORGE FAULKNER, in *Essex-Street*,

M,D,CC,XLV.

DIRECTIONS
TO
SERVANTS

IN GENERAL;

And in particular to

The BUTLER,	PORTER,
COOK,	DAIRY-MAID,
FOOTMAN,	CHAMBER-MAID,
COACHMAN,	NURSE,
GROOM,	LAUNDRESS,
HOUSE-STEWARD,	HOUSE-KEEPER,
and	TUTORESS, or
LAND-STEWARD,	GOVERNESS.

By the Reverend Dr. SWIFT, D.S.P.D.

I have a Thing in the Press, begun above twenty-eight Years ago, and almost finish'd: It will make a Four Shilling Volume; and is such a PERFECTION OF FOLLY, that you shall never hear of it, till it is printed, and then you shall be left to guess. Nay, I have ANOTHER OF THE SAME AGE, which will require a long Time to perfect, and is worse than the former, in which I will serve you the same Way. Letters to and from Dr. Swift, &c. Lett. LXI. alluding to POLITE CONVERSATION and DIRECTIONS TO SERVANTS.

LONDON:

Printed for R. DODSLEY, in *Pall-Mall*, and M. COOPER, in *Pater-Noster-Row*,

MDCCXLV.

[Price One Shilling and Six-Pence.]

The Publisher's Preface

*T*HE *following Treatise of* Directions to Servants *was began some Years ago by the Author, who had not Leisure to finish and put it into proper Order, being engaged in many other Works of greater Use to his Country, as may be seen by most of his Writings. But, as the Author's Design was to expose the Villanies and Frauds of Servants to their Masters and Mistresses, we shall make no Apology for its Publication; but give it our Readers in the same Manner as we find it, in the Original, which may be seen in the Printer's Custody. The few Tautologies that occur in the Characters left unfinished, will make the Reader look upon the Whole as a rough Draught with several Outlines only drawn: However, that there may appear no Daubing or Patch-Work by other Hands, it is thought most adviseable to give it in the Author's own Words.*

It is imagined, that he intended to make a large Volume of this Work; but as Time and Health would not permit him, the Reader may draw from what is here exhibited, Means to detect the many Vices and Faults, which People in that Kind of low Life are subject to.

If Gentlemen would seriously consider this Work, which is written for their Instruction, (although ironically) it would make them better Œconomists, and preserve their Estates and Families from Ruin.

It may be seen by some scattered Papers (wherein were given Hints for a Dedication and Preface, and a List of all Degrees of Servants) that the Author intended to have gone through all their Characters.

This is all that need be said as to this Treatise, which can only be looked upon as a Fragment.

G.F.

Dublin, Nov. 8,

1745.

RULES

All SERVANTS in general.

WHEN your Master or Lady call a Servant by Name, if that Servant be not in the Way, none of you are to answer, for then there will be no End of your Drudgery: And Masters themselves allow, that if a Servant comes when he is called, it is sufficient.

When you have done a Fault, be always pert and insolent, and behave your self as if you were the injured Person; this will immediately put your Master or Lady off their Mettle.

If you see your Master wronged by any of your Fellow-servants, be sure to conceal it, for fear of being called a Tell-tale: However, there is one Exception, in case of a favourite Servant, who is justly hated by the whole Family; who therefore are bound in Prudence to lay all the Faults they can upon the Favourite.

The Cook, the Butler, the Groom, the Market-man, and every other Servant, who is concerned in the Expences of the Family, should act as if his Master's whole Estate ought to be applied to that Servant's particular Business. For Instance, if the Cook computes his Master's Estate to be a thousand Pounds a Year, he reasonably concludes that a thousand Pounds a Year will afford Meat enough, and therefore, he need not be saving; the Butler makes the same Judgment; so may the Groom and the Coachman; and thus every Branch of Expence will be filled to your Master's Honour.

When you are chid before Company, (which with Submission to our Masters and Ladies is an unmannerly Practice) it often happens that some Stranger will have the Good-nature to drop a Word in your Excuse; in such a Case, you have a good

Title to justify your self, and may rightly conclude, that when-ever he chides you afterwards on other Occasions, he may be in the wrong; in which Opinion you will be the better confirmed by stating the Case to your Fellow-servants in your own Way, who will certainly decide in your Favour: Therefore, as I have said before, whenever you are chidden, complain as if you were injured.

It often happens that Servants sent on Messages, are apt to stay out somewhat longer than the Message requires, perhaps two, four, six, or eight Hours, or some such Trifle; for the Temptation to be sure was great, and Flesh and Blood cannot always resist: When you return, the Master storms, the Lady scolds, stripping, cudgelling, and turning off, is the Word. But here you ought to be provided with a Set of Excuses, enough to serve on all Occasions: For Instance, your Uncle came fourscore Miles to Town this Morning, on purpose to see you, and goes back by Break of Day To-morrow: A Brother-Servant, that borrowed Money of you when he was out of Place, was running away to *Ireland:* You were taking Leave of an old Fellow-servant, who was shipping for *Barbados:* Your Father sent a Cow for you to sell, and you could not find a Chapman till Nine at Night: You were taking Leave of a dear Cousin who is to be hanged next *Saturday:* You wrencht your Foot against a Stone, and were forced to stay three Hours in a Shop, before you could stir a Step: Some Nastiness was thrown on you out of a Garret Window, and you were ashamed to come Home before you were cleaned, and the Smell went off: You were pressed for the Sea-service, and carried before a Justice of Peace, who kept you three Hours before he examined you, and you got off with much a-do: A Bailiff by Mistake seized you for a Debtor, and kept you the whole Evening in a Spunging-house: You were told your Master had gone to a Tavern, and come to some Mis-chance, and your Grief was so great that you inquired for his Honour in a hundred Taverns between *Pall-mall* and *Temple-bar.*

Take all Tradesmens Parts against your Master, and when you are sent to buy any Thing, never offer to cheapen it, but generously pay the full Demand. This is highly for your Master's Honour; and may be some Shillings in your Pocket; and you are to consider, if your Master hath paid too much, he can better afford the Loss than a poor Tradesman.

Never submit to stir a Finger in any Business but that for which you were particularly hired. For Example, if the Groom be drunk or absent, and the Butler be ordered to shut the Stable Door, the Answer is ready, An please your Honour, I don't understand Horses; If a Corner of the Hanging wants a single Nail to fasten it, and the Footman be directed to tack it up, he may say, he doth not understand that Sort of Work, but his Honour may send for the Upholsterer.

Masters and Ladies are usually quarrelling with the Servants for not shutting the Doors after them: But neither Masters nor Ladies consider, that those Doors must be open before they can be shut, and that the Labour is double to open and shut the Doors; therefore the best, the shortest, and easiest Way is to do neither. But if you are so often teized to shut the Door, that you cannot easily forget it, then give the Door such a Clap as you go out, as will shake the whole Room, and make every Thing rattle in it, to put your Master and Lady in Mind that you observe their Directions.

If you find yourself to grow into Favour with your Master or Lady, take some Opportunity, in a very mild Way, to give them Warning; and when they ask the Reason, and seem loth to part with you, answer That you would rather live with them, than any Body else, but a poor Servant is not to be blamed if he strives to better himself; that Service is no Inheritance, that your Work is great, and your Wages very small: Upon which, if your Master hath any Generosity, he will add five or ten Shillings a Quarter rather than let you go: But, if you are baulked, and have no Mind to go off, get some Fellow-servant to tell your Master, that he hath prevailed upon you to stay.

Whatever good Bits you can pilfer in the Day, save them to junket with your Fellow-servants at Night, and take in the Butler, provided he will give you Drink.

Write your own Name and your Sweet-heart's with the

Smoak of a Candle on the Roof of the Kitchen, or the Servants Hall, to shew your Learning.

If you are a young sightly Fellow, whenever you whisper your Mistress at the Table, run your Nose full in her Cheek, or if your Breath be good, breathe full in her Face; this I know to have had very good Consequences in some Families.

Never come till you have been called three or four Times; for none but Dogs will come at the first Whistle; And when the Master calls [*Who's there?*] no Servant is bound to come; for [*Who's there*] is no Body's Name.

When you have broken all your earthen Drinking Vessels below Stairs (which is usually done in a Week) the Copper Pot will do as well; it can boil Milk, heat Porridge, hold Small-Beer, or in Case of Necessity serve for a Jordan; therefore apply it indifferently to all these Uses; but never wash or scour it, for Fear of taking off the Tin.

Although you are allowed Knives for the Servants Hall, at Meals, yet you ought to spare them, and make Use only of your Master's.

Let it be a constant Rule, that no Chair, Stool, or Table in the Servants Hall, or the Kitchen, shall have above three Legs, which hath been the antient, and constant Practice in all the Families I ever knew, and is said to be founded upon two Reasons; first, to shew that Servants are ever in a tottering Condition; secondly, it was thought a Point of Humility, that the Servants Chairs and Tables should have at least one Leg fewer than those of their Masters. I grant there hath been an Exception to this Rule, with regard to the Cook, who by old Custom was allowed an easy Chair to sleep in after Dinner; and yet I have seldom seen them with above three Legs. Now this epidemical Lameness of Servants Chairs is by Philosophers imputed to two Causes, which are observed to make the greatest Revolutions in States and Empires; I mean, Love and War. A Stool, a Chair, or a Table, is the first Weapon taken up in a general Romping or Skirmish; and after a Peace, the Chairs, if they be not very strong, are apt to suffer in the Conduct of an Amour; the Cook being usually fat and heavy, and the Butler a little in Drink.

I could never endure to see Maid-Servants so ungenteel as to walk the Streets with their Pettycoats pinned up; it is a foolish Excuse to alledge, their Pettycoats will be dirty, when they have so easy a Remedy as to walk three or four Times down a clean Pair of Stairs after they come home.

When you stop to tattle with some crony Servant in the same Street, leave your own Street-Door open, that you may get in without knocking, when you come back; otherwise your Mistress may know you are gone out, and you will be chidden.

I do most earnestly exhort you all to Unanimity and Concord. But mistake me not: You may quarrel with each other as much as you please, only bear in Mind that you have a common Enemy, which is your Master and Lady, and you have a common Cause to defend. Believe an old Practitioner; whoever out of Malice to a Fellow-servant, carries a Tale to his Master, shall be ruined by a general Confederacy against him.

The general Place of Rendezvous for all Servants, both in Winter and Summer, is the Kitchen; there the grand Affairs of the Family ought to be consulted; whether they concern the Stable, the Dairy, the Pantry, the Laundry, the Cellar, the Nursery, the Dining-room, or my Lady's Chamber: There, as in your own proper Element, you can laugh, and squall, and romp, in full Security.

When any Servant comes home drunk, and cannot appear, you must all join in telling your Master, that he is gone to Bed very sick; upon which your Lady will be so good-natured, as to order some comfortable Thing for the poor Man, or Maid.

When your Master and Lady go abroad together, to Dinner, or on a Visit for the Evening, you need leave only one Servant in the House, unless you have a Black-guard-boy to answer at the Door, and attend the Children, if there be any. Who is to stay at home is to be determined by short and long Cuts, and the Stayer at home may be comforted by a Visit from a Sweet-heart, without Danger of being caught together. These Opportunities must never be missed, because they come but sometimes; and all is safe enough while there is a Servant in the House.

When your Master or Lady comes home, and wants a Servant who happens to be abroad, your Answer must be, that he is but just that Minute stept out, being sent for by a Cousin who is dying.

If your Master calls you by Name, and you happen to answer at the fourth Call, you need not hurry yourself; and if you be chidden for staying, you may lawfully say, you came no sooner, because you did not know what you were called for.

When you are chidden for a Fault, as you go out of the Room, and down Stairs, mutter loud enough to be plainly heard; this will make him believe you are innocent.

Whoever comes to visit your Master or Lady when they are abroad, never burthen your Memory with the Persons Name, for indeed you have too many other Things to remember. Besides, it is a Porter's Business, and your Master's Fault that he doth not keep one; and who can remember Names? and you will certainly mistake them, and you can neither write nor read.

If it be possible, never tell a Lye to your Master or Lady, unless you have some Hopes that they cannot find it out in less than half an Hour. When a Servant is turned off, all his Faults must be told, although most of them were never known by his Master or Lady; and all Mischiefs done by others, charged to him. [Instance them.] And when they ask any of you, why you never acquainted them before? The Answer is, Sir, or Madam, really I was afraid it would make you angry; and besides perhaps you might think it was Malice in me. Where there are little Masters and Misses in a House, they are usually great Impediments to the Diversions of the Servants; the only Remedy is to bribe them with Goody Goodyes, that they may not tell Tales to Papa and Mamma.

I advise you of the Servants, whose Master lives in the Country, and who expect Vales, always to stand Rank and File when a Stranger is taking his Leave; so that he must of Necessity pass between you; and he must have more Confidence, or less Money than usual, if any of you let him escape, and, according as he behaves himself, remember to treat him the next Time he comes.

If you are sent with ready Money to buy any Thing at a Shop, and happen at that Time to be out of Pocket (which is very usual) sink the Money and take up the Goods on your Master's Account. This is for the Honour of your Master and yourself; for he becomes a Man of Credit at your Recommendation.

When your Lady sends for you up to her Chamber, to give you any Orders, be sure to stand at the Door, and keep it open, fiddling with the Lock all the while she is talking to you, and keep the Button in your Hand for fear you should forget to shut the Door after you.

If your Master or Lady happen once in their Lives to accuse you wrongfully, you are a happy Servant, for you have nothing more to do, than for every Fault you commit, while you are in their Service, to put them in Mind of that false Accusation, and protest yourself equally innocent in the present Case.

When you have a Mind to leave your Master, and are too bashful to break the Matter for fear of offending him, your best way is to grow rude and saucy of a sudden, and beyond your usual Behaviour, till he finds it necessary to turn you off; and when you are gone, to revenge yourself, give him and his Lady such a Character to all your Brother-servants, who are out of Place, that none will venture to offer their Service.

Some nice Ladies who are afraid of catching Cold, having observed that the Maids and Fellows below Stairs often forget to shut the Door after them, as they come in or go out into the back Yards, have contrived that a Pulley and Rope with a large Piece of Lead at the End, should be so fixt as to make the Door shut of itself, and require a strong Hand to open it; which is an immense Toil to Servants, whose Business may force them to go in and out fifty Times in a Morning: But Ingenuity can do much, for prudent Servants have found out an effectual Remedy against this insupportable Grievance, by tying up the Pulley in such a Manner, that the Weight of the Lead will have no Effect; however, as to my own Part, I would rather chuse to keep the Door always open, by laying a heavy Stone at the Bottom of it.

The Servants Candlesticks are generally broken, for nothing can last for ever: But, you may find out many Expedients: You may conveniently stick your Candle in a Bottle, or with a Lump of Butter against the Wainscot, in a Powder-horn, or in an old Shoe, or in a cleft Stick, or in the Barrel of a Pistol, or upon its own Grease on a Table, in a Coffee Cup or a Drinking Glass, a Horn Can, a Tea Pot, a twisted Napkin, a Mustard Pot, an Ink-horn, a Marrowbone, a Piece of Dough, or you may cut a Hole in a Loaf, and stick it there.

When you invite the neighbouring Servants to junket with you at home in an Evening, teach them a particular way of tapping or scraping at the Kitchen Window, which you may hear, but not your Master or Lady, whom you must take Care not to disturb or frighten at such unseasonable Hours.

Lay all Faults on a Lap-dog, a favourite Cat, a Monkey, a Parrot, a Magpye, a Child, or on the Servant who was last turned off: By this Rule you will excuse yourself, do no Hurt to any Body else, and save your Master or Lady from the Trouble and Vexation of chiding.

When you want proper Instruments for any Work you are about, use all Expedients you can invent, rather than leave your Work undone. For Instance, if the Poker be out of the Way or broken, stir up the Fire with the Tongs; if the Tongs are not at Hand, use the Muzzle of the Bellows, the wrong End of the Fire-Shovel, the Handle of the Fire-Brush, the End of a Mop, or your Master's Cane. If you want Paper to singe a Fowl, tear the first Book you see about the House. Wipe your Shoes for want of a Clout, with the Bottom of a Curtain, or a Damask Napkin. Strip your Livery Lace for Garters. If the Butler wants a Jordan, in case of need, he may use the great Silver Cup.

There are several Ways of putting out Candles, and you ought to be instructed in them all: You may run the Candle End against the Wainscot, which puts the Snuff out immediately: You may lay it on the Floor, and tread the Snuff out with your Foot; You may hold it upside down until it is

choaked with its own Grease; or cram it into the Socket of the
Candlestick: You may whirl it round in your Hand till it goes
out: When you go to Bed, after you have made Water, you
may dip your Candle End into the Chamber-Pot: You may
spit on your Finger and Thumb, and pinch the Snuff until it
goes out: The Cook may run the Candle's Nose into the Meal
Tub, or the Groom into a Vessel of Oats, or a Lock of Hay,
or a Heap of Litter: The House-maid may put out her Candle
by running it against a Looking-glass, which nothing cleans
so well as Candle Snuff: But the quickest and best of all
Methods, is to blow it out with your Breath, which leaves the
Candle clear and readier to be lighted.

There is nothing so pernicious in a Family as a Tell-tale,
against whom it must be the principal Business of you all
to unite: Whatever Office he serves in, take all Opportunities
to spoil the Business he is about, and to cross him in every
Thing. For Instance, if the Butler be the Tell-tale, break his
Glasses whenever he leaves the Pantry open; or lock the
Cat or the Mastiff in it, who will do as well: Mislay a Fork
or a Spoon, so as he may never find it. If it be the Cook, whenever she turns her Back, throw a Lump of Soot or a Handful
of Salt in the Pot, or smoaking Coals into the Dripping-Pan,
or daub the roast Meat with the Back of the Chimney, or hide
the Key of the Jack. If a Footman be suspected, let the Cook
daub the Back of his new Livery; or when he is going up with
a Dish of Soup, let her follow him softly with a Ladle-full,
and drible it all the Way up Stairs to the Dining-room, and
then let the House-maid make such a Noise, that her Lady may
hear it. The Waiting-maid is very likely to be guilty of this
Fault, in hopes to ingratiate herself. In this Case, the Laundress
must be sure to tear her Smocks in the washing, and yet wash
them but half; and, when she complains, tell all the House
that she sweats so much, and her Flesh is so nasty, that she
fouls a Smock more in one Hour, than the Kitchen-maid doth
in a week.

DIRECTIONS

TO

SERVANTS.

CHAP. I

Directions to the BUTLER.

IN my Directions to Servants, I find from my long Observation, that you, Butler, are the principal Party concerned.

Your Business being of the greatest Variety, and requiring the greatest Exactness, I shall, as well as I can recollect, run through the several Branches of your Office, and order my Instructions accordingly.

In waiting at the Side-board, take all possible Care to save your own Trouble, and your Master's Drink and Glasses: Therefore, first, since those who dine at the same Table are supposed to be Friends, let them all drink out of the same Glass without washing; which will save you much Pains, as well as the Hazard of breaking them. Give no Person any Liquor till he has called for it thrice at least; by which means, some out of Modesty, and others out of Forgetfulness, will call the seldomer, and thus your Master's Liquor be saved.

If any one desires a Glass of Bottled-Ale; first shake the Bottle, to see whether any thing be in it, then taste it, to know what Liquor it is, that you may not be mistaken; and lastly, wipe the Mouth of the Bottle with the Palm of your Hand, to shew your Cleanliness.

Be more careful to have the Cork in the Belly of the Bottle

than in the Mouth; and, if the Cork be musty, or white Fryers in your Liquor, your Master will save the more.

If an humble Companion, a Chaplain, a Tutor, or a dependent Cousin happen to be at Table, whom you find to be little regarded by the Master, and the Company, which no Body is readier to discover and observe than we Servants, it must be the Business of you and the Footman, to follow the Example of your Betters, by treating him many Degrees worse than any of the rest; and you cannot please your Master better, or at least your Lady.

If any one calls for Small-beer towards the end of Dinner, do not give yourself the Pains of going down to the Cellar, but gather the Droppings and Leavings out of the several Cups, and Glasses, and Salvers into one; but turn your Back to the Company, for Fear of being observed: On the contrary, if any one calls for Ale towards the end of Dinner, fill the largest Tankard top-full, by which you will have the greatest Part left to oblige your Fellow-servants without the Sin of stealing from your Master.

There is likewise an honest Perquisite by which you have a Chance of getting every Day the best Part of a Bottle of Wine to your self; for you are not to suppose that Gentlefolks will value the Remainder of a Bottle; therefore, always set a fresh one before them after Dinner, although there hath not been above a Glass drank of the other.

Take special Care that your Bottles be not musty before you fill them, in order to which, blow strongly into the Mouth of every Bottle, and then if you smell nothing but your own Breath, immediately fill it.

If you are sent down in haste to draw any Drink, and find it will not run, do not be at the Trouble of opening a Vent, but blow strongly into the Fosset, and you will find it immediately pour into your Mouth; or take out the Vent, but do not stay to put it in again, for fear your Master should want you.

If you are curious to taste some of your Master's choice Bottles, empty as many of them just below the Neck as will make the Quantity you want; but then take Care to fill them up again with clean Water, that you may not lessen your Master's Liquor.

There is an excellent Invention found out of late Years in the Management of Ale and Small-beer at the Side-board: For Instance, a Gentleman calls for a Glass of Ale, and drinks but half; another calls for Small-beer: You immediately teem out the Remainder of the Ale into the Tankard, and fill the Glass with Small-beer, and so backwards and forwards as long as Dinner lasts; by which you answer three great Ends: First, you save your self the Trouble of washing, and consequently the Danger of breaking your Glasses: Secondly, you are sure not to be mistaken in giving Gentlemen the Liquor they call for: And lastly, by this Method you are certain that nothing is lost.

Because Butlers often forget to bring up their Ale and Beer Time enough, be sure you remember to have up yours two Hours before Dinner; and place them in the sunny Part of the Room, to let People see that you have not been negligent.

Some Butlers have a Way of decanting (as they call it) bottled Ale, by which they lose a good Part of the Bottom: Let your Method be to turn the Bottle directly upside down, which will make the Liquor appear double the Quantity; by this means, you will be sure not to lose one Drop, and the Froth will conceal the Muddiness.

Clean your Plate, wipe your Knives, and rub the foul Table, with the Napkins and Table-cloth used that Day; for, it is but one washing, besides you save wearing out the coarse Rubbers; in Reward of which good Husbandry, my Judgment is, that you may lawfully make use of the finest Damask Napkins to be Night-caps for yourself.

When you clean your Plate, leave the Whiteing plainly to be seen in all the Chinks, for fear your Lady should believe you had not cleaned it.

There is nothing wherein the Skill of a Butler more appears, than the Management of Candles, whereof, although some Part may fall to the Share of other Servants, yet you being the principal Person concerned, I shall direct my Instructions upon this Article to you only, leaving your Fellow-Servants to apply them upon Occasion.

First, to avoid burning Day-light, and to save your Master's Candles, never bring them up until Half an Hour after it be dark, although they be called for ever so often.

Let your Sockets be full of Grease to the Brim, with the old Snuff at the Top, then stick on your fresh Candles. It is true, this may endanger their falling, but the Candles will appear so much the longer and handsomer before Company. At other Times, for Variety, put your Candles loose in the Sockets, to shew they are clean to the Bottom.

When your Candle is too big for the Socket, melt it to a right Size in the Fire; and to hide the Smut, wrap it in Paper half way up.

You cannot but observe the great Extravagance of late Years among the Gentry upon the Article of Candles, which a good Butler ought by all means to discourage, both to save his own Pains and his Master's Money: This may be contrived several Ways: As when you are ordered to put Candles into the Sconces.

Sconces are great Wasters of Candles, and you, who are always to consider the Advantage of your Master, should do your utmost to discourage them: Therefore, your Business must be to press the Candle with both your Hands into the Socket, so as to make it lean in such a manner, that the Grease may drop all upon the Floor, if some Lady's Head-dress or Gentleman's Perriwig be not ready to intercept it: You may likewise stick the Candle so loose that it will fall upon the Glass of the Sconce, and break it into Shatters; this will save your Master many a fair Penny in the Year, both in Candles, and to the Glass-man, and yourself much Labour, for the Sconces spoiled cannot be used.

Never let the Candles burn too low, but give them as a lawful Perquisite to your Friend the Cook, to increase her Kitchen-stuff; or if this be not allowed in your House, give them in Charity to the poor Neighbours, who often run on your Errands.

When you cut Bread for a Toast, do not stand idly watching it, but lay it on the Coals, and mind your other Business; then come back, and if you find it toasted quite through, scrape off the burned Side, and serve it up.

When you dress up your Side-board, set the best Glasses as near the Edge of the Table as you can; by which Means they will cast a double Lustre, and make a much finer Figure; and the Consequence can be at worst but the breaking of half a Dozen, which is a Trifle in your Master's Pocket.

Wash the Glasses with your own Water, to save your Master's Salt.

When any Salt is spilt on the Table, do not let it be lost, but when Dinner is done, fold up the Table-cloth with the Salt in it, then shake the Salt out into the Salt-cellar, to serve next Day: But the shortest and surest Way is, when you remove the Cloth, to wrap the Knives, Forks, Spoons, Salt-cellars, broken Bread, and Scraps of Meat altogether in the Table-cloth, by which you will be sure to lose nothing, unless you think it better to shake them out of the Window among the Beggars, that they may with more Convenience eat the Scraps.

Leave the Dregs of Ale, Wine, and other Liquors, in the Bottles: To rince them is but Loss of Time, since all will be done at once in a general washing; and you will have a better Excuse for breaking them.

If your Master hath many musty, or very foul and crusted Bottles, I advise you in Point of Conscience, that those may be the first you truck at the next Ale-house for Ale or Brandy.

When a Message is sent to your Master, be kind to your Brother-servant who brings it; give him the best Liquor in your Keeping, for your Master's Honour; and with the first Opportunity he will do the same to you.

After Supper, if it be dark, carry your Plate and China together in the same Basket, to save Candle-light; for you know your Pantry well enough to put them up in the Dark.

When Company is expected at Dinner, or in Evenings, be sure to be Abroad, that nothing may be got which is under your Key, by which your Master will save his Liquor, and not wear out his Plate.

I come now to a most important Part of your Oeconomy,

E

the Bottling of a Hogshead of Wine, wherein I recommend three Virtues, Cleanliness, Frugality, and brotherly Love. Let your Corks be of the longest Kind you can get; which will save some Wine in the Neck of every Bottle: As to your Bottles, chuse the smallest you can find, which will increase the Number of Dozens, and please your Master; for a Bottle of Wine is always a Bottle of Wine, whether it hold more or less; and if your Master hath his proper Number of Dozens, he cannot complain.

Every Bottle must be first rinced with Wine, for fear of any Moisture left in the Washing; some out of mistaken Thrift will rince a Dozen Bottles with the same Wine; but I would advise you, for more Caution, to change the Wine at every second Bottle; a Jill may be enough. Have Bottles ready by to save it; and it will be a good Perquisite, either to sell or drink with the Cook.

Never draw your Hogshead too low; nor tilt it for fear of disturbing the Liquor. When it begins to run slow, and before the Wine grows cloudy, shake the Hogshead, and carry a Glass of it to your Master, who will praise your Discretion, and give you all the rest as a Perquisite of your Place: You may tilt the Hogshead the next Day, and in a Fortnight get a Dozen or two of good clear Wine, to dispose of as you please.

In bottling Wine, fill your Mouth full of Corks, together with a large Plug of Tobacco, which will give to the Wine the true Taste of the Weed, so delightful to all good Judges in drinking.

When you are ordered to decant a suspicious Bottle, if a Pint be out, give your Hand a dextrous Shake, and shew it in a Glass, that it begins to be muddy.

When a Hogshead of Wine or any other Liquor is to be bottled off, wash your Bottles immediately before you begin; but, be sure not to drain them, by which good Management your Master will save some Gallons in every Hogshead.

This is the Time that in Honour to your Master, you ought to shew your Kindness to your Fellow-servants, and especially to the Cook. What signifies a few Flaggons out of a whole Hogshead? But make them be drunk in your Presence; for fear they should be given to other Folks, and so your Master be wronged: But, advise them if they get drunk to go to Bed, and leave Word they are sick, which last Caution I would have all the Servants observe, both Male and Female.

If your Master finds the Hogshead to fall short of his Expectation, what is plainer, than that the Vessel leaked: That, the Wine-Cooper had not filled it in proper Time: That the Merchant cheated him with a Hogshead below the common Measure?

When you are to get Water on for Tea after Dinner (which in many Families is Part of your Office) to save Firing, and to make more Haste, pour it into the Tea-kettle, from the Pot where Cabbage or Fish have been boiling, which will make it much wholsomer, by curing the acid corroding Quality of the Tea.

Be saving of your Candles, and let those in the Sconces, the Hall, the Stairs, and in the Lanthorn, burn down into the Sockets, until they go out of themselves, for which your Master and Lady will commend your Thriftiness, as soon as they shall smell the Snuffs.

If a Gentleman leaves his Snuff-box or Pick-tooth-case on the Table after Dinner, and goes away, look upon it as part of your Vails; for so it is allowed by all Servants, and you do no Wrong to your Master or Lady.

If you serve a Country 'Squire, when Gentlemen and Ladies come to dine at your House, never fail to make their Servants drunk, and especially the Coachman, for the Honour of your Master; to which, in all your Actions, you must have a special Regard, as being the best Judge: For the Honour of every Family is deposited in the Hands of the Cook, the Butler, and the Groom, as I shall hereafter demonstrate.

Snuff the Candles at Supper as they stand on the Table, which is much the securest Way; because, if the burning Snuff happens to get out of the Snuffers, you have a Chance that it may fall into a Dish of Soup, Sack-posset, Rice-milk, or the like, where it will be immediately extinguished with very little Stink.

When you have snuffed the Candle, always leave the Snuffers

open, for then the Snuff will of itself burn away to Ashes, and cannot fall out and dirty the Table, when you snuff the Candles again.

That the Salt may lie smooth in the Salt-cellar, press it down with your moist Palm.

When a Gentleman is going away after dining with your Master, be sure to stand full in his View, and follow him to the Door, and as you have Opportunity look full in his Face, perhaps it may bring you a Shilling; but, if the Gentleman hath lain there a Night, get the Cook, the House-maid, the Stable-men, the Scullion, and the Gardener, to accompany you, and to stand in his Way to the Hall in a Line on each Side him: If the Gentleman performs handsomely, it will do him Honour, and cost your Master nothing.

You need not wipe your Knife to cut Bread for the Table, because, in cutting a Slice or two it will wipe itself.

Put your Finger into every Bottle, to feel whether it be full, which is the surest Way; for Feeling hath no Fellow.

When you go down to the Cellar to draw Ale or Small-beer, take care to observe directly the following Method. Hold the Vessel between the Finger and Thumb of your right Hand, with the Palm upwards, then hold the Candle between your Fingers, but a little leaning towards the Mouth of the Vessel, then take out the Spiggot with your Left-hand, and clap the Point of it in your Mouth, and keep your Left-hand to watch Accidents; when the Vessel is full withdraw the Spiggot from your Mouth, well wetted with Spittle, which being of a slimy Consistence will make it stick faster in the Fosset: If any Tallow drops into the Vessel you may easily (if you think of it) remove it with a Spoon, or rather with your Finger.

Always lock up a Cat in the Closet where you keep your *China* Plates, for fear the Mice may steal in and break them.

A good Butler always breaks off the Point of his Bottle-screw in two Days, by trying which is harder, the Point of the Screw, or the Neck of the Bottle: In this Case, to supply the Want of a Screw, after the Stump hath torn the Cork in Pieces, make use of a Silver Fork, and when the Scraps of the

Cork are almost drawn out, flirt the Mouth of the Bottle into the Cistern, three or four times, until you quite clear it.

If a Gentleman dines often with your Master, and gives you nothing when he goes away, you may use several Methods to shew him some Marks of your Displeasure, and quicken his Memory: If he calls for Bread or Drink you may pretend not to hear, or send it to another who called after him: If he asks for Wine, let him stay awhile, and then send him Small-beer; give him always foul Glasses; send him a Spoon when he wants a Knife; wink at the Footman to leave him without a Plate: By these, and the like Expedients, you may probably be a better Man by half a Crown before he leaves the House, provided you watch an Opportunity of standing by when he is going.

If your Lady loves Play, your Fortune is fixed for ever: Moderate Gaming will be a Perquisite of ten shillings a Week; and in such a Family I would rather chuse to be Butler than Chaplain, or even rather than be Steward: It is all ready Money and got without Labour, unless your Lady happens to be one of those, who either obligeth you to find Wax-Candles, or forceth you to divide it with some favourite Servants; but at worst, the old Cards are your own; and, if the Gamesters play deep or grow peevish, they will change the Cards so often, that the old ones will be a considerable Advantage by selling them to Coffee-Houses, or Families who love Play, but cannot afford better than Cards at second-hand: When you attend at this Service, be sure to leave new Packs within the Reach of the Gamesters, which, those who have ill Luck will readily take to change their Fortune; and now and then an old Pack mingled with the rest will easily pass. Be sure to be very officious on Play-nights, and ready with your Candles to light out your Company, and have Salvers of Wine at Hand to give them when they call; but manage so with the Cook, that there be no Supper, because it will be so much saved in your Master's Family; and, because a Supper will considerably lessen your Gains.

Next to Cards there is nothing so profitable to you as Bottles, in which Perquisite you have no Competitors, except the Footmen, who are apt to steal and vend them for Pots of Beer: But you are bound to prevent any such Abuses in your Master's Family: The Footmen are not to answer for what are broken at a general Bottling; and those may be as many as your Discretion will make them.

The Profit of Glasses is so very inconsiderable, that it is hardly worth mentioning: It consists only in a small Present made by the Glassman, and about four Shillings in the Pound added to the Prices for your Trouble and Skill in chusing them. If your Master hath a large Stock of Glasses, and you or your Fellow-servants happen to break any of them without your Master's Knowledge, keep it a Secret till there are not enough left to serve the Table, then tell your Master that the Glasses are gone; this will be but one Vexation to him, which is much better than fretting once or twice a Week; and it is the Office of a good Servant to discompose his Master and his Lady as seldom as he can; and here the Cat and Dog will be of great Use to take the Blame from you. *Note*, That Bottles missing are supposed to be half stolen by Stragglers and other Servants, and the other half broken by Accident, and at a general Washing.

Whet the Backs of your Knives until they are as sharp as the Edge, which will have this Advantage, that when Gentlemen find them blunt on one Side, they may try the other; and to shew you spare no Pains in sharpening the Knives, whet them so long, till you wear out a good Part of the Iron, and even the Bottom of the Silver Handle. This doth Credit to your Master, for it shews good House-keeping, and the Goldsmith may one Day make you a Present.

Your Lady, when she finds the Small-beer or Ale dead, will blame you for not remembering to put the Peg into the Vent-hole. This is a great Mistake, nothing being plainer, than that the Peg keeps the Air in the Vessel, which spoils the Drink, and therefore ought to be let out; but if she insisteth upon it, to prevent the Trouble of pulling out the Vent, and putting it in a Dozen Times a Day, which is not to be born by a good Servant, leave the Spiggot half out at Night, and you will find with only the Loss of two or three Quarts of Liquor, the Vessel will run freely.

When you prepare your Candles, wrap them up in a Piece of brown Paper, and so stick them in the Socket: Let the Paper come half way up the Candle, which looks handsome, if any Body should come in.

Do all in the Dark (as clean Glasses, &c.) to save your Master's Candles.

CHAP. II

Directions to the COOK.

Although I am not ignorant that it hath been a long Time since the Custom began among People of Quality to keep Men cooks, and generally of the *French* Nation; yet because my Treatise is chiefly calculated for the general Run of Knights, Squires, and Gentlemen both in Town and Country, I shall therefore apply to you Mrs. Cook, as a Woman: However, a great Part of what I intend, may serve for either Sex; and your Part naturally follows the former, because the Butler and you are joined in Interest. Your Vails are generally equal, and paid when others are disappointed. You can junket together at Nights upon your own Prog, when the rest of the House are abed; and have it in your Power to make every Fellow-servant your Friend. You can give a good Bit or a good Sup to the little Masters and Misses, and gain their Affections. A Quarrel between you is very dangerous to you both, and will probably end in one of you being turned off; in which fatal Case, perhaps, it will not be so easy in some Time to cotton with another. And now Mrs. Cook, I proceed to give you my Instructions, which I desire you will get some Fellow-servant in the Family to read to you constantly one Night in every Week upon your going to Bed, whether you serve in Town or Country; for my Lessons shall be fitted to both.

If your Lady forgets at Supper that there is any cold Meat in the House, do not you be so officious as to put her in Mind; it is plain she did not want it; and if she recollects it the next Day, say she gave you no Orders, and it is spent; therefore, for fear of telling a Lye, dispose of it with the Butler, or any other Crony, before you go to Bed.

Never send up a Leg of a Fowl at Supper, while there is a Cat or Dog in the House, that can be accused for running away with it: But, if there happen to be neither, you must lay it upon the Rats, or a strange Greyhound.

It is ill Housewifry to foul your Kitchen Rubbers with wiping the Bottoms of the Dishes you send up, since the Table-cloath will do as well, and is changed every Meal.

Never clean your Spits after they have been used; for the Grease left upon them by Meat, is the best Thing to preserve them from Rust; and when you make use of them again, the same Grease will keep the Inside of the Meat moist.

If you live in a rich Family, roasting and boiling are below the Dignity of your Office, and which it becomes you to be ignorant of; therefore leave that Work wholly to the Kitchen Wench, for fear of disgracing the Family you live in.

If you be employed in Marketing, buy your Meat as cheap as you can: but when you bring in your Accounts, be tender of your Master's Honour; and set down the highest Rate; which besides is but Justice; for no body can afford to sell at the same Rate that he buys; and I am confident that you may alway safely swear that you gave no more than what the Butcher and Poulterer asked. If your Lady orders you to set up a Piece of Meat for Supper, you are not to understand that you must set it up *all*; therefore you may give half to yourself and the Butler.

Good Cooks cannot abide what they very justly call fidling Work, where Abundance of Time is spent and little done: Such, for Instance, is the dressing small Birds, requiring a world of Cookery and Clutter; and a second or third Spit; which by the way is absolutely needless; for it would be a very ridiculous Thing indeed, if a Spit which is strong enough to turn a Sirloyn of Beef, should not be able to turn a Lark. However, if your Lady be nice, and is afraid that a large Spit will tear them, place them handsomely in the Dripping-pan, where the Fat of roasted Mutton or Beef falling on the Birds, will serve to baste them; and so save both Time and Butter: for what Cook of any Spirit would lose her Time in picking Larks, Wheatears, and other small Birds; therefore, if you cannot get the Maids, or the young Misses to assist you, e'en make short Work, and either singe or flay them; there is no great Loss in the Skins, and the Flesh is just the same.

If you are employed in Market, do not accept a Treat of a Beef-stake and Pot of Ale from the Butcher, which I think in Conscience is no better than wronging your Master; but do you always take that Perquisite in Money, if you do not go in Trust; or in Poundage when you pay the Bills.

The Kitchen Bellows being usually out of Order with stirring the Fire with the Muzzle to save Tongs and Poker; borrow the Bellows out of your Lady's Bed-chamber, which being least used, are commonly the best in the House: and if you happen to damage or grease them, you have a Chance to keep them entirely for your own Use.

Let a Blackguard Boy be always about the House to send on your Errands, and go to Market for you in rainy Days; which will save your Cloaths, and make you appear more creditable to your Mistress.

If your Mistress allows you the Kitchen-stuff, in return of her Generosity, take care to boil and roast your Meat sufficient. If she keeps it for her own Profit, do her Justice; and rather than let a good Fire be wanting, enliven it now and then with the Dripping and the Butter that happens to turn to Oil.

Send up your Meat well stuck with Scewers, to make it look round and plump; and an Iron Scewer, rightly employed now and then, will make it look handsomer.

When you roast a long Joint of Meat, be careful only about the Middle, and leave the two extreme Parts raw; which may serve another Time, and will also save Firing.

When you scour your Plates and Dishes, bend the Brim inward, so as to make them hold the more.

Always keep a large Fire in the Kitchen when there is a small Dinner, or the Family dines abroad; that the Neighbours seeing the Smoak, may commend your Master's House-keeping: But, when much Company is invited, then be as sparing as possible of your Coals; because a great deal of the Meat being half raw will be saved, and serve for next Day.

Boil your Meat constantly in Pump Water, because you must sometimes want River or Pipe Water, and then your Mistress observing your Meat of a different Colour, will chide you when you are not in Fault.

When you have Plenty of Fowl in the Larder, leave the Door open, in Pity to the poor Cat, if she be a good Mouser.

If you find it necessary to go to market in a wet Day, take out your Mistress's Riding-hood and Cloak to save your Cloaths.

Get three or four Char-women constantly to attend you in the Kitchen, whom you pay at small Charges, only with the broken Meat, a few Coals, and all the Cinders.

To keep troublesome Servants out of the Kitchen, always leave the Winder sticking on the Jack to fall on their Heads.

If a Lump of Soot falls into the Soup, and you cannot con-veniently get it out, scum it well, and it will give the Soup a high *French* Taste.

If you melt your Butter to Oil, be under no Concern, but send it up; for Oil is a genteeler Sauce than Butter.

Scrape the Bottoms of your Pots and Kettles with a Silver Spoon, for fear of giving them a Taste of Copper.

When you send up Butter for Sauce, be so thrifty as to let it be half Water; which is also much wholesomer.

Never make use of a Spoon in any thing that you can do with your Hands, for fear of wearing out your Master's Plate.

When you find that you cannot get Dinner ready at the Time appointed, put the Clock back, and then it may be ready to a Minute.

Let a red hot Coal now and then fall into the Dripping-pan,

that the Smoak of the Dripping may ascend, and give the roast Meat a high Taste.

You are to look upon your Kitchen as your Dressing-room; but, you are not to wash your Hands till you have gone to the Necessary-house, and spitted your Meat, trussed your Pullets, pickt your Sallad, nor indeed till after you have sent up the second Course; for your Hands will be ten times fouled with the many Things you are forced to handle; but when your Work is over, one Washing will serve for all.

There is but one Part of your Dressing that I would admit while the Victuals are boiling, roasting, or stewing, I mean the combing your Head, which loseth no Time, because you can stand over your Cookery, and watch it with one Hand, while you are using your Comb with the other.

If some of the Combings happen to be sent up with the Victuals, you may safely lay the Fault upon any of the Footmen that hath vexed you: As those Gentlemen are sometimes apt to be malicious if you refuse them a Sop in the Pan, or a Slice from the Spit; much more when you discharge a Ladle-full of hot Porridge on their Legs, or send them up to their Masters with a Dish-clout pinned at their Tails.

In roasting and boiling, order the Kitchen-maid to bring none but the large Coals, and save the small ones for the Fires above Stairs; the first are properest for dressing Meat, and when they are out, if you happen to miscarry in any Dish, you may fairly lay the Fault upon want of Coals: Besides, the Cinder-pickers will be sure to speak ill of your Master's House-keeping, where they do not find Plenty of large Cinders mixed with fresh large Coals: Thus you may dress your Meat with Credit, do an Act of Charity, raise the Honour of your Master, and sometimes get Share of a Pot of Ale for your Bounty to the Cinder-women.

As soon as you have sent up the second Course, you have nothing to do in a great Family until Supper: Therefore, scoure your Hands and Face, put on your Hood and Scarfe, and take your Pleasure among your Cronies, till Nine or Ten at Night——But dine first.

Let there be always a strict Friendship between you and the

Butler, for it is both your Interests to be united: The Butler often wants a comfortable Tit-bit, and you much oftener a cool Cup of good Liquor. However, be cautious of him, for he is sometimes an inconstant Lover, because he hath great Advantage to allure the Maids with a Glass of Sack, or White Wine and Sugar.

When you roast a Breast of Veal, remember your Sweetheart the Butler loves a Sweet-bread; therefore set it aside till Evening: You can say, the Cat or the Dog has run away with it, or you found it tainted, or fly-blown; and besides, it looks as well on the Table without the Sweet-bread as with it.

When you make the Company wait long for Dinner, and the Meat be overdone, (which is generally the Case) you may lawfully lay the Fault on your Lady, who hurried you so to send up Dinner, that you were forced to send it up too much boiled and roasted.

When you are in haste to take down your Dishes, tip them in such a manner, that a Dozen will fall together upon the Dresser, just ready for your Hand.

To save Time and Trouble, cut your Apples and Onions with the same Knife, for well-bred Gentry love the Taste of an Onion in every thing they eat.

Lump three or four Pounds of Butter together with your Hands, then dash it against the Wall just over the Dresser, so as to have it ready to pull by Pieces as you have occasion for it.

If you have a Silver Saucepan for the Kitchen Use, let me advise you to batter it well, and keep it always black; make room for the Saucepan by wriggling it on the Coals, &c.: This will be for your Master's Honour, because it shews there has been constant good Housekeeping: And in the same manner, if you are allowed a large Silver Spoon for the Kitchen, have the Bole of it be worn out with continual scraping and stirring, and often say merrily, This Spoon owes my Master no Service.

When you send up a Mess of Broth, Water-gruel, or the like, to your Master in a Morning, do not forget with your Thumb and two Fingers to put Salt on the Side of the Plate;

for if you make use of a Spoon, or the End of a Knife, there may be Danger that the Salt would fall, and that would be a Sign of ill Luck. Only remember to lick your Thumb and Fingers clean, before you offer to touch the Salt.

If your Butter, when it is melted, tastes of Brass, it is your Master's Fault, who will not allow you a Silver Sauce-pan; besides, the less of it will go further, and new tinning is very chargeable: If you have a Silver Sauce-pan, and the Butter smells of Smoak, lay the Fault upon the Coals.

If your Dinner miscarries in almost every Dish, how could you help it: You were teized by the Footmen coming into the Kitchen; and, to prove it true, take Occasion to be angry, and throw a Ladle-full of Broth on one or two of their Liveries; besides, *Friday* and *Childermas-day* are two cross Days in the Week, and it is impossible to have good Luck on either of them; therefore on those two Days you have a lawful Excuse.

CHAP. III

Directions to the FOOTMAN.

YOUR Employment being of a mixt Nature, extends to a great Variety of Business, and you stand in a fair way of being the Favourite of your Master or Mistress, or of the young Masters and Misses; you are the fine Gentleman of the Family, with whom all the Maids are in Love. You are sometimes a Pattern of Dress to your Master, and sometimes he is so to you. You wait at Table in all Companies, and consequently have the Opportunity to see and know the World, and to understand Men and Manners; I confess your Vails are but few, unless you are sent with a Present, or attend the Tea in the Country; but you are called Mr. in the Neighbourhood, and sometimes pick up a Fortune, perhaps your Master's Daughter; and I have known many of your Tribe to have good

Commands in the Army. In Town you have a Seat reserved for you in the Play-house, where you have an Opportunity of becoming Wits and Criticks: You have no profest Enemy except the Rabble, and my Lady's Waiting-woman, who are sometimes apt to call you Skipkennel. I have a true Veneration for your Office, because I had once the Honour to be one of your Order, which I foolishly left by demeaning myself with accepting an Employment in the Custom-house.—But that you, my Brethren, may come to better Fortunes, I shall here deliver my Instructions, which have been the Fruits of much Thought and Observation, as well as of seven Years Experience.

In order to learn the Secrets of other Families, tell your Brethren those of your Master's; thus you will grow a favourite both at home and abroad, and regarded as a Person of Importance.

Never be seen in the Streets with a Basket or Bundle in your Hands, and carry nothing but what you can hide in your Pocket, otherwise you will disgrace your Calling: To prevent which, always retain a Blackguard Boy to carry your Loads; and if you want Farthings, pay him with a good Slice of Bread or Scrap of Meat.

Let a Shoe-boy clean your own Shoes first, for fear of fouling the Chambers, and then let him clean your Master's; keep him on purpose for that Use and to run of Errands, and pay him with Scraps. When you are sent on an Errand, be sure to hedge in some Business of your own, either to see your Sweet-heart, or drink a Pot of Ale with some Brother-Servant, which is so much Time clear gained.

There is a great Controversy about the most convenient and genteel Way of holding your Plate at Meals; some stick it between the Frame and the Back of the Chair, which is an excellent Expedient, where the Make of the Chair will allow it: Others, for fear the Plate should fall, grasp it so firmly, that their Thumb reacheth to the Middle of the Hollow; which however, if your Thumb be dry, is no secure Method; and therefore in that Case, I advise your wetting the Bowl of it with your Tongue: As to that absurd Practice of letting the

Back of the Plate lye leaning on the Hollow of your Hand, which some Ladies recommend, it is universally exploded, being liable to so many Accidents. Others again, are so refined, that they hold their Plate directly under the left Arm-pit, which is the best Situation for keeping it warm; but this may be dangerous in the Article of taking away a Dish, where your Plate may happen to fall upon some of the Company's Heads. I confess myself to have objected against all these Ways, which I have frequently tried; and therefore I recommend a Fourth, which is to stick your Plate up to the Rim inclusive, in the left Side between your Waistcoat and your Shirt: This will keep it at least as warm as under your Arm-pit, or Ockster, (as the *Scots* call it) this will hide it so, as Strangers may take you for a better Servant, too good to hold a Plate; this will secure it from falling; and thus disposed, it lies ready for you to whip it out in a Moment, ready warmed, to any Guest within your Reach, who may want it. And lastly, there is another Convenience in this Method, that if any Time during your waiting, you find yourselves going to cough or sneeze, you can immediately snatch out your Plate, and hold the hollow Part close to your Nose or Mouth, and, thus prevent spirting any Moisture from either, upon the Dishes or the Ladies Head-dress: You see Gentlemen and Ladies observe a like Practice on such an Occasion, with a Hat or a Handkerchief; yet a Plate is less fouled and sooner cleaned than either of these; for, when your Cough or Sneeze is over, it is but return-ing your Plate to the same Position, and your Shirt will clean it in the Passage.

Take off the largest Dishes, and set them on with one Hand, to shew the Ladies your Vigour and Strength of Back; but always do it between two Ladies, that if the Dish happens to slip, the Soup or Sauce may fall on their Cloaths, and not daub the Floor: By this Practice, two of our Brethren, my worthy Friends, got considerable Fortunes.

Learn all the new-fashion Words, and Oaths, and Songs, and Scraps of Plays that your Memory can hold. Thus, you will become the Delight of nine Ladies in ten, and the Envy of ninety nine Beaux in a hundred.

Take Care, that at certain Periods, during Dinner especially, when Persons of Quality are there, you and your Brethren be all out of the Room together, by which you will give yourselves some Ease from the Fatigue of waiting, and at the same Time leave the Company to converse more freely, without being constrained by your Presence.

When you are sent on a Message, deliver it in your own Words, altho' it be to a Duke or a Dutchess, and not in the Words of your Master or Lady; for how can they understand what belongs to a Message as well as you, who have been bred to the Employment: But never deliver the Answer till it is called for, and then adorn it with your own Style.

When Dinner is done, carry down a great Heap of Plates to the Kitchen, and when you come to the Head of the Stairs, trundle them all before you: There is not a more agreeable Sight or Sound, especially if they be Silver; besides the Trouble they save you, and there they will lie ready near the Kitchen Door, for the Scullion to wash them.

If you are bringing up a Joint of Meat in a Dish, and it falls out of your Hand, before you get into the Dining Room, with the Meat on the Ground, and the Sauce spilled, take up the Meat gently, wipe it with the Lap of your Coat, then put it again into the Dish, and serve it up; and when your Lady misses the Sauce, tell her, it is to be sent up in a Plate by itself.

When you carry up a Dish of Meat, dip your Fingers in the Sauce, or lick it with your Tongue, to try whether it be good, and fit for your Master's Table.

You are the best Judge of what Acquaintance your Lady ought to have, and therefore, if she sends you on a Message of Compliment or Business to a Family you do not like, deliver the Answer in such a Manner, as may breed a Quarrel between them not to be reconciled: Or, if a Footman comes from the same Family on the like Errand, turn the Answer she orders you to deliver, in such a Manner, as the other Family may take it for an Affront.

When you are in Lodgings, and no Shoe-boy to be got, clean your Master's Shoes with the Bottom of the Curtains, a clean Napkin, or your Landlady's Apron.

Ever wear your Hat in the House, but when your Master calls; and as soon as you come into his Presence, pull it off to shew your Manners.

Never clean your Shoes on the Scraper, but in the Entry, or at the Foot of the Stairs, by which will have the Credit of being at home, almost a Minute sooner, and the Scraper will last the longer.

Never ask Leave to go abroad, for then it will be always known that you are absent, and you will be thought an idle rambling Fellow; whereas, if you go out, and no body observes, you have a Chance of coming home without being missed, and you need not tell your Fellow-servants where you are gone, for they will be sure to say, you were in the House but two Minutes ago, which is the Duty of all Servants.

Snuff the Candles with your Fingers, and throw the Snuff on the Floor, then tread it out to prevent stinking: This Method will very much save the Snuffers from wearing out. You ought also to snuff them close to the Tallow, which will make them run, and so encrease the Perquisite of the Cook's Kitchen-Stuff; for she is the Person you ought in Prudence to be well with.

While Grace is saying after Meat, do you and your Brethren take the Chairs from behind the Company, so that when they go to sit again, they may fall backwards, which will make them all merry; but be you so discreet as to hold your Laughter till you get to the Kitchen, and then divert your Fellow-servants.

When you know your Master is most busy in Company, come in and pretend to settle about the Room; and if he chides, say, you thought he rung the Bell. This will divert him from plodding on Business too much, or spending himself in Talk, or racking his Thoughts, all which are hurtful to his Constitution.

If you are ordered to break the Claw of a Crab or a Lobster, clap it between the Sides of the Dining Room Door between the Hinges: Thus you can do it gradually without mashing the Meat, which is often the Case by using the Street-Door-Key, or the Pestle.

F

When you take a foul Plate from any of the Guests, and observe the foul Knife and Fork lying on the Plate, shew your Dexterity, take up the Plate, and throw off the Knife and Fork on the Table, without shaking off the Bones or broken Meat that are left: Then the Guest, who hath more Time than you, will wipe the Fork and Knife already used.

When you carry a Glass of Liquor to any Person who hath called for it, do not bob him on the Shoulder, or cry Sir, or Madam, here's the Glass, that would be unmannerly, as if you had a Mind to force it down one's Throat; but stand at the Person's right Shoulder, and wait his Time; and if he strikes it down with his Elbow by Forgetfulness, that was his Fault and not yours.

When your Mistress sends you for a Hackney Coach in a wet Day, come back in the Coach to save your Cloaths and the Trouble of walking; it is better the Bottom of her Petty-coats should be daggled with your dirty Shoes, than your Livery be spoiled, and yourself get a Cold.

There is no Indignity so great to one of your Station, as that of lighting your Master in the Streets with a Lanthorn; and therefore, it is very honest Policy to try all Arts how to evade it: Besides, it shews your Master to be either poor or covetous, which are the two worst Qualities you can meet with in any Service. When I was under these Circumstances, I made use of several wise Expedients, which I here recommend to you: Sometimes I took a Candle so long, that it reached to the very Top of the Lanthorn, and burned it: But, my Master after a good Beating, ordered me to paste the Top with Paper. I then used a middling Candle, but stuck it so loose in the Socket, that it leaned towards one Side, and burned a whole Quarter of the Horn. Then I used a Bit of Candle of half an Inch, which sunk in the Socket, and melted the Solder, and forced my Master to walk half the Way in the Dark. Then he made me stick two Inches of Candle in the Place where the Socket was; after which, I pretended to stumble, put out the Candle, and broke all the Tin Part to Pieces: At last, he was forced to make use of a Lanthorn-boy out of perfect good Husbandry.

It is much to be lamented, that Gentlemen of our Employment have but two Hands to carry Plates, Dishes, Bottles, and the like out of the Room at Meals; and the Misfortune is still the greater, because one of those Hands is required to open the Door, while you are encumbred with your Load: Therefore, I advise, that the Door may be always left at jarr, so as to open it with your Foot, and then you may carry out Plates and Dishes from your Belly up to your Chin, besides a good Quantity of Things under your Arms, which will save you many a weary Step; but take Care that none of the Burthen falls until you are out of the Room, and if possible, out of Hearing.

If you are sent to the Post-Office with a Letter in a cold rainy Night, step to the Ale-house, and take a Pot, until it is supposed you have done your Errand; but take the next fair Opportunity to put the Letter in carefully, as becomes an honest Servant.

If you are ordered to make Coffee for the Ladies after Dinner, and the Pot happens to boil over, while you are running up for a Spoon to stir it, or are thinking of something else, or struggling with the Chamber-maid for a Kiss, wipe the Sides of the Pot clean with a Dishclout, carry up your Coffee boldly, and when your Lady finds it too weak, and examines you whether it hath not run over, deny the Fact absolutely, swear you put in more Coffee than ordinary, that you never stirred an Inch from it, that you strove to make it better than usual, because your Mistress had Ladies with her, that the Servants in the Kitchen will justify what you say: Upon this, you will find that the other Ladies will pronounce your Coffee to be very good, and your Mistress will confess that her Mouth is out of Taste, and she will for the future suspect herself, and be more cautious in finding Fault. This I would have you do from a Principle of Conscience, for Coffee is very unwholesome; and out of Affection to your Lady, you ought to give it her as weak as possible: And upon this Argument, when you have a Mind to treat any of the Maids with a Dish of fresh Coffee, you may, and ought to subtract a third Part of the Powder, on account of your Lady's Health, and getting her Maids Good-will.

If your Master sends you with a small trifling Present to one of his Friends, be as careful of it as you would be of a Diamond Ring: Therefore, if the Present be only Half a Dozen Pippins, send up the Servant who received the Message to say, that you were ordered to deliver them with your own Hands. This will shew your Exactness and Care to prevent Accidents or Mistakes; and the Gentleman or Lady cannot do less than give you a Shilling: So when your Master receives the like Present, teach the Messenger who brings it to do the same, and give your Master Hints that may stir up his Generosity; for Brother Servants should assist one another, since it is all for your Master's Honour, which is the chief Point to be consulted by every good Servant, and of which he is the best Judge.

When you step but a few Doors off to tattle with a Wench, or take a running Pot of Ale, or to see a Brother Footman going to be hanged, leave the Street Door open, that you may not be forced to knock, and your Master discover you are gone out; for a Quarter of an Hour's Time can do his Service no Injury.

When you take away the remaining Pieces of Bread after Dinner, put them on foul Plates, and press them down with other Plates over them, so as no body can touch them; and so, they will be a good Perquisite to the Blackguard Boy in ordinary.

When you are forced to clean your Master's Shoes with your own Hand, use the Edge of the sharpest Case Knife, and dry them with the Toes an Inch from the Fire, because wet Shoes are dangerous; and besides, by these Arts you will get them the sooner for yourself.

In some Families the Master often sends to the Tavern for a Bottle of Wine, and you are the Messenger: I advise you, therefore, to take the smallest Bottle you can find; but however, make the Drawer give you a full Quart, then you will get a good Sup for yourself, and your Bottle will be filled.

As for a Cork to stop it, you need be at no Trouble, for the Thumb will do as well, or a Bit of dirty chewed Paper.

In all Disputes with Chairmen and Coachmen, for demanding too much, when your Master sends you down to chaffer with them, take Pity of the poor Fellows, and tell your Master that they will not take a Farthing less: It is more for your Interest to get Share of a Pot of Ale, than to save a Shilling for your Master, to whom it is a Trifle.

When you attend your Lady in a dark Night, if she useth her Coach, do not walk by the Coach Side, so as to tire and dirt yourself, but get up into your proper Place, behind it, and so hold the Flambeau sloping forward over the Coach Roof, and when it wants snuffing, dash it against the Corners.

When you leave your Lady at Church on *Sundays*, you have two Hours safe to spend with your Companions at the Alehouse, or over a Beef-Stake and a Pot of Beer at Home with the Cook, and the Maids; and, indeed, poor Servants have so few Opportunities to be happy, that they ought not to lose any.

Never wear Socks when you wait at Meals, on the Account of your own Health, as well as of them who sit at Table; because as most Ladies like the Smell of young Mens Toes, so it is a sovereign Remedy against the Vapours.

Chuse a Service, if you can, where your Livery Colours are least tawdry and distinguishing: Green and Yellow immediately betray your Office, and so do all Kinds of Lace, except Silver, which will hardly fall to your Share, unless with a Duke, or some Prodigal just come to his Estate. The Colours you ought to wish for, are Blue, or Filemot, turned up with Red; which with a borrowed Sword, a borrowed Air, your Master's Linen, and a natural and improved Confidence, will give you what Title you please, where you are not known.

When you carry Dishes or other Things out of the Room at Meals, fill both your Hands as full as possible; for, although you may sometimes spill, and sometimes let fall, yet you will find at the Year's End, you have made great Dispatch, and saved abundance of Time.

If your Master or Mistress happens to walk the Streets, keep on one Side, and as much on the Level with them as you can, which People observing, will either think you do not belong to them, or that you are one of their Companions; but, if either of them happen to turn back and speak to you, so that you are under the Necessity to take off your Hat, use but your Thumb and one Finger, and scratch your Head with the rest.

In Winter Time light the Dining-Room Fire but two Minutes before Dinner is served up, that your Master may see, how saving you are of his Coals.

When you are ordered to stir up the Fire, clean away the Ashes from between the Bars with the Fire-Brush.

When you are ordered to call a Coach, although it be Mid-night, go no further than the Door, for Fear of being out of the Way when you are wanted; and there stand bawling, Coach, Coach, for half an Hour.

Although you Gentlemen in Livery have the Misfortune to be treated scurvily by all Mankind, yet you make a Shift to keep up your Spirits, and sometimes arrive at considerable Fortunes. I was an intimate Friend to one of our Brethren, who was Footman to a Court-Lady: She had an honourable Employment, was Sister to an Earl, and the Widow of a Man of Quality. She observed something so polite in my Friend, the Gracefulness with which he tript before her Chair, and put his Hair under his Hat, that she made him many Advances; and one Day taking the Air in her Coach with *Tom* behind it, the Coachman mistook the Way, and stopt at a priviledged Chapel, where the Couple were marryed, and *Tom* came home in the Chariot by his Lady's Side: But he unfortunately taught her to drink Brandy, of which she died, after having pawned all her Plate to purchase it, and *Tom* is now a Journeyman Malster.

Boucher, the famous Gamester, was another of our Fraternity, and when he was worth 50,000*l.* he dunned the Duke of B——*m* for an Arrear of Wages in his Service: And I could instance many more, particularly another, whose Son had one of the chief Employments at Court; and is sufficient to give you the following Advice, which is to be pert and sawcy to all

Mankind, especially to the Chaplain, the Waiting-woman, and the better Sort of Servants in a Person of Quality's Family, and value not now and then a Kicking, or a Caning; for your Insolence will at last turn to good Account; and from wearing a Livery, you may probably soon carry a Pair of Colours.

When you wait behind a Chair at Meals, keep constantly wriggling the Back of the Chair, that the Person behind whom you stand, may know you are ready to attend him.

When you carry a Parcel of *China* Plates, if they chance to fall, as it is a frequent Misfortune, your Excuse must be, that a Dog ran across you in the Hall; that the Chamber-maid accidentally pushed the Door against you; that a Mop stood across the Entry, and tript you up; that your Sleeve stuck against the Key, or Button of the Lock.

When your Master and Lady are talking together in their Bed-chamber, and you have some Suspicion that you or your Fellow-servants are concerned in what they say, listen at the Door for the publick Good of all the Servants, and join all to take proper Measures for preventing any Innovations that may hurt the Community.

Be not proud in Prosperity: You have heard that Fortune turns on a Wheel; if you have a good Place, you are at the Top of the Wheel. Remember how often you have been stripped, and kicked out of Doors, your Wages all taken up beforehand, and spent in translated red-heeled Shoes, second-hand Toupees, and repaired Lace Ruffles, besides a swinging Debt to the Ale-wife and the Brandy-shop. The neighbouring Tapster, who before would beckon you over to a savoury Bit of Ox-cheek in the Morning, give it you gratis, and only score you up for the Liquor, immediately after you were packt off in Disgrace, carried a Petition to your Master, to be paid out of your Wages, whereof not a Farthing was due, and then pursued you with Bailiffs into every blind Cellar. Remember how soon you grew shabby, thread-bare and out-at-heels; was forced to borrow an old Livery Coat, to make your Appearance while you were looking for a Place; and sneak to every House where you have an old Acquaintance to steal you a Scrap, to keep Life and Soul together; and upon the whole, were in the lowest

Station of Human Life, which, as the old Ballad says, is that of a Skipkennel turned out of Place: I say, remember all this now in your flourishing Condition. Pay your Contributions duly to your late Brothers the Cadets, who are left to the wide World: Take one of them as your Dependant, to send on your Lady's Messages when you have a Mind to go to the Ale-house; slip him out privately now and then a Slice of Bread, and a Bit of cold Meat, your Master can afford it; and if he be not yet put upon the Establishment for a Lodging, let him lye in the Stable, or the Coach-house, or under the Back-stairs, and recommend him to all the Gentlemen who frequent your House, as an excellent Servant.

To grow old in the Office of a Footman, is the highest of all Indignities: Therefore, when you find Years coming on, without Hopes of a Place at Court, a Command in the Army, a Succession to the Stewardship, an Employment in the Revenue (which two last you cannot obtain without Reading and Writing) or running away with your Master's Niece or Daughter; I directly advise you to go upon the Road, which is the only Post of Honour left you: There you will meet many of your old Comrades, and live a short Life and a merry one, and make a Figure at your Exit, wherein I will give you some Instructions.

The last Advice I shall give you, relates to your Behaviour when you are going to be hanged; which, either for robbing your Master, for House-breaking, or going upon the High-way, or in a drunken Quarrel, by killing the first Man you meet, may very probably be your Lot, and is owing to one of these three Qualities; either a Love of good Fellowship, a Generosity of Mind, or too much Vivacity of Spirits. Your good Behaviour on this Article, will concern your whole Community: At your Tryal deny the Fact with all Solemnity of Imprecations: A hundred of your Brethren, if they can be admitted, will attend about the Bar, and be ready upon Demand to give you a good Character before the Court: Let nothing prevail on you to confess, but the Promise of a Pardon for discovering your Comrades: But, I suppose all this to be in vain, for if you escape now, your Fate will be the same another Day. Get a Speech to

be written by the best Author of *Newgate:* Some of your kind
Wenches will provide you with a *Holland* Shirt, and white Cap
crowned with a crimson or black Ribbon: Take Leave chearfully
of all your Friends in *Newgate:* Mount the Cart with Courage:
Fall on your Knees: Lift up your Eyes: Hold a Book in
your Hands although you cannot read a Word: Deny the Fact
at the Gallows: Kiss and forgive the Hangman, and so Farewel:
You shall be buried in Pomp, at the Charge of the Fraternity:
The Surgeon shall not touch a Limb of you; and your Fame
shall continue until a Successor of equal Renown succeeds in
your Place.

CHAP. IV.

Directions to the COACHMAN.

YOU are strictly bound to nothing, but to step into the
Box, and carry your Master or Lady.

Let your Horses be so well trained, that when you
attend your Lady at a Visit, they will wait until you slip into a
neighbouring Ale-house, to take a Pot with a Friend.

When you are in no Humour to drive, tell your Master
that the Horses have got a Cold; that they want Shoeing; that
Rain does them Hurt, and roughens their Coat, and rots the
Harness. This may likewise be applied to the Groom.

If your Master dines with a Country Friend, drink as much
as you can get; because it is allowed, that a good Coachman
never drives so well as when he is drunk, and then shew your
Skill, by driving to an Inch by a Precipice; and say you never
drive so well as when drunk.

If you find any Gentleman fond of one of your Horses, and
willing to give you a Consideration beside the Price; perswade
your Master to sell him, because he is so vicious that you
cannot undertake to drive with him, and is foundered into the
Bargain.

Get a Blackguard-boy to watch your Coach at the Church Door on *Sundays*, that you and your Brother-Coachmen may be merry together at the Ale-house, while your Master and Lady are at Church.

Take Care that your Wheels be good; and get a new Set bought as often as you can, whether you are allowed the old as your Perquisite or not: In one Case it will turn to your honest Profit, and in the other it will be a just Punishment on your Master's Covetousness; and probably the Coach-maker will consider you too.

CHAP. V.

Directions to the GROOM.

YOU are the Servant upon whom the Care of your Master's Honour in all Journies entirely depends: Your Breast is the sole Repository of it. If he travels the Country, and lodgeth at Inns, every Dram of Brandy, every Pot of Ale extraordinary that you drink, raiseth his Character; and therefore, his Reputation ought to be dear to you; and, I hope, you will not stint yourself in either. The Smith, the Sadler's Journeyman, the Cook at the Inn, the Ostler and the Boot-catcher, ought all by your Means to partake of your Master's Generosity: Thus, his Fame will reach from one County to another; and what is a Gallon of Ale, or a Pint of Brandy in his Worship's Pocket? And, although he should be in the Number of those who value their Credit less than their Purse, yet your Care of the former ought to be so much the greater. His Horse wanted two Removes; your Horse wanted Nails; his Allowance of Oats and Beans was greater than the Journey required; a third Part may be retrenched, and turned into Ale or Brandy; and thus his Honour may be preserved by your Discretion, and less Expence to him; or, if he travels with no other Servant, the Matter is easily made up in the Bill between you and the Tapster.

Therefore, as soon as you alight at the Inn, deliver your Horses to the Stable-boy, and let him gallop them to the next Pond; then call for a Pot of Ale, for it is very fit that a Christian should drink before a Beast. Leave your Master to the Care of the Servants in the Inn, and your Horses to those in the Stable: Thus both he and they are left in the properest Hands; but you are to provide for yourself; therefore get your Supper, drink freely, and go to Bed without troubling your Master, who is in better Hands than yours. The Ostler is an honest Fellow, loves Horses in his Heart, and would not wrong the dumb Creatures for the World. Be tender of your Master, and order the Servants not to wake him too early. Get your Breakfast before he is up, that he may not wait for you; make the Ostler tell him the Roads are very good, and the Miles short; but advise him to stay a little longer until the Weather clears up, for he is afraid there will be Rain, and he will be Time enough after Dinner.

Let your Master mount before you, out of Good-manners. As he is leaving the Inn, drop a good Word in Favour of the Ostler, what Care he took of the Cattle; and add, that you never saw civiller Servants. Let your Master ride on before, and do you stay until the Landlord hath given you a Dram; then gallop after him thro' the Town or Village with full Speed, for fear he should want you, and to shew your Horsemanship.

If you are a Piece of a Farrier, as every good Groom ought to be, get Sack, Brandy, or Strong-beer to rub your Horses Heels every Night, and be not sparing, for (if any be spent) what is left, you know how to dispose of it.

Consider your Master's Health, and rather than let him take long Journies, say the Cattle are weak, and fallen in their Flesh with hard Riding; tell him of a very good Inn five Miles nearer than he intended to go; or leave one of his Horses Fore Shoes loose in the Morning; or contrive that the Saddle may pinch the Beast in his Withers; or keep him without Corn all Night and Morning, so that he may tire on the Road; or wedge a thin Plate of Iron between the Hoof and the Shoe, to make him halt; and all this in perfect Tenderness to your Master.

When you are going to be hired, and the Gentleman asks you, Whether you are apt to be drunk? Own freely, that you love a Cup of good Ale; but that it is your Way, drunk or sober, never to neglect your Horses.

When your Master hath a Mind to ride out for the Air, or for Pleasure, if any private Business of your own makes it inconvenient for you to attend him; give him to understand, that the Horses want bleeding or purging; that his own Pad hath got a Surfeit; or, that the Saddle wants stuffing; and his Bridle is gone to be mended: This you may honestly do, because it will be no Injury to the Horses or your Master; and at the same time shews the great Care you have of the poor dumb Creatures.

If there be a particular Inn in the Town whither you are going, and where you are well acquainted with the Ostler or Tapster, and the People of the House; find Fault with the other Inns, and recommend your Master thither; it may probably be a Pot and a Dram or two more in your Way, and to your Master's Honour.

If your Master sends you to buy Hay, deal with those who will be the most liberal to you; for Service being no Inheritance, you ought not to let slip any lawful and customary Perquisite. If your Master buys it himself, he wrongs you; and to teach him his Duty, be sure to find fault with that Hay as long as it lasts; and, if the Horses thrive with it, the Fault is yours.

Hay and Oats in the Management of a skilful Groom, will make excellent Ale as well as Brandy; but this I only hint.

When your Master dines, or lies at a Gentleman's House in the Country, altho' there be no Groom, or he be gone abroad, or that the Horses have been quite neglected; be sure to employ one of the Servants to hold the Horse when your Master mounts. This I would have you do, when your Master only alights, to call in for a few Minutes: For Brother-servants must always befriend one another, and this also concerns your Master's Honour; because he cannot do less than give a Piece of Money to him who holds his Horse.

In long Journies, ask your Master Leave to give Ale to the Horses; carry two Quarts full to the Stable, pour Half a Pint into a Bowl, and if they will not drink it, you and the Ostler must do the best you can; perhaps they may be in a better Humour at the next Inn, for I would have you never fail to make the Experiment.

When you go to air your Horses in the Park, or the Fields, give them to a Horse-boy, or one of the Blackguards, who being lighter than you, may be trusted to run Races with less Damage to the Horses, and teach them to leap over Hedges and Ditches, while you are drinking a friendly Pot with your Brother Grooms: But sometimes you and they may run Races yourselves for the Honour of your Horses, and of your Masters.

Never stint your Horses at home in Hay and Oats, but fill the Rack to the Top, and the Manger to the Brim: For you would take it ill to be stinted yourself, although perhaps, they may not have the Stomach to eat; consider, they have no Tongues to ask. If the Hay be thrown down, there is no Loss, for it will make Litter and save Straw.

When your Master is leaving a Gentleman's House in the Country, where he hath lain a Night; then consider his Honour: Let him know how many Servants there are of both Sexes, who expect Vails; and give them their Cue to attend in two Lines as he leaves the House; but, desire him not to trust the Money with the Butler, for fear he should cheat the rest: This will force your Master to be more generous; and then you may take Occasion to tell your Master, that Squire such a one, whom you lived with last, always gave so much apiece to the common Servants, and so much to the House-keeper, and the rest, naming at least double to what he intended to give; but, be sure to tell the Servants what a good Office you did them: This will gain you Love, and your Master Honour.

You may venture to be drunk much oftener than the Coachman, whatever he pretends to alledge in his own Behalf, because you hazard no Body's Neck but your own; for, the Horse will probably take so much Care of himself, as to come off with only a Strain or a Shoulder-slip.

When you carry your Master's Riding-Coat in a Journey,

wrap your own in it, and buckle them up close with a Strap, but turn you Master's Inside out, to preserve the Outside from Wet and Dirt; thus, when it begins to rain, your Master's Coat will be first ready to be given him; and, if it get more Hurt than yours, he can afford it better, for your Livery must always serve its Year's Apprenticeship.

When you come to your Inn with the Horses wet and dirty after hard Riding, and are very hot, make the Ostler immediately plunge them into Water up to their Bellies, and allow them to drink as much as they please; but, be sure to gallop them full-speed a Mile at least, to dry their Skins and warm the Water in their Bellies. The Ostler understands his Business, leave all to his Discretion, while you get a Pot of Ale and some Brandy at the Kitchen Fire to comfort your heart.

If your Horse drop a Fore-Shoe, be so careful to alight and take it up: Then ride with all the Speed you can (the Shoe in your Hand that every Traveller may observe your Care) to the next Smith on the Road, make him put it on immediately, that your Master may not wait for you, and that the poor Horse may be as short a Time as possible without a Shoe.

When your Master lies at a Gentleman's House, if you find the Hay and Oats are good, complain aloud of their Badness; this will get you the Name of a diligent Servant; and be sure to cram the Horses with as much Oats as they can eat, while you are there, and you may give them so much the less for some Days at the Inns, and turn the Oats into Ale. When you leave the Gentleman's House, tell your Master what a covetous Huncks that Gentleman was, that you got nothing but Butter-milk or Water to drink; this will make your Master out of Pity allow you a Pot of Ale the more at the next Inn: But, if you happen to get drunk in a Gentleman's House, your Master cannot be angry, because it cost him nothing; and so you ought to tell him as well as you can in your present Condition, and let him know it is both for his and the Gentleman's Honour to make a Friend's Servant welcome.

A Master ought always to love his Groom, to put him into a handsome Livery, and to allow him a Silver-laced Hat. When you are in this Equipage, all the Honours he receives on the Road are owing to you alone: That he is not turned out of the Way by every Carrier, is caused by the Civility he receives at second Hand from the Respect paid to your Livery.

You may now and then lend your Master's Pad to a Brother Servant, or your favourite Maid, for a short Jaunt, or hire him for a Day, because the Horse is spoiled for want of Exercise: And if your Master happens to want his Horse, or hath a Mind to see the Stable, curse that Rogue the Helper who is gone out with the Key.

When you want to spend an Hour or two with your Companions at the Ale-House, and that you stand in need of a reasonable Excuse for your Stay, go out of the Stable Door, or the back Way, with an old Bridle, Girth, or Stirrup Leather in your Pocket, and on your Return, come home by the Street Door with the same Bridle, Girth, or Stirrup Leather dangling in your Hand, as if you came from the Saddler's, where you were getting the same mended; (if you are not missed all is well), but, if you are met by your Master, you will have the Reputation of a careful Servant. This I have known practised with good Success.

CHAP. VI.

Directions to the HOUSE STEWARD, *and* LAND STEWARD.

L ORD *Peterborough*'s Steward that pulled down his House, sold the Materials, and charged my Lord with Repairs. Take Money for Forbearance from Tenants. Renew Leases and get by them, and sell Woods. Lend my Lord his own Money. (*Gilblas* said much of this, to whom I refer.)

CHAP. VII.

Directions to the PORTER.

IF your Master be a Minister of State, let him be at Home to none but his Pimp, or Chief Flatterer, or one of his Pension-ary Writers, or his hired Spy, and Informer, or his Printer in ordinary, or his City Sollicitor, or a Land-Jobber, or his Inventor of new Funds, or a Stock-Jobber.

CHAP. VIII.

Directions to the CHAMBER-MAID.

THE Nature of your Employment differs according to the Quality, the Pride, or the Wealth of the Lady you serve; and this Treatise is to be applied to all Sorts of Families; so, that I find myself under great Difficulty to adjust the Business for which you are hired. In a Family where there is a tolerable Estate, you differ from the House-Maid, and in that View I give my Directions. Your particular Province is your Lady's Chamber, where you make the Bed, and put Things in Order; and if you live in the Country, you take Care of Rooms where Ladies lie who come into the House, which brings in all the Vails that fall to your Share. Your usual Lover, as I take it, is the Coachman; but, if you are under Twenty, and tolerably handsome, perhaps a Footman may cast his Eyes on you.

Get your favourite Footman to help you in making your Lady's Bed; and, if you serve a young Couple, the Footman and you, as you are turning up the Bed-Cloaths, will make the prettiest Observations in the World; which, whispered about, will be very entertaining to the whole Family, and get among the Neighbourhood.

Do not carry down the necessary Vessels for the Fellows to see, but empty them out of the Window, for your Lady's Credit. It is highly improper for Men Servants to know that fine Ladies have Occasion for such Utensils; and do not scour the Chamber pot, because the Smell is wholesome.

If you happen to break any China with the Top of the Whisk on the Mantle-tree or the Cabinet, gather up the Fragments, put them together as well as you can, and place them behind the rest, so that when your Lady comes to discover them, you may safely say they were broke long ago, before you came to the Service. This will save your Lady many an Hour's Vexation.

It sometimes happens that a Looking-Glass is broken by the same Means, while you are looking another Way, as you sweep the Chamber, the long End of the Brush strikes against the Glass, and breaks it to Shivers. This is the extremest of all Misfortunes, and all Remedy desperate in Appearance, because it is impossible to be concealed. Such a fatal Accident once happened in a great Family where I had the Honour to be a Footman; and I will relate the Particulars, to shew the Ingenuity of the poor Chamber-maid on so sudden and dreadful an Emergency, which perhaps may help to sharpen your Invention, if your evil Star should ever give you the like Occasion. The poor Girl had broken a large Japan Glass of great Value, with a Stroke of her Brush: She had not considered long, when by a prodigious Presence of Mind, she locked the Door, stole into the Yard, brought a Stone of three Pound Weight into the Chamber, laid it on the Hearth just under the Looking-Glass, then broke a Pane in the Sash Window that looked into the same Yard, so shut the Door, and went about her other Affairs. Two Hours after, the Lady goes into the Chamber, sees the Glass broken, the Stone lying under, and a whole Pane in the Window destroyed; from all which Circumstances, she concluded just as the Maid could have wished, that some idle Straggler in the Neighbourhood, or perhaps one of the Out-Servants, had through Malice,

G

Accident, or Carelessness, flung in the Stone and done the Mischief. Thus far all Things went well, and the Girl concluded herself out of Danger: But, it was her ill Fortune, that a few Hours after in came the Parson of the Parish, and the Lady (naturally) told him the Accident, which you may believe had much discomposed her; but the Minister, who happened to understand Mathematicks, after examining the Situation of the Yard, the Window, and the Chimney, soon convinced the Lady, that the Stone could never reach the Looking-Glass without taking three Turns in its Flight from the Hand that threw it; and the Maid being proved to have swept the Room the same Morning, was strictly examined, but constantly denied that she was guilty upon her Salvation, offering to take her Oath upon the Bible, before his Reverence, that she was innocent as the Child unborn; yet the poor Wench was turned off, which I take to have been hard Treatment, considering her Ingenuity: However, this may be a Direction to you in the like Case, to contrive a Story that will better hang together. For Instance, you might say, that while you were at Work with the Mop, or Brush, a Flash of Lightning came suddenly in at the Window, which almost blinded you; that you immediately heard the ringing of broken Glass on the Hearth; that, as soon as you recovered your Eyes, you saw the Looking-Glass all broken to Pieces: Or, you may alledge, that observing the Glass a little covered with Dust, and going very gently to wipe it, you suppose the Moisture of the Air had dissolved the Glue or Cement, which made it fall to the Ground: Or, as soon as the Mischief is done, you may cut the Cords that fastened the Glass to the Wainscot, and so let it fall flat on the Ground; run out in a Fright, tell your Lady, curse the Upholsterer; and declare how narrowly you escaped, that it did not fall upon your Head. I offer these Expedients, from a Desire I have to defend the Innocent; for Innocent you certainly must be, if you did not break the Glass on purpose, which I would by no Means excuse, except upon great Provocations.

Oil the Tongs, Poker, and Fire-shovel up to the Top, not only to keep them from rusting, but likewise to prevent meddling People from wasting your Master's Coals with stirring the Fire.

When you are in haste, sweep the Dust into a Corner of the Room, but leave your Brush upon it, that it may not be seen, for that would disgrace you.

Never wash your Hands, or put on a clean Apron, until you have made your Lady's Bed, for fear of rumpling your Apron, or fouling your Hands again.

When you bar the Window-shuts of your Lady's Bed-chamber at Nights, leave open the Sashes, to let in the fresh Air, and sweeten the Room against Morning.

In the Time when you leave the Windows open for Air, leave Books, or something else on the Window-seat, that they may get Air too.

When you sweep your Lady's Room, never stay to pick up foul Smocks, Handkerchiefs, Pinners, Pin-cushions, Tea-spoons, Ribbons, Slippers, or whatever lieth in your Way; but sweep all into a Corner, and then you may take them up in a Lump, and save Time.

Making Beds in hot Weather is a very laborious Work, and you will be apt to sweat; therefore, when you find the Drops running down from your Forehead, wipe them off with a Corner of the Sheet, that they may not be seen on the Bed.

When your Lady sends you to wash a *China*-cup, and it happen to fall, bring it up, and swear you did but just touch it with your Hand, when it broke into *three Halves*: And here I must inform you, as well as your fellow Servants, that you ought never to be without an Excuse; it doth no Harm to your Master, and it lessens your Fault: As in this Instance; I do not commend you for breaking the Cup; it is certain you did not break it on purpose, and the Thing is possible, that it might break in your Hand.

You are sometimes desirous to see a Funeral, a Quarrel, a Man going to be hanged, a Wedding, a Bawd carted, or the like: As they pass by in the Street, you lift up the Sash suddenly; there by Misfortune it sticks: This was no Fault of yours; young Women are curious by Nature; you have no Remedy, but to cut the Cord; and lay the Fault upon the Carpenter, unless no Body saw you, and then you are as innocent as any Servant in the House.

Wear your Lady's Smock when she has thrown it off; it will do you Credit, save your own Linen, and be not a Pin the worse.

When you put a clean Pillow-case on your Lady's Pillow, be sure to fasten it well with three corking Pins, that it may not fall off in the Night.

When you spread Bread and Butter for Tea, be sure that all the Holes in the Loaf be left full of Butter, to keep the Bread moist against Dinner; and let the Mark of your Thumb be seen only upon one End of every Slice, to shew your Cleanliness.

When you are ordered to open or lock any Door, Trunk, or Cabinet, and miss the proper Key, or cannot distinguish it in the Bunch; try the first Key that you can thrust in, and turn it with all your Strength until you open the Lock, or break the Key; for your Lady will reckon you a Fool to come back and do nothing.

CHAP. IX.

Directions to the WAITING MAID.

TWO Accidents have happened to lessen the Comforts and Profits of your Employment; First, that execrable Custom got among Ladies, of trucking their old Cloaths for *China*, or turning them to cover easy Chairs, or making them into patch-work for Screens, Stools, Cushions, and the like. The Second is, the Invention of small Chests and Trunks, with Lock and Key, wherein they keep the Tea and Sugar, without which it is impossible for a Waiting-maid to live: For, by this means, you are forced to buy brown Sugar, and pour Water upon the Leaves, when they have lost all their Spirit and Taste: I cannot contrive any perfect Remedy against either of these two Evils. As to the former, I think there should be a general Confederacy of all the Servants in every Family, for the publick Good, to drive those *China* Hucksters from the Doors; and as to the latter, there is no other Method to relieve your selves, but by a false Key, which is a Point both difficult and dangerous to compass; but, as to the Circumstance of Honesty in procuring one, I am under no Doubt, when your Mistress gives you so just a Provocation, by refusing you an ancient and legal Perquisite. The Mistress of the Tea-shop may now and then give you half an Ounce, but that will be only a Drop in the Bucket: Therefore, I fear you must be forced, like the rest of your Sisters, to run in Trust, and pay for it out of your Wages, as far as they will go, which you can easily make up other ways, if your Lady be handsome, or her Daughters have good Fortunes.

If you are in a great Family, and my Lady's Woman, my Lord may probably like you, although you are not half so handsome as his own Lady. In this Case, take Care to get as much out of him as you can; and never allow him the smallest Liberty, not the squeezing of your Hand, unless he puts a Guinea into it; so, by degrees, make him pay accordingly for every new Attempt, doubling upon him in proportion to the Concessions you allow, and always struggling, and threatning to cry out, or tell your Lady, although you receive his Money: Five Guineas for handling your Breast is a cheap Pennyworth, although you seem to resist with all your Might; but never allow him the last Favour under a hundred Guineas, or a Settlement of twenty Pounds a Year for Life.

In such a Family, if you are handsome, you will have the Choice of three Lovers; the Chaplain, the Steward, and my Lord's Gentleman. I would first advise you to chuse the Steward; but, if you happen to be young with Child by my Lord, you must take up with the Chaplain. I like my Lord's Gentleman the least of the three; for he is usually vain and sawcy from the Time he throws off his Livery; and, if he misseth a Pair of Colours, or a Tide-waiter's Place, he hath no Remedy but the Highway.

I must caution you particularly against my Lord's eldest

Son: If you are dextrous enough, it is odds that you may draw
him in to marry you, and make you a Lady: If he be a common
Rake, or a Fool, (and he must be one or the other) but, if the
former, avoid him like *Satan*, for he stands in less Awe of a
Mother, than my Lord doth of a Wife; and, after ten thousand
Promises, you will get nothing from him, but a big Belly,
or a Clap, and probably both together.

When your Lady is ill, and after a very bad Night, is getting
a little Nap in the Morning, if a Footman comes with a Message
to enquire how she doth, do not let the Compliment be lost,
but shake her gently until she wakes; then deliver the Message,
receive her Answer, and leave her to sleep.

If you are so happy as to wait on a young Lady with a great
Fortune, you must be an ill Manager if you cannot get five
or six hundred Pounds for disposing of her. Put her often
in Mind, that she is rich enough to make any Man happy;
that there is no real Happiness but in Love; that she hath
Liberty to chuse wherever she pleaseth, and not by the Direction of Parents, who never give Allowances for an innocent
Passion; that there are a World of handsome, fine, sweet
young Gentlemen in Town, who would be glad to die at her
Feet; that the Conversation of two Lovers is a Heaven upon
Earth; that Love like Death equals all Conditions; that if she
should cast her Eyes upon a young Fellow below her in Birth
and Estate, his marrying her, would make him a Gentleman;
that you saw Yesterday on the *Mall*, the prettiest Ensign;
and, that if you had forty thousand Pounds it should be at
his Service. Take care that every Body should know what
Lady you live with; how great a Favourite you are; and, that
she always takes your Advice. Go often to St. *James's* Park, the
fine Fellows will soon discover you, and contrive to slip a
Letter into your Sleeve or your Bosom: Pull it out in a Fury,
and throw it on the Ground, unless you find at least two
Guineas along with it; but in that Case, seem not to find it,
and to think he was only playing the Wag with you: When
you come home, drop the Letter carelessly in your Lady's
Chamber; she finds it, is angry; protest you knew nothing
of it, only you remember, that a Gentleman in the Park

struggled to kiss you, and you believe it was he that put the Letter in your Sleeve or Pettycoat; and, indeed, he was as pretty a Man as ever she saw: That she may burn the Letter if she pleaseth. If your Lady be wise, she will burn some other Paper before you, and read the Letter when you are gone down. You must follow this Practice as often as you safely can; but, let him who pays you best with every Letter, be the handsomest Man. If a Footman presumes to bring a Letter to the House, to be delivered to you, for your Lady, although it come from your best Customer, throw it at his Head; call him impudent Rogue and Villain, and shut the Door in his Face; run up to your Lady, and as a Proof of your Fidelity, tell her what you have done.

I could enlarge very much upon this Subject, but I trust to your own Discretion.

If you serve a Lady who is a little disposed to Gallantries, you will find it a Point of great Prudence how to manage: Three Things are necessary. First, how to please your Lady; Secondly, how to prevent Suspicion in the Husband, or among the Family; and lastly, but principally, how to make it most for your own Advantage. To give you full Directions in this important Affair, would require a large Volume. All Assignations at home are dangerous, both to your Lady and your self; and therefore contrive as much as possible, to have them in a third Place; especially if your Lady, as it is a hundred odds, entertains more Lovers than one, each of whom is often more jealous than a thousand Husbands; and, very unlucky Rencounters may often happen under the best Management. I need not warn you to employ your good Offices chiefly in favour of those, whom you find most liberal; yet, if your Lady should happen to cast an Eye upon a handsome Footman, you should be generous enough to bear with her Humour, which is no Singularity, but a very natural Appetite: It is still the safest of all home Intrigues, and was formerly the least suspected, until of late Years it hath grown more common. The great danger is, lest this Kind of Gentry, dealing too often in bad Ware, may happen not to be sound; and then, your Lady and you are in a very bad Way, although not altogether desperate.

But, to say the Truth, I confess it is a great Presumption in me, to offer you any Instructions in the Conduct of your Lady's Amours, wherein your whole Sisterhood is already so expert, and deeply learned; although it be much more difficult to compass, than that Assistance which my Brother Footmen give their Masters, on the like Occasion; and therefore, I leave this Affair to be treated by some abler Pen.

When you lock up a Silk Mantua, or laced Head in a Trunk or Chest, leave a Piece out, that when you open the Trunk again, you may know where to find it.

CHAP. X.

Directions to the HOUSE-MAID.

IF your Master and Lady go into the Country for a Week or more, never wash the Bed-chamber or Dining-room, until just the Hour before you expect them to return: Thus, the Rooms will be perfectly clean to receive them, and you will not be at the Trouble to wash them so soon again.

I am very much offended with those Ladies, who are so proud and lazy, that they will not be at the Pains of stepping into the Garden to pluck a Rose, but keep an odious Implement sometimes in the Bed-chamber itself, or at least in a dark Closet adjoining, which they make Use of to ease their worst Necessities; and, you are the usual Carriers away of the Pan, which maketh not only the Chamber, but even their Cloaths offensive, to all who come near. Now, to cure them of this odious Practice, let me advise you, on whom this Office lies, to convey away this Utensil, that you will do it openly, down the great Stairs, and in the Presence of the Footmen; and, if any Body knocks, to open the Street-door, while you have the Vessel filled in your Hands: This, if any Thing can, will make your Lady take the Pains of evacuating her Person in the proper Place, rather than expose her Filthiness to all the Men Servants in the House.

Leave a Pail of dirty Water with the Mop in it, a Coal-box, a Bottle, a Broom, a Chamber-pot, and such other unsightly Things, either in a blind Entry, or upon the darkest Part of the Back-stairs, that they may not be seen; and, if People break their Shins by trampling on them, it is their own Fault.

Never empty the Chamber-pots until they are quite full: If that happens in the Night, empty them into the Street; if, in the Morning, into the Garden; for it would be an endless Work to go a dozen Times from the Garret and upper Rooms, down to the Back-sides; but, never wash them in any other Liquor except their own: What cleanly Girl would be dabbling in other Folks Urine? And besides, the Smell of Stale, as I observed before, is admirable against the Vapours; which, a hundred to one, may be your Lady's Case.

Brush down the Cobwebs with a Broom that is wet and dirty, which will make them stick the faster to it, and bring them down more effectually.

When you rid up the Parlour Hearth in a Morning, throw the last Night's Ashes into a Sieve; and what falls through, as you carry it down, will serve instead of Sand for the Room and the Stairs.

When you have scoured the Brasses and Irons in the Parlour Chimney, lay the foul wet Clout upon the next Chair, that your Lady may see you have not neglected your Work: Observe the same Rule, when you clean the Brass Locks, only with this addition, to leave the Marks of your Fingers on the Doors, to shew you have not forgot.

Leave your Lady's Chamber-pot in the Bed-chamber Window, all Day to air.

Bring up none but large Coals to the Dining-room and your Lady's Chamber; they make the best Fires, and, if you find them too big, it is easy to break them on the Marble Hearth.

When you go to Bed, be sure take care of Fire; and therefore blow the Candle out with your Breath, and then thrust it under your Bed. *Note.* The Smell of the Snuff is very good against Vapours.

Persuade the Footman who got you with Child, to marry you before you are six Months gone; and, if your Lady asks you, why you would take a Fellow who was not worth a Groat? Let your Answer be, That Service is no Inheritance.

When your Lady's Bed is made, put the Chamber-pot under it, but in such a manner, as to thrust the Valance along with it, that it may be full in Sight, and ready for your lady when she hath Occasion to use it.

Lock up a Cat or a Dog in some Room or Closet, so as to make such a Noise all over the House, as may frighten away the Thieves, if any should attempt to break or steal in.

When you wash any of the Rooms towards the Street, over Night, throw the foul Water out of the Street Door; but, be sure not to look before you, for fear those on whom the Water lights, might think you uncivil, and that you did it on purpose. If he who suffers, breaks the Windows in revenge, and your Lady chides you, and gives positive Orders that you should carry the Payl down, and empty it in the Sink, you have an easy Remedy. When you wash an upper Room, carry down the Payl so as to let the Water dribble on the Stairs all the way down to the Kitchen; by which, not only your Load will be lighter, but you will convince your Lady, that it is better to throw the Water out of the Windows, or down the Street-Door Steps: Besides, this latter Practice will be very diverting to you and the Family in a frosty Night, to see a hundred People falling on their Noses or Back-sides before your Door, when the Water is frozen.

Polish and brighten the Marble Hearths and Chimney-pieces with a Clout dipt in Grease; nothing makes them shine so well; and, it is the Business of the Ladies to take Care of their Pettycoats.

If your Lady be so nice that she will have the Room scoured with Freestone, be sure to leave the Marks of the Freestone six Inches deep round the Bottom of the Wainscot, that your Lady may see your Obedience to her Orders.

CHAP. XI.

Directions to the DAIRY-MAID.

FATIGUE of making Butter; Put scalding Water in your Churn, although in Summer, and churn close to the Kitchen Fire, and with Cream of a Week old. Keep Cream for your Sweet-heart.

CHAP. XII.

Directions to the CHILDRENS-MAID.

IF a Child be sick, give it whatever it wants to eat or drink, although particularly forbid by the Doctor: For what we long for in Sickness, will do us good; and throw the Physick out of the Window; the Child will love you the better; but bid it not tell. Do the same to your Lady when she longs for any thing in Sickness, and engage it will do her good.

If your Mistress comes to the Nursery, and offers to whip a Child, snatch it out of her Hands in a Rage, and tell her she is the cruellest Mother you ever saw: She will chide, but love you the better. Tell the Children Stories of Spirits, when they offer to cry, &c.

Be sure to wean the Children, &c.

CHAP. XIII.

Directions to the NURSE.

IF you happen to let the Child fall, and lame it, be sure never confess it; and, if it dies, all is safe.

Contrive to be with Child, as soon as you can, while you are giving Suck, that you may be ready for another Service, when the Child you nurse dies, or is weaned.

CHAP. XIV.

Directions to the LAUNDRESS.

IF you singe the Linnen with the Iron, rub the Place with Flour, Chalk, or white Powder; and if nothing will do, wash it so long, till it be either not to be seen, or torn to Rags. Always wash your own Linnen first.

About tearing Linnen in washing.

When your Linnen is pinned on the Line, or on a Hedge, and it rains, whip it off, although you tear it, &c. But the Place for hanging them, is on young Fruit Trees, especially in Blossom; the Linnen cannot be torn, and the Trees give them a fine Smell.

CHAP. XV.

Directions to the HOUSE-KEEPER.

YOU must always have a favourite Footman whom you can depend upon; and order him to be very watchful when the Second Course is taken off, that it be brought safely to your Office, that you and the Steward may have a Tit-bit together.

CHAP. XVI.

Directions to the TUTORESS, *or* GOVERNESS.

SAY the Children have sore Eyes; Miss *Betty* won't take to her Book, &c.

Make the Misses read *French* and *English* Novels, and *French* Romances, and all the Comedies writ in King *Charles* II. and King *William*'s Reigns, to soften their Nature, and make them tender-hearted, &c.

FINIS.

Some Considerations in the Choice of a Recorder

SOME
CONSIDERATIONS
Humbly offered to the Right Honourable the
LORD-MAYOR,
The COURT of ALDERMEN, and COMMON
COUNCIL of the Honourable City of *Dublin*,
in the Choice of a RECORDER.

THE Office of Recorder to this City, being vacant by the
Death of a very worthy Gentleman, it is said that five
or six Persons are solliciting to succeed him in the Employment. I am a Stranger to all their Persons, and to most of
their Characters; which latter, I hope, will, at this Time, be
canvassed with more Decency, than it sometimes happens
upon the like Occasions.

THEREFORE, as I am wholly impartial, I can with more
Freedom deliver my Thoughts, how the several Persons and
Parties concerned ought to proceed, in electing a Recorder
for this great and antient City.

AND, *first*, as it is a very natural, so I can, by no Means,
think it an unreasonable Opinion, that the Sons, or near
Relations of Aldermen, and other deserving Citizens, should
be duly regarded as proper Competitors for any Employment
in the City's Disposal, provided they be equally qualified with
other Candidates; and provided, that such Employments
require no more than common Abilities, and common Honesty.
But in the Choice of a Recorder, the Case is entirely different:
He ought to be a Person of good Abilities in his Calling, of an
unspotted Character, an able Practitioner, one who hath

occasionally merited of this City before; he ought to be of some Maturity in Years, a Member of Parliament, and likely to continue so, regular in his Life, firm in his Loyalty to the *Hanover* Succession, indulgent to tender Consciences; but, at the same time, a firm Adherer to the established Church. If he be such a one who hath already sate in Parliament, it ought to be inquired of what Weight he was there? Whether he voted on all Occasions for the Good of his Country, and particularly for advancing the Trade and Freedom of this City? Whether he be engaged in any Faction, either national or religious? And *lastly*, Whether he be a Man of Courage, not to be drawn from his Duty by the Frowns or Menaces of Power, nor capable to be corrupted by Allurements or Bribes? These, and many other Particulars, are of infinitely more Consequence, than that single Circumstance of being descended by a direct, or collateral Line from any Alderman, or distinguished Citizen alive or dead.

THERE is not a Dealer, or Shop-keeper in this City, of any Substance, whose Thriving, less or more, may not depend upon the good or ill Conduct of a Recorder. He is to watch every Motion in Parliament, that may, in the least, affect the Freedom, Trade, or Welfare of it.

IN this approaching Election, the Commoners, as they are a numerous Body, so they seem to be most concerned in Point of Interest, and their Interest ought to be most regarded; because it altogether depends upon the true Interest of the City; they have no private Views, and giving their Votes, as I am informed, by balotting, they lye under no Awe, or Fear of disobliging Competitors. It is, therefore, hoped, that they will duly consider which of the Candidates is most likely to advance the Trade of themselves and their Brother Citizens, to defend their Liberties both in and out of Parliament, against any Attempts of Encroachment or Oppression: And so GOD direct them in the Choice of a Recorder, who may for many Years supply that important Office with Skill, Diligence, Courage, and Fidelity. And let all the People say *Amen*.

Preface to Mrs. Barber's Poems

SWIFT'S Prefatory Letter to Poems on Several Occasions by Mrs. Mary Barber 1734

To the Right Honourable *John*, Earl of *Orrery*.

My Lord,

I LATELY receiv'd a Letter from Mrs. *Barber*; wherein she desires my Opinion about dedicating her Poems to your Lordship; and seems in Pain to know how far she may be allow'd to draw your Character, which is a Right claim'd by all Dedicators. And she thinks this the more incumbent on her, from the surprising Instances of your Generosity and Favour that she hath already receiv'd, and which she hath been so unfashionable to publish where-ever she goes. This makes her apprehend, that all she can say to your Lordship's Advantage, will be interpreted as the mere Effect of Flattery, under the Style and Title of Gratitude.

I sent her Word, that I could be of no Service to her upon this Article: Yet I confess, my Lord, that all those who are thoroughly acquainted with her, will impute her Encomiums to a sincere, but overflowing Spirit of Thankfulness, as well as to the humble Opinion she hath of herself. Altho' the World in general may possibly continue in its usual Sentiments, and list her in the common Herd of Dedicators.

Therefore, upon the most mature Deliberation, I concluded that the Office of setting out your Lordship's Character, will not come properly from her Pen, for her own Reasons: I mean the great Favours you have already conferr'd upon her. And God forbid, that your Character should not have a much stronger Support. You are hourly gaining the Love, Esteem, and Respect of wise and good Men: And in due Time, if Mrs. *Barber* can but have a little Patience, you will bring them all over in both Kingdoms to a Man: I confess, the Number is not great; but that is not your Lordship's Fault, and therefore, in Reason, you ought to be contented.

I guess the Topicks she intends to insist on: Your Learning, your Genius, your Affability, Generosity, the Love you bear to your native Country, and your Compassion for this; the Goodness of your Nature, your Humility, Modesty, and Condescension, your most agreeable Conversation, suited to all Tempers, Conditions, and Understandings: Perhaps she may be so weak to add the Regularity of your Life, that you believe a God and Providence, that you are a firm Christian, according to the Doctrine of the Church establish'd in both Kingdoms.

These and other Topicks I imagine Mrs. *Barber* designs to insist on, in the Dedication of her Poems to your Lordship; but I think she will better shew her Prudence by omitting them all. And yet, my Lord, I cannot disapprove of her Ambition, so justly plac'd in the Choice of a Patron; and at the same Time declare my Opinion, that she deserveth your Protection on account of her Wit and good Sense, as well as of her Humility, her Gratitude, and many other Virtues. I have read most of her Poems; and believe your Lordship will observe, that they generally contain something new and useful, tending to the Reproof of some Vice or Folly, or recommending some Virtue. She never writes on a Subject with general unconnected Topicks, but always with a Scheme and Method driving to some particular End; wherein many Writers in Verse, and of some Distinction, are so often known to fail. In short, she seemeth to have a true poetical Genius, better cultivated than could well be expected, either from her Sex, or the Scene she hath acted in, as the Wife of a Citizen. Yet I am assured, that no Woman was ever more useful to her Husband in the Way of his Business. Poetry hath only been her favourite Amusement; for which she hath one Qualification, that I wish all good Poets possess'd a Share of, I mean, that she is ready to take Advice, and submit to have her Verses corrected, by those who are generally allow'd to be the best Judges.

I have, at her Intreaty, suffer'd her to take a Copy of this Letter, and given her the Liberty to make it public. For which I ought to desire your Lordship's Pardon: But she was of Opinion it might do her some Service; and therefore I comply'd. I am, my Lord, with the truest Esteem and Respect,

Your *Lordship*'s

Most Obedient Servant,

JONATHAN SWIFT.

Dublin, August 20,
1733.

Advice to the Freemen of Dublin

ADVICE

TO THE

Free-Men of the City of *Dublin* in the Choice of a Member to Represent them in PARLIAMENT.

THose few Writers, who since the Death of Alderman *Burton*, have employed their Pens in giving Advice to our Citizens how they should proceed in electing a new Representative for the next Sessions, having laid aside their Pens; I have reason to hope, that all true Lovers of their Country in general, and particularly those who have any Regard for the Priviledges and Liberties of this great and ancient City, will think a second and a third time before they come to a final Determination upon what Person they resolve to fix their Choice.

I am told there are only two Persons who set up for Candidates; one, is the present Lord Mayor[1], and the other[2], a Gentleman, of good Esteem, an Alderman of the City, a Merchant of Reputation, and possess'd of a considerable Office[3] under the Crown. The Question is, which of these two Persons it will be most for the Advantage of the City to elect? I have but little Acquaintance with either, so that my Inquiries will be very impartial, and drawn only from the general Character and Situation of both.

[1] Humphrey French.   [2] John Macarel.   [3] Register to the Barracks.

In order to this, I must offer my Countrymen and Fellow Citizens, some Reasons, why I think they ought to be more than ordinarily careful at this Juncture upon whom they bestow their Votes.

To perform this with more Clearness, it may be proper to give you a short State of our unfortunate Country.

We consist of two Parties, I do not mean Popish and Protestant, High and Low Church, Episcopal and Sectarians, Whig and Tory; but of these *English* who happen to be born in this Kingdom, (whose Ancestors reduced the whole Nation under the Obedience of the *English* Crown,) and the Gentlemen sent from the other Side to possess most of the chief Employments here: This latter Party is very much enlarged and strengthened by the whole Power in the Church, the Law, the Army, the Revenue, and the Civil Administration deposited in their Hands. Although out of political Ends, and to save Appearances, some Employments are still deposited (yet gradually in a smaller Number to Persons born here: This Proceeding fortified with good Words and many Promises, is sufficient to flatter and feed the Hopes of Hundreds, who will never be one Farthing the better, as they might easily be convinced, if they were qualifyed to think at all.

Civil Employments of all kinds, have been for several Years past, with great Prudence made precarious, and during Pleasure; by which Means the Possessors are, and must inevitably be for ever dependant: Yet those very few of any Consequence, which are dealt with so sparing a Hand to Persons born among us, are enough to keep Hope alive in great Numbers who desire to mend their Condition by the Favour of those in Power.

Now, my dear Fellow-Citizens, how is it possible you can conceive, that any Person who holds an Office of some Hundred Pounds a Year, which may be taken from him whenever Power shall think fit, will if he should be chosen a Member for any City, do the least thing when he sits in the House, that he knows or fears may be displeasing to those who gave him or continue him in that Office. Believe me, these are no times to expect such an exalted Degree of Virtue from mortal Men. *Blazing stars* are much more frequently seen than such heroical Worthies. And I could sooner hope to find ten thousand Pounds by digging in my Garden than such a *Phoenix* by searching among the present Race of Mankind.

I cannot forbear thinking it a very erroneous as well as modern Maxim of Politicks in the *English* Nation, to take every Opportunity of depressing *Ireland*, whereof an hundred Instances may be produced in Points of the highest Importance, and within the Memory of every middle-aged Man. Although many of the greatest Persons among that Party which now prevails, have formerly upon that Article much differed in their Opinion from their present Successors.

But so the Fact stands at present. It is plain, that the Court and Country Party here (I mean in the House of Commons) very seldom agree in any thing but their Loyalty to His present Majesty, their Resolutions to make him and his Viceroy easy in the Government, to the utmost of their Power, under the present Condition of the Kingdom. But the Persons sent from *England*, who (to a Trifle) are possessed of the sole executive Power in all its Branches, with their few Adherents in Possession who were born here, and Hundreds of Expectants, Hopers, and Promissees, put on quite contrary Notions with regard to *Ireland*. They count upon a universal Submission to whatever shall be demanded; wherein they act safely, because none of themselves, except the Candidates, feel the least of our Pressures.

I remember a Person of Distinction some Days ago affirmed in a good deal of mixt Company, and of both Parties. That the Gentry from *England* who now enjoy OUR highest Employments of all kinds, can never be possibly Losers of one Farthing by the greatest Calamities that can befal this Kingdom, except a Plague that would sweep away a Million of our *Hewers of Wood, and Drawers of Water:* Or an Invasion that would fright our Grandees out of the Kingdom. For this Person argued, that while there was a Penny left in the Treasury, the Civil and Military List must be paid; and that the episcopal Revenues which are usually farmed out at six times below the real Value, could hardly fail. He insisted further, that as Money diminished, the Price of all Necessaries for Life must of Consequence do so too, which would be for the Advantage of all Persons in Employment, as well as of my Lords the Bishops, and to the Ruin of every Body else. Among the Company there wanted not Men in Office, besides one or two Expectants; yet I did not observe any of them disposed to return an Answer: But the Consequences drawn were these; That the great Men in Power sent hither from the other Side were by no means upon the same Foot with his Majesty's other Subjects of *Ireland*. They had no common Ligament to bind them with us; they suffered not with our Sufferings, and if it were possible for us to have any Cause of Rejoycing, they could not rejoyce with us.

Suppose a Person born in this Kingdom, shall happen by his Services for the *English* Interest, to have an Employment conferred on him worth 400 l. a Year; and that he hath likewise an Estate in Land, worth 400 l. a Year more: Suppose him to sit in Parliament: Then, suppose a Land-Tax to be brought in of 5s. a Pound for ten Years; I tell you how this Gentleman will compute. He has 400 l. a Year in Land: The Tax he must pay yearly is 100 l. by which in ten Years, he will pay only 1000 l. But if he gives his Vote against this Tax, he will lose 4000 l. by being turned out of his Employment; together with the Power and Influence he hath, by Virtue or Colour of his Employment; and thus the Ballance will be against him three Thousand Pounds.

I desire, my Fellow-Citizens, you will please to call to mind how many Persons you can vouch for among your Acquaintance, who have so much Virtue and Self-denial, as to lose 400 l. a Year for Life; together with the Smiles and Favour of Power, and the Hopes of higher Advancement, meerly out of a generous Love of his Country.

The Contentions of Parties in *England*, are very different from those among us. The Battle there is fought for Power and Riches; and so it is indeed among us: But, whether a great Employment be given to *Tom* or to *Peter*, they were both born in *England*, the Profits are to be spent there. All Employments (except a very few) are bestowed on the Natives: They do not send to *Germany, Holland, Sweden,* or *Denmark,* much less to *Ireland,* for Chancellors, Bishops, Judges, or other Officers. Their Salaries, whether well or ill got, are employed at home; and whatever their Morals or Politicks be, the Nation is not the poorer.

The House of Commons in *England,* have frequently endeavoured to limit the Number of Members who should be allowed to have Employments under the Crown: several Acts have been made to that Purpose, which many wise Men think are not yet effectual enough, and many of them are rendered ineffectual, by leaving the Power of Re-election: Our House of Commons consists, I think, of about three Hundred Members; if one Hundred of these should happen to be made up of Persons already provided for, joined with Expecters, Compliers, easy to be perswaded, such as will give a Vote for a Friend who is in hopes to get something; if they be merry Companions, without Suspicion, of a natural Bashfulness, not apt or able to look forwards; if good Words, Smiles, and Caresses, have any Power over them, the larger Part of a second Hundred may be very easily brought in at a most reasonable Rate.

There is an *Englishman*[1] of no long Standing among us, but in an Employment of great Trust, Power, and Profit. This excellent Person did lately publish, at his own Expence, a Pamphlet printed in *England* by Authority, to justify the Bill for a general *Excise,* or Inland Duty, in order to introduce that blessed Scheme among us. What a tender Care must such an *English* Patriot for *Ireland* have of our Interest, if he should condescend to sit in our Parliament. I will bridle my Indignation. However, methinks I long to see that Mortal, who would with Pleasure blow us up all at a Blast: But, he duly receives his Thousand Pounds a Year; makes his Progresses like a King[2], is received in Pomp at every Town and Village where he travels, and shines in the *English* News-Papers.

I will now apply what I have said to you, my Brethren

[1] *Edward Thompson,* Esq: Member of Parliament for *York,* and a Commissioner of the Revenue in *Ireland.*

[2] Mr. *Thompson* was presented with his Freedom of several Corporations in *Ireland.*

and Fellow-Citizens. Count upon it, as a Truth next to your Creed, that no one Person in Office, of which he is not Master for Life, whether born here, or in *England*, will ever hazard that Office for the Good of this Country. One of your Candidates is of this Kind, and I believe him to be an honest Gentleman, as the Word *Honest* is generally understood. But he loves his Employment better than he does you, or his Country, or all the Countries upon Earth. Will you contribute and give him City Security, to pay him the Value of his Employment, if it should be taken from him, during his Life, for voting on all Occasions with the honest Country Party in the House; although I much question, whether he would do it, even upon that Condition.

Wherefore, since there are but two Candidates, I intreat you will fix on the present Lord-Mayor. He hath shewn more Virtue, more Activity, more Skill, in one Year's Government of the City, than a Hundred Years can equal. He hath endeavoured, with great Success, to banish Frauds, Corruptions, and all other Abuses from amongst you.

A Dozen such Men in Power, would be able to reform a Kingdom. He hath no Employment under the Crown; nor is likely to get or sollicite for any; his Education having not turned him that Way. I will assure for no Man's future Conduct; but he who hath hitherto practised the Rules of Virtue with so much Difficulty, in so great and busy a Station, deserves your Thanks, and the best Returns you can make him; and you, my Brethren, have no other to give him; than that of representing you in Parliament. Tell not me of your Engagements and Promises to another. Your Promises were Sins of Inconsideration at best; and you are bound to repent and annul them. That Gentleman, though with good Reputation, is already engaged on the other Side. He hath 400 l. a Year under the Crown, which he is too wise to part with, by sacrificing so good an Establishment to the empty Names of Virtue, and Love of his Country. I can assure you, the *DRAPIER* is in the Interests of the present Lord-Mayor, whatever you may be told to the Contrary. I have lately heard him declare so in publick Company, and offer some of these very Reasons in Defence of his Opinion; although he hath a Regard and Esteem for the other Gentleman, but would not hazard the Good of the City and the Kingdom, for a Compliment.

The Lord-Mayor's Severity to some unfair Dealers, should not turn the honest Men among them against him. Whatever he did, was for the Advantage of those very Trades whose dishonest Members he punished. He hath hitherto been above Temptation, to act wrong; and therefore, as Mankind goes, he is the most likely to act right as a Representative of your City, as he constantly did in the Government of it.

I

Observations on the Case of the Woollen Manufacturers

OBSERVATIONS

Occasioned by reading a Paper, entitled,

The CASE of the WOOLLEN MANUFACTURERS of Dublin, &c.

THE Paper called The Case of the Woollen Manufacturers, &c. is very well drawn up. The reasonings of the author are just, the facts true, and the consequences natural. But his censure of those seven vile citizens, who import such a quantity of silk stuffs, and woollen cloth from England, is an hundred times gentler than enemies to their country deserve; because I think no punishment in this world can be great enough for them, without immediate repentance and amendment. But, after all, the writer of that paper hath very lightly touched one point of the greatest importance, and very poorly answered the main objection, that the *clothiers are defective both in the quality and quantity of their goods.*

For my own part, when I consider the several societies of handicrafts-men in all kinds, as well as shopkeepers, in this city, after eighteen years experience of their dealings, I am at a loss to know in which of these societies the most or least honesty is to be found. For instance, when any trade comes first into my head, upon examination I determine it exceeds all others in fraud. But after I have considered them all round, as far as my knowledge or experience reacheth, I am at a loss to determine, and to save trouble I put them all upon a par. This I chiefly apply to those societies of men who get their livelihood by the labour of their hands. For, as to shopkeepers, I cannot deny that I have found some few honest men among them, taking the word *honest* in the largest and most charitable sense. But as to handicrafts-men, although I shall endeavour to believe it possible to find a fair dealer among their clans, yet I confess it hath never been once my good fortune to employ one single workman, who did not cheat me at all times to the utmost of his power in the materials, the work, and the price. One universal maxim I have constantly observed among them, that they would rather gain a shilling by cheating you, than twenty in the honest way of dealing, although they were sure to lose your custom, as well as that of others, whom you might probably recommend to them.

This, I must own, is the natural consequence of poverty and oppression. These wretched people catch at any thing to save them a minute longer from drowning. Thus Ireland is the poorest of all civilized countries in Europe, with every natural advantage to make it one of the richest.

As to the grand objection, which this writer flubbers over in so careless a manner, because indeed it was impossible to find a satisfactory answer, I mean the knavery of our woollen manufacturers in general, I shall relate some facts which I had more opportunities to observe than usually fall in the way of men who are not of the trade. For some years, the masters and wardens, with many of their principal workmen and shopkeepers, came often to the Deanry to relate their grievances, and to desire my advice as well as my assistance. What reasons might move them to this proceeding, I leave to public conjecture. The truth is, that the woollen manufacture of this kingdom sate always nearest my heart. But the greatest difficulty lay in these perpetual differences between the shopkeepers and the workmen they employed. Ten or a dozen of these latter often came to the Deanry with their complaints, which I often repeated to the shopkeepers. As, that they brought their prices too low for a poor weaver to get his bread by; and instead of ready money for their labour on Saturdays, they gave them only such a quantity of cloth or stuff, at the highest rate, which the poor men were often forced to sell one-third below the rate, to supply their urgent necessities. On the other side, the shopkeepers complained of idleness, and want of skill, or care, or honesty, in their workmen; and probably their accusations on both sides were just.

Whenever the weavers, in a body, came to me for advice, I gave it freely, that they should contrive some way to bring their goods into reputation; and give up that abominable principle of endeavouring to thrive by imposing bad ware at high prices to their customers, whereby no shopkeeper can reasonably expect to thrive. For, besides the dread of God's anger (which is a motive of small force among them) they may be sure that no buyer of common sense will return to the same shop where he was once or twice defrauded. That gentlemen and ladies, when they found nothing but deceit in the sale of Irish cloths and stuffs, would act as they ought to do, both in prudence and resentment, in going to those very bad citizens the writer mentions, and purchase English goods.

I went farther, and proposed that ten or a dozen of the most substantial woollen drapiers should join in publishing an advertisement, signed with their names, to the following purpose: That for the better encouragement of all gentlemen, &c. the persons undernamed did bind themselves mutually to sell their several cloths and stuffs (naming each kind) at the lowest rate, right merchantable goods, of such a breadth, which they would warrant to be good according to the several prices: and that if a child of ten years old were sent with money, and directions what cloth or stuff to buy, he should not be wronged in any one article. And that whoever should think himself ill used in any of the said shops, he should have his money again from the seller, or upon his refusal, from the rest of the said subscribers, who, if they found the buyer discontented with the cloth or stuff, should be obliged to refund the money; and if the seller refused to repay them, and take his goods again, should publicly advertise that they would answer for none of his goods any more. This would be to establish credit, upon which all trade dependeth.

I proposed this scheme several times to the corporation of weavers, as well as to the manufacturers, when they came to apply for my advice at the Deanry-house. I likewise went to the shops of several woollen-drapiers upon the same errand, but always in vain; for they perpetually gave me the deaf ear, and avoided entering into discourse upon that proposal: I suppose, because they thought it was in vain, and that the spirit of fraud had gotten too deep and universal a possession to be driven out by any arguments from interest, reason, or conscience.

Some Reasons against the Bill for settling the Tythe of Hemp by a Modus

SOME
REASONS
AGAINST THE

Bill for ſettling the Tyth of *Hemp*,
Flax, &c. by a *Modus*.

DUBLIN:

Printed by GEORGE FAULKNER in *Eſſex-Street*,
oppoſite to the Bridge. M DCC XXIV.

ADVERTISEMENT.

IN the Year 1734, a Bill was brought into the House of Commons to settle a Modus, instead of the Tyth on Flax, &c. upon which many eminent Clergymen, who opposed that Scheme, applied themselves to Dr. SWIFT to write against it, which he readily consented to, upon their giving him some Hints; and, in two Days after, the following Reasons were presented to several Members of Parliament, and had so good an Effect, that the Bill was dropped.

R E A S O N S

The BILL for fettling the Tyth of HEMP, FLAX, &c. by a MODUS.

T HE Clergy did little expect to have any Cause of Complaint against the present House of Commons; who in the last Sessions, were pleased to throw out a Bill sent them from the Lords, which that Reverend Body apprehended would be very injurious to them, if it passed into a Law: And who, in the present Sessions, defeated the Arts and Endeavours of *Schismaticks* to repeal the *Sacramental Test*.

For, although it hath been allowed on all Hands, that the former of those Bills might, by its necessary Consequences, be very displeasing to the Lay-Gentlemen of the Kingdom, for many Reasons purely secular; and, that this last Attempt for repealing the *Test*, did much more affect, at present, the Temporal Interest than the Spiritual; yet the whole Body of the lower Clergy have, upon both those Occasions, expressed equal Gratitude to that honourable House, for their Justice and Steadiness, as if the Clergy alone were to receive the Benefit.

It must needs be, therefore, a great Addition to the Clergy's Grief, that such an Assembly as the present House of Commons should now, with an Expedition more than usual, agree to a Bill for encouraging the Linen-Manufacture; with a Clause, whereby the Church is to lose two Parts in Three, of the legal Tyth in Flax and Hemp.

Some Reasons, why the Clergy think such a Law will be a great Hardship upon them, are, I conceive, those that follow.

I shall venture to enumerate them with all Deference due to that honourable Assembly.

First; The Clergy suppose that they have not, by any Fault or Demerit, incurred the Displeasure of the Nation's Representatives: Neither can the declared Loyalty of the present Set, from the highest Prelate to the lowest Vicar, be in the least disputed: Because, there are hardly ten Clergymen through the whole Kingdom, for more than nineteen Years past, who have not been either preferred entirely upon Account of their declared Affection to the *Hanover* Line; or higher promoted as the due Reward of the same Merit.

There is not a Landlord in the whole Kingdom, residing some Part of the Year at his Country Seat, who is not, in his own Conscience, fully convinced, that the Tythes of his Minister have gradually sunk, for some Years past, one Third, or at least one Fourth of their former Value, exclusive of all *Non*-Solvencies.

The Payment of Tythes in this Kingdom is subject to so many Frauds, Brangles, and other Difficulties, not only from *Papists* and *Dissenters*, but even from those who profess themselves *Protestants*; that by the Expence, the Trouble, and Vexation of collecting or bargaining for them, they are, of all other Rents, the most precarious, uncertain, and ill paid.

The Landlords in most Parishes expect, as a Compliment, that they shall pay little more than half the Value of their Tythes for the Lands they hold in their own Hands, which often consist of large Domains: And it is the Minister's Interest to make them easy upon that Article, when he considers, what Influence those Gentlemen have upon their Tenants.

The Clergy cannot but think it extremely severe, that, in a Bill for encouraging the Linen Manufacture, they alone must be the Sufferers, who can least afford it: If, as I am told, there be a Tax of three thousand Pounds a Year, paid by the Publick, for a further Encouragement to the said Manufacture; are not the Clergy equal Sharers in the Charge with the rest of their Fellow Subjects? What satisfactory Reason can be therefore given, why they alone should bear the whole additional

Weight, unless it will be alledged, that their Property is not upon an equal Foot with the Properties of other Men. They acquire their own small Pittance, by at least as honest Means as their Neighbours the Landlords possess their Estates; and have been always supposed, except in rebellious or fanatical Times, to have as good a Title: For, no Families now in Being, can shew a more antient. Indeed, if it be true, that some Persons (I hope they were not many) were seen to laugh when the Rights of the Clergy were mentioned; in this Case, an Opinion may possibly be soon advanced, that they have no Rights at all. And this is likely enough to gain Ground, in Proportion as the Contempt of all Religion shall increase; which is already in a very forward Way.

It is said, there will be also added in this Bill, a Clause for diminishing the Tyth of Hopps, in order to cultivate that useful Plant among us: And here likewise the Load is to lie entirely on the Shoulders of the Clergy, while the Landlords reap all the Benefit. It will not be easy to foresee where such Proceedings are like to stop: Or whether by the same Authority, in civil Times, a Parliament may not as justly challenge the same Power, in reducing all Things tythable, not below the tenth Part of the Product (which is, and ever will be, the Clergy's equitable Right) but from a tenth Part to the sixtieth or eightieth, and from thence to nothing.

I have heard it granted by skilful Persons, that the Practice of taxing the Clergy by Parliament, without their own Consent, is a new Thing, not much above the Date of seventy Years: Before which Period, in Times of Peace, they always taxed themselves. But Things are extremely altered at present: It is not now sufficient to tax them in common with their Fellow-Subjects, without imposing an additional Tax upon them, from which, or from any thing equivalent, all their Fellow-Subjects are exempt; and this in a Country professing Christianity.

The greatest Part of the Clergy throughout this Kingdom, have been stripped of their Glebes by the Confusion of Times, by Violence, Fraud, Oppression, and other unlawful Means; all which Glebes are now in the Hands of the Laity. So that they now are generally forced to lie at the Mercy of Landlords, for a small Piece of Ground in their Parishes, at a most exorbitant Rent, and usually for a short Term of Years; whereon to build an House, and enable them to reside. Yet, in spight of these Disadvantages, I am a Witness, that they are generally more constant Residents than their Brethren in *England*; where the meanest Vicar hath a convenient Dwelling, with a Barn, a Garden, and a Field or two for his Cattle; besides the Certainty of his little Income from honest Farmers, able and willing not only to pay him his Dues, but likewise to make him Presents, according to their Ability, for his better Support. In all which Circumstances, the Clergy of *Ireland* meet with a Treatment directly contrary.

It is hoped the honourable House will consider that it is impossible for the most ill-minded, avaricious, or cunning Clergyman, to do the least Injustice to the meanest Cottager in his Parish, in any Bargain for Tythes, or other Ecclesiastical Dues. He can, at the utmost, only demand to have his Tyth fairly laid out; and does not once in an hundred Times obtain his Demand. But every Tenant, from the poorest Cottager to the most substantial Farmer, can, and generally doth, impose upon the Minister by Fraud, by Theft, by Lyes, by Perjuries, by Insolence, and sometimes by Force; notwithstanding the utmost Vigilance and Skill of himself and his Proctor. Insomuch, that it is allowed, that the Clergy in general receive little more than one half of their legal Dues; not including the Charges they are at in collecting or bargaining for them.

The Land Rents of *Ireland* are computed to about two Millions, whereof one Tenth amounts to two hundred thousand Pounds. The beneficed Clergymen, excluding those of this City, are not reckoned to be above five hundred; by which Computation, they should each of them possess two hundred Pounds a Year, if those Tythes were equally divided, although in well cultivated Corn Countries it ought to be more; whereas they hardly receive one half of that Sum; with great Defalcations, and in very bad Payments. There are indeed a few Glebes in the North pretty considerable; but if these and all the rest were in like manner equally divided, they would not add five

Pounds a Year to every Clergyman. Therefore, whether the Condition of the Clergy in general among us be justly lyable to Envy, or able to bear a heavy Burthen, which neither the Nobility, nor Gentry, nor Tradesmen, nor Farmers, will touch with one of their Fingers; this, I say, is submitted to the honourable House.

One terrible Circumstance in this Bill, is that of turning the Tyth of *Flax* and *Hemp* into what the Lawyers call a *Modus*, or a certain Sum in lieu of a tenth Part of the Product. And by this Practice of claiming a *Modus* in many Parishes by ancient Custom, the Clergy in both Kingdoms have been almost incredible Sufferers. Thus, in the present Case, the Tyth of a tolerable Acre of *Flax*, which by a Medium is worth twelve Shillings, is by the present Bill reduced to four Shillings. Neither is this the worst Part in a *Modus*; every determinate Sum must, in Process of Time, sink from a fourth to a four-and-twentieth Part, or a great deal lower, by that necessary Fall attending the Value of Money, which is now at least nine Tenths lower all over *Europe* than it was four hundred Years ago, by a gradual Decline; and even a third Part at least within our own Memories, in purchasing almost every Thing required for the Necessities or Conveniences of Life; as any Gentleman can attest, who hath kept House for twenty Years past. And this will equally affect poor Countries as well as rich. For, although I look upon it as an Impossibility that this Kingdom should ever thrive under its present Disadvantages, which without a Miracle must still increase; yet, when the whole Cash of the Nation shall sink to fifty thousand Pounds; we must in all our Traffick Abroad either of Import or Export, go by the general Rate at which Money is valued in those Countries that enjoy the common Privileges of human Kind. For this Reason, no Corporation (if the Clergy may presume to call themselves one) should by any Means grant away their Properties in Perpetuity upon any Consideration whatsoever. Which is a Rock that many Corporations have split upon, to their great Impoverishment, and sometimes to their utter Undoing. Because they are supposed to subsist for ever; and because no Determination

K

of Money is of any certain perpetual intrinsick Value. This is known enough in *England*, where Estates let for ever, some hundred Years ago, by several antient noble Families, do not at this present pay their Posterity a twentieth Part of what they are now worth at an easy Rent.

A Tax affecting one Part of a Nation, which already bears its full Share in all Parliamentary Impositions, cannot possibly be just, except it be inflicted as a Punishment uopn that Body of Men which is taxed, for some great Demerit or Danger to the Publick apprehended from those upon whom it is laid: Thus the *Papists* and *Non-jurors* have been doubly taxed for refusing to give proper Securities to the Government; which cannot be objected against the Clergy. And therefore, if this Bill should pass; I think it ought to be with a Preface, shewing wherein they have offended, and for what Disaffection or other Crime they are punished.

If an additional Excise upon Ale, or a Duty upon Flesh and Bread, were to be enacted, neither the Victualler, Butcher, or Baker would bear any more of the Charge, than for what themselves consumed; but it would be an equal general Tax through the whole Kingdom: Whereas, by this Bill, the Clergy alone are avowedly condemned to be deprived of their ancient, inherent, undisputed Rights, in order to encourage a Manufacture by which all the rest of the Kingdom are supposed to be Gainers.

This Bill is directly against *Magna Charta*, whereof the first Clause is for confirming the inviolable Rights of Holy Church; as well as contrary to the Oath taken by all our Kings at their Coronation, where they swear to defend and protect the Church in all her Rights.

A Tax laid upon Employments is a very different Thing. The Possessors of Civil and Military Employments are no Corporation; neither are they any Part of our Constitution: Their Salaries, Pay, and Perquisites are all changeable at the Pleasure of the Prince who bestows them, although the Army be paid from Funds raised and appropriated by the Legislature. But the Clergy, as they have little Reason to expect, so they desire no more than their antient legal Dues; only indeed with

the Removal of many grievous Impediments in the Collection
of them; which it is to be feared they must wait for until more
favourable Times. It is well known, that they have already
of their own Accord shewn great Indulgence to their People
upon this very Article of *Flax*, seldom taking above a fourth
Part of their Tyth for small Parcels, and oftentimes nothing
at all from new Beginners; waiting with Patience until the
Farmers were able, and until greater Quantities of Land were
employed in that Part of Husbandry; never suspecting that
their good Intentions should be perverted in so singular
a Manner to their Detriment, by that very Assembly, which,
during the time that Convocations (which are an original
Part of our Constitution, ever since Christianity became
National among us) are thought fit to be suspended, GOD
knows for what Reason, or from what Provocations; I
say from that very Assembly, who, during the Intervals of
Convocations, should rather be supposed to be Guardians of
the Rights and Properties of the Clergy, than to make the least
Attempt upon either.

I have not heard, upon Enquiry, that any of those Gentlemen, who, among us without Doors, are called the Court-
Party, discover the least Zeal in this Affair. If they had
Thoughts to interpose, it might be conceived they would
shew their Displeasure against this Bill, which must very much
lessen the Value of the King's Patronage upon Promotion
to vacant Sees; in the Disposal of Deanries, and other considerable Preferments in the Church, which are in the
Donation of the Crown; whereby the Viceroys will have fewer
good Preferments to bestow on their Dependents, as well as
upon the Kindred of Members, who may have a sufficient
Stock of that Sort of Merit, whatever it may be, which may
in future Times most prevail.

The *Dissenters*, by not succeeding in their Endeavours to
procure a Repeal of the *Test*, have lost nothing, but continue
in a full Enjoyment of their Toleration; while the Clergy
without giving the least Offence, are by this Bill deprived of a
considerable Branch of their antient legal Rights, whereby the

Schismatical Party will have the Pleasure of gratifying their Revenge. *Hoc Graii voluere.*

The Farmer will find no Relief by this *Modus*, because, when his present Lease shall expire, his Landlord will infallibly raise the Rent, in an equal Proportion, upon every Part of Land where Flax is sown, and have so much a better Security for Payment, at the Expence of the Clergy.

If we judge by things past, it little avails that this Bill is to be limited to a certain Time of ten, twenty, or thirty Years. For no Landlord will ever consent, that a Law shall expire, by which he finds himself a Gainer; and of this there are many Examples, as well in *England* as in this Kingdom.

The great End of this Bill is, by proper Encouragement, to extend the Linen Manufacture into those Counties where it hath hitherto been little cultivated: But this Encouragement *of lessening the Tyth of Flax and Hemp* is one of such a Kind as, it is to be feared, will have a directly contrary Effect. Because, if I am rightly informed, no set of Men hath, for their Number and Fortunes, been more industrious and successful than the Clergy, in introducing that Manufacture into Places which were unacquainted with it; by persuading their People to sow *Flax* and *Hemp*; by procuring Seed for them and by having them instructed in the Management thereof; and this they did not without reasonable Hopes of increasing the Value of their Parishes after some time, as well as of promoting the Benefit of the Publick. But if this *Modus* should take Place, the Clergy will be so far from gaining that they will become Losers by any extraordinary Care, by having their best arable Lands turned to *Flax* and *Hemp*, which are reckoned great Impoverishers of Land. They cannot therefore be blamed, if they should shew as much Zeal to prevent its being introduced or improved in their Parishes, as they hitherto have shewed in the introducing and improving it. This, I am told, some of them have already declared, at least so far as to resolve not to give themselves any more Trouble than other Men about promoting a Manufacture, by the Success of which, they only of all Men are to be Sufferers. Perhaps the giving them even a further Encouragement than the Law doth, as it now stands, to a Set of Men, who might on many Accounts be so useful to this Purpose, would be no bad Method of having the great End of the Bill more effectually answered: But this is what they are far from desiring; all they petition for is no more than to continue on the same footing with the rest of their Fellow-Subjects.

If this *Modus* of paying by the Acre be to pass into a Law, it were to be wished that the same Law would appoint one or more sworn Surveyors in each Parish to measure the Lands on which *Flax* and *Hemp* are sown, as also would settle the Price of surveying, and determine whether the Incumbent or Farmer is to pay for each annual Survey. Without something of this Kind, there must constantly be Disputes between them; and the neighbouring Justices of Peace must be teized as often as those Disputes happen.

I had written thus far, when a Paper was sent to me, with several Reasons against the Bill, some whereof, although they have been already touched, are put in a better Light, and the rest did not occur to me. I shall deliver them in the Author's own Words.

N.B. *Some Alterations have been made in the Bill about the* Modus, *since the above Paper was writt; but they are of little Moment.*

Some further Reasons against the Bill for settling the Tyth of Hemp, Flax, *&c.*

I. THAT Tyths are the Patrimony of the Church: And if not of Divine Original, yet at least of great Antiquity.

II. That all Purchases and Leases of Tythable Lands, for many Centuries past, have been made and taken, subject to the Demand of Tyths; and those Lands sold and taken just so much the cheaper on that Account.

III. That if any Lands are exempted from Tyths; or the legal Demands of such Tyths lessened by Act of Parliament, so much Value is taken from the Proprietor of the Tyths, and vested in the Proprietor of the Lands, or his Head-Tenants.

IV. That no innocent unoffending Person can be so deprived of his Property without the greatest Violation of common Justice.

V. That to do this upon a Prospect of encouraging the Linen, or any other Manufacture, is acting upon a very mistaken and unjust Supposition, inasmuch as the Price of the Lands so occupied will be no way lessened to the Farmer by such a Law.

VI. That the Clergy are content chearfully to bear (as they now do) any Burthen in common with their Fellow-Subjects, either for the Support of his Majesty's Government, or the Encouragement of the Trade of the Nation; but think it very hard, that they should be singled out to pay heavier Taxes than others, at a Time when, by the Decrease of the Value of their Parishes, they are less able to bear them.

VII. That the Legislature hath heretofore distinguished the Clergy by Exemptions, and not by additional Loads, and the present Clergy of the Kingdom hope they have not deserved worse of the Legislature than their Predecessors.

VIII. That by the original Constitution of these Kingdoms, the Clergy had the sole Right of taxing themselves, and were in Possession of that Right as low as the Restoration: And if that Right be now devolved upon the Commons by the Cession of the Clergy, the Commons can be considered in this Case in no other Light than as the Guardians of the Clergy.

IX. That besides those Tyths always in the Possession of the Clergy; there are some Portions of Tyths lately come into their Possession by Purchase; that if this Clause should take Place, they would not be allowed the Benefit of these Purchases, upon an equal Foot of Advantage with the rest of their Fellow Subjects. And that some Tyths, in the Hands of Impropriators, are under Settlements and Mortgages.

X. That the Gentlemen of this House should consider, that loading the Clergy is loading their own younger Brothers and

Children, with this additional Grievance; that it is taking from the younger and poorer to give to the elder and richer. And,

Lastly, That if it were at any Time just and proper to do this, it would however be too severe to do it now, when all the Tyths of the Kingdom are known for some Years past, to have sunk almost above one-third Part in their Value.

Any Income in the Hands of the Clergy, is at least as useful to the Publick, as the same Income in the Hands of the Laity.

It were more reasonable to grant the Clergy, in three Parts of the Nation, an additional Support, than to diminish the present Subsistance.

Great Employments are and will be in the Hands of *Englishmen*; nothing left for the younger Sons of *Irishmen* but *Vicarages*, *Tide-waiters Places*, *&c.* therefore no Reason to make them worse.

The *Modus* upon the *Flax* in *England* affects only Lands reclaimed since the Year 1690, and is at the Rate of five Shillings the *English* Acre, which is equivalent to eight Shillings and eight Pence *Irish*, and that to be paid before the Farmer removeth it from the Field. *Flax* is a Manufacture of little Consequence in *England*, but is the Staple in *Ireland*; and if it increases (as it probably will) must in many Places jostle out Corn, because it is more gainful.

The Clergy of the established Church have no Interest like those of the Church of *Rome*, distinct from the true Interest of their Country; and therefore ought to suffer under no distinct Impositions or Taxes of any Kind.

The Bill for settling the *Modus* of *Flax* in *England* was brought in, in the first Year of the Reign of King *George* I. when the Clergy lay very unjustly under the Imputation of some Disaffection; and to encourage the bringing in of some Fens in *Lincolnshire*, which were not to be continued under *Flax*; but it left all Lands where *Flax* had been sown before that Time, under the same Condition of Tything, in which they were before the passing of that Bill: Whereas this Bill takes away what the Clergy are actually possessed of.

That the Woollen Manufacture is the Staple of *England*, as the Linen is that of *Ireland*, yet no Attempt was ever made in

England to reduce the Tyth of Wool for the Encouragement of that Manufacture. This Manufacture hath already been remarkably favoured by the Clergy, who have hitherto been generally content with less than half, some with six Pence a Garden, and some have taken nothing.

Employments, they say, have been taxed; the Reasons for which Taxation will not hold with regard to Property, at least until Employments become Inheritances. The Commons always have had so tender a regard to Property, that they never would suffer any Law to pass, whereby any particular Persons might be aggrieved without their own Consent.

A Letter on the Fishery

A LETTER ON THE FISHERY

Dublin, March 23, 1734.

SIR,

I RETURN you my hearty Thanks for your Letter and Discourse upon the Fishery; you discover in both a true Love of your Country, and (except your Civilities to me) a very good Judgment, good Wishes to this ruined Kingdom, and a perfect Knowledge of the Subject you treat: But you are more temperate than I, and consequently much wiser; for Corruptions are apt to make me impatient and give Offence, which you prudently avoid. Ever since I began to think, I was enraged at the Folly of *England*, in suffering the *Dutch* to have almost the whole Advantage of our Fishery just under our Noses. The last Lord *Wemys* told me, he was Governor of a Castle in *Scotland*, near which the *Dutch* used to fish: He sent to them in a civil Manner, to desire they would send him some Fish, which they brutishly refused; whereupon he ordered three or four Cannon to be discharged from the Castle (for their Boats were in reach of the Shot) and immediately they sent him more than he wanted. The *Dutch* are like a Knot of Sharpers among a Parcel of honest Gentlemen, who think they understand Play, and are bubbled of their Money.

I LOVE them for the Love they have to their Country; which, however, is no Virtue in them, because it is their private Interest, which is directly contrary to *England*. In the Queen's Time, I did often press the Lord Treasurer *Oxford*, and others of the Ministry, upon this very Subject, but the Answer was, We must not offend the *Dutch*; who were at that very Time opposing us in all our Steps towards a Peace. I laughed to see the Zeal that Ministry had about the Fishing of *Newfoundland*, (I think) while no Care was taken against the *Dutch* fishing just at our Doors. As to my Native Country, (as you call it) I happened indeed by a perfect Accident to be born here, my Mother being left here from returning to her House at *Leicester*, and I was a Year old before I was sent to *England*;

thus I am a *Teague*, or an *Irishman*, or what People please, although the best Part of my Life was in *England*. What I did for this Country was from perfect Hatred of Tyranny and Oppression, for which I had a Proclamation against me of 300 *l*. which my old Friend, my Lord *Carteret*, was forced to consent to, the very first or second Night of his Arrival hither. The Crime was, that of writing against the Project of one *Wood*, an Ironmonger, to coin One hundred and eight Thousand Pounds in Halfpence, not worth a sixth Part of the Money; which was laid before the People in so plain a Manner, that they all refused it, and so the Nation was preserved from immediate Ruin. I have done some small Services to this Kingdom, but I can do no more: I have too many Years upon me, and have too much Sickness. I am out of Favour at Court, where I was well received during two Summers six and seven Years ago. The governing People here do not love me; for, as corrupt as *England* is, it is an Habitation of Saints in Comparison of *Ireland*. We are all Slaves, and Knaves, and Fools, and all but Bishops and People in Employments, Beggars. The Cash of *Ireland* does not amount to Two hundred thousand Pounds. The few honest Men amongst us are dead-hearted, poor, and out of Favour and Power. I talked to two or three Gentlemen of this House of Commons now sitting here, mentioned your Scheme, shewed how very advantageous it would be to *Ireland*; they agreed with me, but said, that if such an Affair were proposed, the Members would all go out, as a Thing they had no Concern in. I believe the People of *Lapland*, or the *Hotten-tots*, are not so miserable a People as we; for Oppression supported by Power will infallibly introduce slavish Principles. I am afraid, that even in *England*, your Proposal will come to nothing; there is not Virtue enough left among Mankind. If your Scheme should pass into a Law, it will become a Jobb; your sanguine Temper will cool, Rogues will be the Gainers; Party and Faction will intermingle, and defeat the most essential Parts of the whole Design; Standing-Armies in Time of Peace, Projects of Excise, and Bribing-Elections, are all you are like to be employed in; not forgetting Septennial

Parliaments, directly against the old Whig-Principles, which always have been mine.

A GENTLEMAN of this Kingdom, about three Years ago, joined with some others in a Fishery here in the Northern Parts; they advanced only Two hundred Pounds by Way of Tryal; they got Men from *Orkney* to cure the Fish, who understood it well; but, the vulgar Folks of *Ireland* are so lazy and so knavish, that it turned to no Account, nor would any Body join with them, and so the Matter fell, and they lost two Thirds of their Money. Oppressed Beggars are always Knaves, and, I believe, there are hardly any other among us; they had rather gain a Shilling by Knavery, than five Pounds by honest Dealing. They lost 30,000 *l.* a Year for ever, in the Time of the Plague[1], at *Marseilles*, when the *Spaniards* would have bought all their Linen from *Ireland*; but, the Merchants and the Weavers sent over such abominable Linen that it was all returned back, and sold for a fourth Part Value. This is our Condition, which you may please to pity, but never can mend. I wish you good Success with all my Heart. I have always loved good Projects, but have always found them to miscarry. I am, Sir, with true Esteem for your good Intentions, your most obedient humble Servant.

P. S. I would subscribe my Name, if I had not a very bad one, so I leave you to guess it. If I can be of any Service to you in this Kingdom, I shall be glad you will employ me.

[1] *In the Year* 1720.

Reasons why we should not Lower the Coins Etc.

REASONS

Why we should not

Lower the COINS

Now current in this

KINGDOM.

Occasioned by a Paper Entitled,

REMARKS on the Coins current *in this*
KINGDOM.

To which is added,

The Rev. Dean SWIFT'*s*

OPINION,

Delivered by him, in an Assembly of above One hundred
and Fifty eminent Merchants who met at the Guild Hall,
on *Saturday* the 24th of *April*, 1736, in order to draw up
their Petition, and Present it to his Grace the Lord-Lieutenant against lowering said Coin.

Dublin: Printed and sold by *E. Waters* in *Dame-street*.

THE REV. DEAN *SWIFT'S* REASONS AGAINST LOWERING THE GOLD AND SILVER COIN

GENTLEMEN,

I Beg you will consider, and very well weigh in your hearts what I am going to say, and what I have often said before. There are several Bodies of Men, among whom the Power of this Kingdom is divided. 1st, *The Lord-Lieutenant, Lords-Justices and Council,* next to these, *my Lords the Bishops; there is likewise my Lord Chancellor, and my Lords the Judges of the Land, with other eminent Persons in the Law, who have Employments and great Salaries annexed. To these must be added the Commissioners of the Revenue, with all their under Officers: And lastly, their Honours of the Army, of all Degrees.*

Now, *Gentlemen,* I beg you again to consider, that none of these Persons above-named, can ever suffer the loss of one Farthing *by all the Miseries under which the Kingdom groans at present.* For, first, until the Kingdom be *intirely Ruined* the Lord Lieutenant and Lords-Justices must have their *Salaries.* My Lords the Bishops, whose Lands are set a fourth part value, will be sure of their *Rents* and their *Fines.* My Lords the Judges, and Those of other *Employments* in the Courts, must likewise have their *Salaries.* The Gentlemen of the Revenue will pay Themselves; and as to the Officers of the Army, *the Consequences of not paying Them, is obvious enough:* Nay, so far will those *Persons* I have already mentioned be from suffering, that, on the contrary, their *Revenues* being no way lessen'd by the fall of Money, and the *prices* of all *Commodities* considerably sunk thereby, they must be great *Gainers.* Therefore, *Gentlemen,* I do entreat you, that, as long as you live, you will look upon all *Persons* who are for lowering the Gold, or any other Coin, *as no Friends to this poor Kingdom,* but such who find their private account in what will be most detrimental to *Ireland.* And, *as the Absentees* are in the strongest views, our greatest *Enemies*, first, by consuming above one half of the *Rents of this Nation Abroad*. And, secondly, by turning the Weight, by their Absence, so much on the Popish side, by weakning the Protestant Interest. Can there be a greater folly than to pave a Bridge of Gold at your own Expence, to support them in their Luxury and Vanity abroad, while hundreds of thousands are starving at home, for want of Employment.

Concerning that Universal Hatred, which Prevails against the Clergy

CONCERNING THAT UNIVERSAL HATRED, WHICH PREVAILS AGAINST THE CLERGY

MAY 24, M DCC XXXVI.

I HAVE been long considering and conjecturing, what could be the causes of that great disgust, of late, against the Clergy of both kingdoms, beyond what was ever known 'till that Monster and Tyrant, Henry VIII. who took away from them, against law, reason, and justice, at least two thirds of their legal possessions; and whose successors (except Queen Mary) went on with their rapine, till the accession of King James I. That detestable Tyrant Henry VIII. although he abolished the Pope's power in England, as universal bishop, yet what he did in that article, however just it were in itself, was the mere effect of his irregular appetite, to divorce himself from a wife he was weary of, for a younger and more beautiful woman, whom he afterwards beheaded. But, at the same time, he was an entire defender of all the Popish doctrines, even those which were the most absurd. And, while he put people to death for denying him to be head of the church, he burned every offender against the doctrines of the Roman Faith; and cut off the head of Sir Thomas More, a person of the greatest virtue this kingdom ever produced, for not directly owning him to be head of the church. Among all the princes who ever reigned in the world there was never so infernal a beast as Henry the VIII. in every vice of the most odious kind, without any one appearance of virtue: But cruelty, lust, rapine, and atheism, were his peculiar talents. He rejected the power of the Pope for no other reason, than to give his full swing to commit sacrilege, in which no Tyrant, since Christianity became national, did ever equal him by many degrees. The abbeys, endowed with lands by the mistaken notion of well-disposed men, were indeed too numerous, and hurtful to the kingdom; and, therefore, the legislature might, after the Reformation, have justly applied them to some pious or public uses.

In a very few centuries after Christianity became national in most parts of Europe, although the Church of Rome had already introduced many corruptions in religion; yet the piety of early Christians, as well as new converts, was so great, and particularly of princes, as well as noblemen and other wealthy persons, that they built many religious houses, for those who were inclined to live in a recluse or solitary manner, endowing those monasteries with land. It is true, we read of monks some ages before, who dwelt in caves and cells, in desert places. But, when public edifices were erected and endowed, they began gradually to degenerate into idleness, ignorance, avarice, ambition, and luxury, after the usual fate of all human institutions. The popes, who had already aggrandized themselves, laid hold of the opportunity to subject all religious houses with their priors and abbots, to their peculiar authority; whereby these religious orders became of an interest directly different from the rest of mankind, and wholly at the pope's devotion. I need say no more on this article, so generally known and so frequently treated, or of the frequent endeavours of some other princes, as well as our own, to check the growth, and wealth, and power of the regulars.

In later times, this mistaken piety, of erecting and endowing abbeys, began to decrease. And therefore, when some new invented sect of monks and friars began to start up, not being able to procure grants of land, they got leave from the pope to appropriate the tithes and glebes of certain parishes, as contiguous or near as they could find, obliging themselves to send out some of their body to take care of the people's souls: And if some of those parishes were at too great a distance from the abbey, the monks appointed to attend them were paid for the cure, either a small stipend of a determined sum, or sometimes a third part, or what are now call'd the vicarial tithes.

As to the church-lands, it hath been the opinion of many writers, that, in England, they amounted to a third part of the whole kingdom. And therefore, if that wicked Prince above mentioned, when he had cast off the Pope's Power, had introduced some reformation in religion, he could not have been blamed for taking away the abbey lands by authority of parliament. But, when he continued the most cruel persecutor of all those who differed in the least article of the Popish religion, which was then the national, and established faith, his seizing on those lands, and applying them to profane uses, was absolute sacrilege, in the strongest sense of the word; having been bequeathed by princes and pious men to sacred uses.

In the reign of this Prince, the Church and Court of Rome had arrived to such a height of corruption, in doctrine and discipline, as gave great offence to many wise, learned, and pious men through most parts of Europe; and several countries agreed to make some reformation in religion. But, although a proper and just reformation were allowed to be necessary, even to preserve Christianity itself, yet the passions and vices of men had mingled themselves so far, as to pervert and confound all the good endeavours of those who intended well: And thus the reformation, in every country where it was attempted, was carried on in the most impious and scandalous manner that can possibly be conceived. To which unhappy proceedings we owe all the just reproaches that Roman Catholics have cast upon us ever since. For, when the northern kingdoms and states grew weary of the Pope's tyranny, and when their preachers, beginning with the scandalous abuses of indulgences, and proceeding farther to examine several points of faith, had credit enough with their princes, who were in some fear lest such a change might affect the peace of their countries, because their bishops had great influence on the people, by their wealth and power; these politic teachers had a ready answer to this purpose: 'Sir, Your Majesty need not 'be in any pain or apprehension: Take away the lands, and sink 'the authority of the bishops: Bestow those lands on your 'courtiers, on your nobles, and your great officers in your 'army; and then you will be secure of the people.' This advice was exactly followed. And, in the Protestant monarchies abroad, little more than the shadow of Episcopacy is left; but, in the republics, is wholly extinct.

In England the Reformation was brought in after a somewhat different manner, but upon the same principle of robbing the church. However, Henry VIII. with great dexterity, discovered an invention to gratify his insatiable thirst for blood, on both religions, ✱ ✱ ✱

A Proposal for giving Badges to Beggars

A

PROPOSAL

FOR GIVING

BADGES

TO THE

BEGGARS

IN ALL THE

Parishes of *DUBLIN*.

By the Dean of St. PATRICK's.

M. B. Drapier

DUBLIN:
Printed by GEORGE FAULKNER, Bookseller, in
Essex-Street, opposite to the Bridge,
M DCC XXX VII.

A

PROPOSAL

FOR GIVING

BADGES

TO THE

BEGGARS

IN ALL THE

Parishes of *DUBLIN*.

BY THE

DEAN of St. *PATRICK*'s

LONDON,

Printed for T. COOPER at the *Globe* in *Pater Noster Row*.
MDCCXXXVII.

Price Six Pence.

A

PROPOSAL

FOR GIVING

BADGES, &c.

IT hath been a general Complaint, that the Poor-House, especially since the new Constitution by Act of Parliament, hath been of no Benefit to this City, for the Ease of which it was wholly intended. I had the Honour to be a Member of it many Years before it was new modelled by the Legislature; not from any personal Regard, but meerly as one of the two Deans, who are of Course put into most Commissions that relate to the City; and I have likewise the Honour to have been left out of several Commissions upon the Score of Party, in which my Predecessors, Time out of Mind, have always been Members.

THE first Commission was made up of about fifty Persons, which were the Lord Mayor, Aldermen, and Sheriffs, and some few other Citizens: The Judges, the two Arch-Bishops, the two Deans of the City, and one or two more Gentlemen. And I must confess my Opinion, that the dissolving the old Commission, and establishing a new one of near three Times the Number, have been the great Cause of rendering so good a Design not only useless, but a Grievance instead of a Benefit to the City. In the present Commission all the City-Clergy are included, besides a great Number of 'Squires, not only those who reside in *Dublin*, and the Neighbourhood, but several who live at a great Distance, and cannot possibly have the least Concern for the Advantage of the City.

At the few General Meetings that I have attended since the new Establishment, I observed very little was done except one or two Acts of extream Justice, which I then thought might as well have been spared: And I have found the Court of Assistants usually taken up in little Brangles about Coachmen, or adjusting Accounts of Meal and Small-Beer; which, however necessary, might sometimes have given Place to Matters of much greater Moment, I mean some Schemes recommended to the General Board, for answering the chief Ends in erecting and establishing such a Poor-House, and endowing it with so considerable a Revenue: And the principal End I take to have been that of maintaining the Poor and Orphans of the City, where the Parishes are not able to do it; and clearing the Streets from all Strollers, Foreigners, and sturdy Beggars, with which, to the universal Complaint and Admiration, *Dublin* is more infested since the Establishment of the Poor-House, than it was ever known to be since its first Erection.

As the whole Fund for supporting this Hospital is raised only from the Inhabitants of the City; so there can be hardly any Thing more absurd than to see it misemployed in maintaining Foreign Beggars and Bastards, or Orphans, whose Country Landlords never contributed one Shilling towards their Support. I would engage, that half this Revenue, if employed with common Care, and no very great Degree of common Honesty, would maintain all the real Objects of Charity in this City, except a small Number of Original Poor in every Parish, who might without being burthensome to the Parishioners find a tolerable Support.

I HAVE for some Years past applied my self to several Lord Mayors, and to the late Arch-Bishop of *Dublin*, for a Remedy to this Evil of Foreign Beggars; and they all appeared ready to receive a very plain Proposal, I mean, that of badging the Original Poor of every Parish, who begged in the Streets; that, the said Beggars should be confined to their own Parishes; that, they should wear their Badges well sown upon one of their Shoulders, always visible, on Pain of being whipt and turned out of Town; or whatever legal Punishment may be thought proper and effectual. But, by the wrong Way of thinking in some Clergymen, and the Indifference of others, this Method was perpetually defeated to their own continual disquiet, which they do not ill deserve; and if the Grievance affected only them, it would be of less Consequence; because the Remedy is in their own Power. But, all Street-walkers, and Shop-keepers, bear an equal Share in this hourly Vexation.

I NEVER heard more than one Objection against this Expedient of badging the Poor, and confining their Walks to their several Parishes. The Objection was this: What shall we do with the Foreign Beggars? Must they be left to starve? I answered, No; but they must be driven or whipt out of Town; and let the next Country Parish do as they please, or rather after the Practice in *England*, send them from one Parish to another, until they reach their own Homes. By the old Laws of *England* still in Force, and I presume by those of *Ireland*, every Parish is bound to maintain its own Poor; and the Matter is of no such Consequence in this Point as some would make it, whether a Country Parish be rich or poor. In the remoter and poorer Parishes of the Kingdom, all Necessaries for Life proper for poor People are comparatively cheaper; I mean Butter-milk, Oatmeal, Potatoes, and other Vegetables; and every Farmer or Cottager, who is not himself a Beggar, can sometimes spare a Sup or a Morsel, not worth the fourth Part of a Farthing, to an indigent Neighbour of his own Parish, who is disabled from Work. A Beggar Native of the Parish is known to the 'Squire, to the Church Minister, to the Popish Priest, or the Conventicle Teachers, as well as to every Farmer: He hath generally some Relations able to live, and contribute something to his Maintenance. None of which Advantages can be reasonably expected on a Removal to Places where he is altogether unknown. If he be not quite maimed, he and his Trull, and Litter of Brats (if he hath any) may get half their Support by doing some Kind of Work in their Power, and thereby be less burthensome to the People. In short, all Necessaries of Life grow in the Country, and not in Cities, and are cheaper where they grow; nor is it equal

M

that Beggars should put us to the Charge of giving them Victuals, and the Carriage too.

BUT, when the Spirit of wandring takes him, attended by his Female, and their Equipage of Children, he becomes a Nuisance to the whole Country: He and his Female are Thieves, and teach the Trade of stealing to their Brood at four Years old; and if his Infirmities be counterfeit, it is dangerous for a single Person unarmed to meet him on the Road. He wanders from one County to another, but still with a View to this Town, whither he arrives at last, and enjoys all the Priviledges of a *Dublin* Beggar.

I DO not wonder that the Country 'Squires should be very willing to send up their Colonies; but why the City should be content to receive them, is beyond my Imagination.

IF the City were obliged by their Charter to maintain a thousand Beggars, they could do it cheaper by eighty per Cent. a hundred Miles off, than in this Town, or any of its Suburbs.

THERE is no Village in *Connaught*, that in Proportion shares so deeply in the Daily encreasing Miseries of *Ireland*, as its Capital City; to which Miseries there hardly remained any Addition, except the perpetual Swarms of Foreign Beggars, who might be banished in a Month without Expence, and with very little Trouble.

As I am personally acquainted with a great Number of Street Beggars, I find some weak Attempts have been made in one or two Parishes to promote the wearing of Badges; and my first Question to those who ask an Alms is, *Where is your Badge?* I have in several Years met with about a Dozen who were ready to produce them, some out of their Pockets, others from under their Coat, and two or three on their Shoulders, only covered with a Sort of Capes which they could lift up or let down upon Occasion. They are too lazy to work; they are not afraid to steal, nor ashamed to beg, and yet are too proud to be seen with a Badge, as many of them have confessed to me, and not a few in very injurious Terms, particularly the Females. They all look upon such an Obligation as a high Indignity done to their Office. I appeal to all indifferent

People whether such Wretches deserve to be relieved. As to my self, I must confess, this absurd Insolence hath so affected me, that for several Years past, I have not disposed of one single Farthing to a Street Beggar, nor intend to do so until I see a better Regulation; and I have endeavoured to persuade all my Brother-walkers to follow my Example, which most of them assure me they do. For, if Beggary be not able to beat out Pride, it cannot deserve Charity. However, as to Persons in Coaches and Chairs, they bear but little of the Persecution we suffer, and are willing to leave it intirely upon us.

To say the Truth, there is not a more undeserving vicious Race of human Kind than the Bulk of those who are reduced to Beggary, even in this beggarly Country. For, as a great Part of our publick Miseries is originally owing to our own Faults (but, what those Faults are I am grown by Experience too wary to mention) so I am confident, that among the meaner People, nineteen in twenty of those who are reduced to a starving Condition, did not become so by what Lawyers call the Work of GOD, either upon their Bodies or Goods; but meerly from their own Idleness, attended with all Manner of Vices, particularly Drunkenness, Thievery, and Cheating.

WHOEVER inquires, as I have frequently done, from those who have asked me an Alms, what was their former Course of Life, will find them to have been Servants in good Families, broken Tradesmen, Labourers, Cottagers, and what they call decayed Housekeepers; but (to use their own Cant) reduced by Losses and Crosses, by which nothing can be understood but Idleness and Vice.

As this is the only Christian Country where People contrary to the old Maxim, are the Poverty and not the Riches of the Nation; so, the Blessing of Increase and Multiply is by us converted into a Curse: And, as Marriage hath been ever countenanced in all free Countries, so we should be less miserable if it were discouraged in ours, as far as can be consistent with Christianity. It is seldom known in *England*, that the Labourer, the lower Mechanick, the Servant, or the Cottager, thinks of marrying until he hath saved up a Stock of Money sufficient to carry on his Business; nor takes a Wife without a suitable Portion; and as seldom fails of making a yearly Addition to that Stock, with a View of providing for his Children. But, in this Kingdom the Case is directly contrary, where many thousand Couples are yearly married, whose whole united Fortunes, bating the Rags on their Backs, would not be sufficient to purchase a Pint of Butter-milk for their Wedding Supper, nor have any Prospect of supporting their *honourable State* but by Service, or Labour, or Thievery. Nay, their *Happiness* is often deferred until they find Credit to borrow, or cunning to steal a Shilling to pay their Popish Priest, or infamous Couple-Beggar. Surely no miraculous Portion of Wisdom would be required to find some kind of Remedy against this destructive Evil, or at least, not to draw the Consequences of it upon our decaying City, the greatest Part whereof must of Course in a few Years become desolate, or in Ruins.

In all other Nations, that are not absolutely barbarous, Parents think themselves bound by the Law of Nature and Reason to make some Provision for their Children; but the Reasons offered by the Inhabitants of *Ireland* for marrying, is, that they may have Children to maintain them when they grow old and unable to work.

I am informed that we have been for some Time past extremely obliged to *England* for one very beneficial Branch of Commerce: For, it seems they are grown so Gracious as to transmit us continually Colonies of Beggars, in Return of a Million of Money they receive yearly from hence. That I may give no Offence, I profess to mean real *English* Beggars in the literal Meaning of the Word, as it is usually understood by Protestants. It seems, the Justices of the Peace and Parish Officers in the Western Coasts of *England*, have a good while followed the Trade of exporting hither their supernumerary Beggars, in order to advance the *English* Protestant Interest among us; and, these they are so kind to send over Gratis, and Duty-free. I have had the Honour more than once to attend large Cargoes of them from *Chester* to *Dublin:* And I was then so ignorant as to give my Opinion, that our City should receive them into Bridewell, and after a Month's Residence, having been well whipt twice a Day, fed with Bran and Water, and put to hard Labour, they should be returned honestly back with Thanks as cheap as they came: Or, if that were not approved of, I proposed, that whereas one *English* Man is allowed to be of equal intrinsick Value with twelve born in *Ireland*, we should in Justice return them a Dozen for One, to dispose of as they pleased. But to return.

As to the native Poor of this City, there would be little or no Damage in confining them to their several Parishes. For Instance; a Beggar of the Parish of St. *Warborough*'s, or any other Parish here, if he be an Object of Compassion, hath an equal Chance to receive his Proportion of Alms from every charitable Hand; because the Inhabitants, one or other, walk through every Street in Town, and give their Alms, without considering the Place, wherever they think it may be well disposed of: And, these Helps, added to what they get in Eatables by going from House to House, among the Gentry and Citizens, will, without being very burthensome, be sufficient to keep them alive.

It is true, the Poor of the Suburb Parishes will not have altogether the same Advantage, because they are not equally in the Road of Business and Passengers: But here it is to be considered, that the Beggars there have not so good a Title to Publick Charity, because most of them are Strollers from the Country, and compose a principal Part of that great Nuisance, which we ought to remove.

I should be apt to think, that few Things can be more irksome to a City-Minister, than a Number of Beggars which do not belong to his District, whom he hath no Obligation to take Care of, who are no Part of his Flock, and who take the Bread out of the Mouths of those, to whom it properly belongs. When I mention this Abuse to any Minister of a City-Parish, he usually lays the Fault upon the Beadles, who he says are bribed by the Foreign Beggars; and as those Beadles often keep Ale-Houses, they find their Account in such Customers. This Evil might easily be remedyed, if the Parishes would make some small Addition to the Salaries of a Beadle, and be more careful in the Choice of those Officers.

But, I conceive there is one effectual Method, in the Power of every Minister to put in Practice; I mean, by making it the Interest of all his own original Poor, to drive out Intruders: For, if the Parish-Beggars were absolutely forbidden by the Minister and Church-Officers, to suffer Strollers to come into the Parish, upon Pain of themselves being not permitted to beg Alms at the Church-Doors, or at the Houses and Shops of the Inhabitants; they would prevent Interlopers more effectually than twenty Beadles.

AND, here I cannot but take Notice of the great Indiscretion in our City-Shopkeepers, who suffer their Doors to be daily besieged by Crowds of Beggars, (as the Gates of a Lord are by Duns,) to the great Disgust and Vexation of many Customers, whom I have frequently observed to go to other Shops, rather than suffer such a Persecution; which might easily be avoided, if no Foreign Beggars were allowed to infest them.

WHEREFORE, I do assert, that the Shopkeepers who are the greatest Complainers of this Grievance, (lamenting that for every Customer, they are worried by fifty Beggars,) do very well deserve what they suffer, when a 'Prentice with a Horse-Whip is able to lash every Beggar from the Shop, who is not of the Parish, and doth not wear the Badge of that Parish on his Shoulder, well fastned and fairly visible; and if this Practice were universal in every House, to all the sturdy Vagrants, we should in a few Weeks clear the Town of all Mendicants, except those who have a proper Title to our Charity: As for the Aged and Infirm, it would be sufficient to give them nothing, and then they must starve or follow their Brethren.

IT was the City that first endowed this Hospital, and those who afterwards contributed, as they were such who generally inhabited here; so they intended what they gave to be for the Use of the City's Poor. The Revenues which have since been raised by Parliament, are wholly paid by the City, without the least Charge upon any other Part of the Kingdom; and therefore nothing could more defeat the original Design, than to misapply those Revenues on strolling Beggars, or Bastards from the Country, which bears no Share in the Charges we are at.

IF some of the Out-Parishes be over-burthened with Poor, the Reason must be, that the greatest Part of those Poor are Strollers from the Country, who nestle themselves where they can find the cheapest Lodgings, and from thence infest every Part of the Town, out of which they ought to be whipped as a most insufferable Nuisance, being nothing else but a profligate Clan of Thieves, Drunkards, Heathens, and Whoremongers, fitter to be rooted out off the Face of the Earth, than suffered to levy a vast annual Tax upon the City, which shares too deep in the publick Miseries brought on us by the Oppressions we lye under from our Neighbours, our Brethren, our Countrymen, our Fellow Protestants, and Fellow Subjects.

SOME Time ago I was appointed one of a Committee to inquire into the State of the Workhouse; where we found that a Charity was bestowed by a great Person for a certain Time, which in its Consequences operated very much to the Detriment of the House: For, when the Time was elapsed, all those who were supported by that Charity, continued on the same Foot with the rest of the Foundation; and being generally a Pack of profligate vagabond Wretches from several Parts of the Kingdom, corrupted all the rest; so partial, or treacherous, or interested, or ignorant, or mistaken, are generally all Recommenders, not only to Employments, but even to Charity it self.

I KNOW it is complained, that the Difficulty of driving Foreign Beggars out of the City is charged upon the *Bellowers* (as they are called) who find their Accounts best in suffering those Vagrants to follow their Trade through every Part of the Town. But, this Abuse might easily be remedied and very much to the Advantage of the whole City, if better Salaries were given to those who execute that Office in the several Parishes, and would make it their Interest to clear the Town of those Caterpillars, rather than hazard the Loss of an Employment that would give them an honest Livelihood. But, if that should fail, yet a general Resolution of never giving Charity to a Street Beggar out of his own Parish, or without a visible Badge, would infallibly force all Vagrants to depart.

THERE is generally a Vagabond Spirit in Beggars, which ought to be discouraged and severely punished. It is owing to the same Causes that drove them into Poverty; I mean, Idleness, Drunkenness, and rash Marriages without the least Prospect of supporting a Family by honest Endeavours; which never came into their Thoughts. It is observed, that hardly one Beggar in twenty looks upon himself to be relieved by receiving Bread or other Food; and they have in this Town been frequently seen to pour out of their Pitcher good Broth that hath been given them, into the Kennel; neither do they much regard Cloaths, unless to sell them; for, their Rags are Part of their Tools with which they work: They want only Ale, Brandy, and other strong Liquors, which cannot be had without Money; and Money, as they conceive, always abounds in the Metropolis.

I HAD some other Thoughts to offer upon this Subject. But, as I am a Desponder in my Nature, and have tolerably well discovered the Disposition of our People, who never will move a Step towards easing themselves from any one single Grievance; it will be thought, that I have already said too much, and to little or no Purpose; which hath often been the Fate, or Fortune of the Writer.

J. SWIFT.

April 22,
1737.

Letter to the Printer of Thoughts on the Tillage of Ireland

A

LETTER

TO THE

PRINTER.

Mr. Faulkner,

*I*Received from you, a Manuscript, sent, as you tell me, by some unknown Hand, entitled, A Discourse upon the Tillage of Ireland; of which you desire my Judgment: In Answer, I do assure you, I think it extremely well writ, and might be of the greatest Advantage to the Kingdom, if there were Virtue enough among us to follow the Author's Advice, as I heartily wish.

> I am, Sir,
>
> Your assured Friend,
>
> and Servant,
>
> J. SWIFT.

Deanry-House,
Dec. 13, 1737.

Dr. Swift's Will

THE

LAST WILL

AND

TESTAMENT

OF

JONATHAN SWIFT, *D. D.*

Attested by Jo. WYNNE, Jo. ROCHFORT,
and WILLIAM DUNKIN.

Taken out of the Perogative Court of
Dublin.

DUBLIN Printed:
LONDON Reprinted; and sold by M. COOPER
in *Pater-noster-row.*
MDCCXLVI.

Dr. SWIFT's

WILL.

IN the Name of God, *Amen*. I JONATHAN SWIFT, Doctor in Divinity, and Dean of the Cathedral Church of St. *Patrick, Dublin*, being at this Present of sound Mind, although weak in Body, do here make my last Will and Testament, hereby revoking all my former Wills.

Imprimis: I bequeath my Soul to GOD, (in humble Hopes of his Mercy through JESUS CHRIST) and my Body to the Earth. And, I desire that my Body may be buried in the great Isle of the said Cathedral, on the South Side, under the Pillar next to the Monument of Primate *Narcissus Marsh*, three Days after my Decease, as privately as possible, and at Twelve o'Clock at Night: And, that a Black Marble of   Feet square, and seven Feet from the Ground, fixed to the Wall, may be erected, with the following Inscription in large Letters, deeply cut, and strongly gilded. HIC DEPOSITUM EST CORPUS *JONATHAN SWIFT*, S.T.D. HUJUS ECCLESIÆ CATHEDRALIS DECANI, UBI SÆVA INDIGNATIO ULTERIUS COR LACERARE NEQUIT. ABI VIATOR, ET IMITARE, SI POTERIS, STRENUUM PRO VIRILI LIBERTATIS VINDICATOREM. OBIIT ANNO (1745) MENSIS (OCTOBRIS) DIE (19) ÆTATIS ANNO (78).

Item: I give and bequeath to my Executors all my worldly Substance, of what Nature or Kind soever (excepting such Part thereof as is herein after particularly devised) for the following Uses and Purposes, that is to say, to the Intent that they, or the Survivors or Survivor of them, their Executors, or Administrators, as soon as conveniently may be after my Death, shall turn it all into ready Money, and lay out the

same in purchasing Lands of Inheritance in Fee-simple, situate
in any Province of *Ireland*, except *Connaught*, but as near to
the City of *Dublin*, as conveniently can be found, and not
incumbered with, or subject to any Leases for Lives renew-
able, or any Terms for Years longer than Thirty-one: And I
desire that a yearly Annuity of Twenty Pounds *Sterling*, out of
the annual Profits of such Lands when purchased, and out of
the yearly Income of my said Fortune, devised to my Executors
as aforesaid, until such Purchase shall be made, shall be
paid to *Rebecca Dingley* of the City of *Dublin*, Spinster, during
her Life, by two equal half-yearly Payments, on the Feasts of
All-Saints, and St. *Philip* and St. *Jacob*, the first Payment to be
made on such of the said Feasts as shall happen next after my
Death. And that the Residue of the yearly Profits of the said
Lands when purchased, and until such Purchase be made, the
Residue of the yearly Income and Interest of my said Fortune
devised as aforesaid to my Executors, shall be laid out in purchasing a Piece of Land, situate near Dr. *Steven*'s Hospital, or
if it cannot be there had, somewhere in or near the City of
Dublin, large enough for the Purposes herein after mentioned,
and in building thereon an Hospital large enough for the
Reception of as many Idiots and Lunaticks as the annual
Income of the said Lands and worldly Substance shall be
sufficient to maintain: And, I desire that the said Hospital
may be called St. *Patrick*'s Hospital, and may be built in such
a manner, that another Building may be added unto it, in case
the Endowment thereof should be enlarged; so that the
additional Building may make the whole Edifice regular and
compleat. And my further Will and Desire is, that when the
said Hospital shall be built, the whole yearly Income of the
said Lands and Estate, shall, for ever after, be laid out in
providing Victuals, Cloathing, Medicines, Attendance, and
all other Necessaries for such Idiots and Lunaticks, as shall
be received into the same; and in repairing and enlarging
the Building, from Time to Time, as there may be Occasion.
And, if a sufficient Number of Idiots and Lunaticks cannot
readily be found, I desire that Incurables may be taken into
the said Hospital to supply such Deficiency: But that no

Person shall be admitted into it, that laboureth under any infectious Disease: And that all such Idiots, Lunaticks and Incurables, as shall be received into the said Hospital, shall constantly live and reside therein, as well in the Night as in the Day; and that the Salaries of Agents, Receivers, Officers, Servants, and Attendants, to be employed in the Business of the said Hospital, shall not in the Whole exceed one Fifth Part of the clear yearly Income, or Revenue thereof. And, I further desire that my Executors, the Survivors or Survivor of them, or the Heirs of such, shall not have Power to demise any Part of the said Lands so to be purchased as aforesaid, but with Consent of the Lord Primate, the Lord High Chancellor, the Lord Archbishop of *Dublin*, the Dean of *Christ-Church*, the Dean of St. *Patrick*'s, the Physician to the State, and the Surgeon-General, all for the Time being, or the greater Part of them, under their Hands in Writing; and that no Leases of any Part of the said Lands, shall ever be made other than Leases for Years not exceeding Thirty-one, in Possession, and not in Reversion or Remainder, and not dispunishable of Waste, whereon shall be reserved the best and most improved Rents, that can reasonably and moderately, without racking the Tenants, be gotten for the same, without Fine. Provided always, and it is my Will and earnest Desire, that no Lease of any Part of the said Lands, so to be purchased as aforesaid, shall ever be made to, or in Trust for any Person any way concerned in the Execution of this Trust, or to, or in Trust for any Person any way related or allied, either by Consanguinity or Affinity, to any of the Persons who shall at that Time be concerned in the Execution of this Trust: And, that if any Leases shall happen to be made contrary to my Intention above expressed, the same shall be utterly void and of no Effect. And I further desire, until the Charter herein after mentioned be obtained, my Executors, or the Survivors or Survivor of them, his Heirs, Executors, or Administrators, shall not act in the Execution of this Trust, but with the Consent and Approbation of the said seven additional Trustees, or the greater Part of them, under their Hands in Writing, and shall, with such Consent and Approbation, as aforesaid, have Power, from time to time, to make Rules, Orders, and Regulations for the Government and Direction of the said Hospital. And, I make it my Request to my said Executors, that they may in convenient Time apply to his Majesty for a Charter to incorporate them, or such of them as shall be then living, and the said additional Trustees, for the better Management and Conduct of this Charity, with a Power to purchase Lands; and to supply by Election such Vacancies happening in the Corporation, as shall not be supplied by Succession, and such other Powers as may be thought expedient for the due Execution of this Trust, according to my Intention herein before expressed. And when such Charter shall be obtained, I desire that my Executors, or the Survivors or Survivor of them, or the Heirs of such Survivor, may convey to the Use of such Corporation in Fee-simple for the Purposes aforesaid, all such Lands and Tenements, as shall be purchased in manner above mentioned. Provided always, and it is my Will and Intention, that my Executors, until the said Charter, and afterwards the Corporation to be hereby incorporated, shall out of the yearly Profits of the said Lands when purchased, and out of the yearly Income of my said Fortune devised to my Executors as aforesaid, until such Purchase be made, have Power to reimburse themselves for all such Sums of their own Money, as they shall necessarily expend in the Execution of this Trust. And that until the said Charter be obtained, all Acts which shall at any Time be done in Execution of this Trust by the greater Part of my Executors then living, with the Consent of the greater Part of the said additional Trustees, under their Hands in Writing, shall be as valid and effectual, as if all my Executors had concurred in the same.

Item: Whereas I purchased the Inheritance of the Tythes of the Parish of *Effernock* near *Trim* in the County of *Meath*, for Two Hundred and Sixty Pounds *Sterling*; I bequeath the said Tythes to the Vicars of *Laracor* for the Time being, that is to say, so long as the present Episcopal Religion shall continue to be the National Established Faith and Profession in this Kingdom: But whenever any other Form of Christian

Religion shall become the Established Faith in this Kingdom, I leave the said Tythes of *Effernock* to be bestowed, as the Profits come in, to the Poor of the said Parish of *Laracor*, by a weekly Proportion, and by such Officers as may then have the Power of distributing Charities to the Poor of the said Parish, while Christianity under any Shape shall be tolerated among us, still excepting professed *Jews, Atheists* and *Infidels*.

Item: Whereas I have some Leases of certain Houses in St. *Kevin's-street*, near the Deanry-House, built upon the Dean's Ground, and one other House now inhabited by *Henry Land*[1], in *Deanry-lane* alias *Mitre-alley*, some of which Leases are let for forty-one Years, or forty at least, and not yet half expired, I bequeath to Mrs. *Martha Whiteway* my Lease or Leases of the said Houses; I also bequeath to the said *Martha*, my Lease of forty Years of *Goodman's* Holding, for which I receive Ten Pounds *per Annum*; which are two Houses, or more lately built; I bequeath also to the said *Martha* the Sum of Three Hundred Pounds *Sterling*, to be paid her by my Executors out of my ready Money, or Bank Bills, immediately after my Death, as soon as the Executors meet. I leave, moreover, to the said *Martha*, my repeating Gold Watch, my yellow Tortoise Shell Snuff Box, and her Choice of four Gold Rings, out of seven which I now possess.

Item: I bequeath to Mrs. *Mary Swift* alias *Harrison*, Daughter of the said *Martha*, my plain Gold Watch made by *Quare*, to whom also I give my *Japan* Writing Desk, bestowed to me by my Lady *Worseley*, my square Tortoise Shell Snuff Box, richly lined and inlaid with Gold, given to me by the Right Honourable *Henrietta* now Countess of *Oxford*, and the Seal with a *Pegasus*, given to me by the Countess of *Granville*.

Item: I bequeath to Mr. *Ffolliot Whiteway*, eldest son of the aforesaid *Martha*, who is bred to be an Attorney, the Sum of Sixty Pounds, as also Five Pounds to be laid out in the Purchase of such Law Books as the Honourable Mr. Justice *Lyndsay*, Mr. *Stannard*[2], or Mr. *McAullay*[3] shall judge proper for him.

[1] Sexton of St. *Patrick's* Cathedral.
[2] *Eaton Stannard*, Esq; Recorder of the City of *Dublin*.
[3] *Alexander McAullay*, Esq; Counsellor at Law, and made Judge of the Consistorial Court, Nov. 1745.

Item: I bequeath to Mr. *John Whiteway*, youngest Son of the said *Martha*, who is to be brought up a Surgeon, the Sum of One Hundred Pounds, in order to qualify him for a Surgeon, but under the Direction of his Mother; which said Sum of One Hundred Pounds is to be paid to Mrs. *Whiteway*, in Behalf of her said Son *John*, out of the Arrears which shall be due to me from my Church Livings, (except those of the Deanry Tythes, which are now let to the Reverend Doctor *Wilson*) as soon as the said Arrears can be paid to my Executors. I also leave the said *John* Five Pounds to be laid out in buying such Physical or Chirurgical Books as Doctor *Grattan* and Mr. *Nichols*[1] shall think fit for him.

Item: I bequeath to Mrs. *Anne Ridgeway*[2], now in my Family, the Profits of the Lease of two Houses let to *John Cownly*, for forty Years, of which only eight or nine are expired, for which the said *Cownly* payeth me Nine Pounds *Sterling* for Rent yearly. I also bequeath to the said *Anne*, the Sum of One Hundred Pounds *Sterling*, to be paid her by my Executors in six Weeks after my Decease, out of whatever Money or Bank Bills I may possess when I die: As also three Gold Rings, the Remainder of the seven above mentioned, after Mrs. *Whiteway* hath made her Choice of four; and all my small Pieces of Plate, not exceeding in Weight one Ounce and one third Part of an Ounce.

Item: I bequeath to my dearest Friend *Alexander Pope* of *Twittenham*, Esq; my Picture in Miniature, drawn by *Zinck*, of *Robert* late Earl of *Oxford*.

Item: I leave to *Edward* now Earl of *Oxford*, my Seal of *Julius Cæsar*, as also another Seal, supposed to be a young *Hercules*, both very choice Antiques, and set in Gold: Both which I chuse to bestow to the said Earl, because they belonged to her late Most Excellent Majesty Queen *Anne*, of ever Glorious, Immortal, and truly Pious Memory, the real Nursing Mother of all her Kingdoms.

Item: I leave to the Reverend Mr. *James Stopford*, Vicar of

---

[1] *John Nichols*, Esq; Surgeon General.

[2] Daughter to Mrs. Brent, and who for many years had been the Dean's faithful, domestick Friend.

Finglass, my Picture of King *Charles* the First, drawn by *Vandike*, which was given to me by the said *James*; as also my large Picture of Birds, which was given to me by *Thomas* Earl of *Pembroke*.

Item: I bequeath to the Reverend Mr. *Robert Grattan*, Prebendary of St. *Audeon*'s, my Gold Bottle Screw, which he gave me, and my strong Box, on Condition of his giving the sole Use of the said Box to his Brother Dr. *James Grattan*, during the Life of the said Doctor, who hath more Occasion for it, and the second best Beaver Hat I shall die possessed of.

Item: I bequeath to Mr. *John Grattan*, Prebendary of *Clonmethan*, my Silver Box in which the Freedom of the City of *Cork* was presented to me; in which I desire the said *John* to keep the Tobacco he usually cheweth, called Pigtail.

Item: I bequeath all my Horses and Mares to the Reverend Mr. *John Jackson*, Vicar of *Santry*, together with all my Horse Furniture: Lamenting that I had not Credit enough with any Chief Governor (since the Change of Times) to get some additional Church Preferment for so virtuous and worthy a Gentleman. I also leave him my third best Beaver Hat.

Item: I bequeath to the Reverend Doctor *Francis Wilson*, the Works of *Plato* in three Folio Volumes, the Earl of *Clarendon*'s History in three Folio Volumes, and my best Bible; together with thirteen small *Persian* Pictures in the Drawing Room, and the small Silver Tankard given to me by the Contribution of some Friends, whose Names are engraved at the Bottom of the said Tankard.

Item: I bequeath to the Earl of *Orrery* the enamelled Silver Plates to distinguish Bottles of Wine by, given to me by his excellent Lady, and the Half-length Picture of the late Countess of *Orkney* in the Drawing Room.

Item: I bequeath to *Alexander M'Aullay*, Esq; the Gold Box in which the Freedom of the City of *Dublin* was presented to me, as a Testimony of the Esteem and Love I have for him, on Account of his great Learning, fine natural Parts, unaffected Piety and Benevolence, and his truly honourable Zeal in Defence of the legal Rights of the Clergy, in Opposition to all their unprovoked Oppressors.

Item: I bequeath to *Deane Swift*, Esq; my large Silver Standish, consisting of a large Silver Plate, an Ink Pot, a Sand Box and Bell of the same Mettal.

Item: I bequeath to Mrs. *Mary Barber* the Medal of Queen *Anne* and Prince *George*, which she formerly gave me.

Item: I leave to the Reverend Mr. *John Worral*[1] my best Beaver Hat.

Item: I bequeath to the Reverend Doctor *Patrick Delany* my Medal of Queen *Anne* in Silver, and on the Reverse the Bishops of *England* kneeling before her Most Sacred Majesty.

Item: I bequeath to the Reverend Mr. *James King*, Prebendary of *Tipper*, my large gilded Medal of King *Charles* the First, and on the Reverse a Crown of Martyrdom, with other Devices. My Will, nevertheless, is, that if any of the above named Legatees should die before me, that then, and in that Case, the respective Legacies to them bequeathed, shall revert to myself, and become again subject to my Disposal.

Item: Whereas I have the Lease of a Field in Trust for me, commonly called the *Vineyard*, let to the Reverend Doctor *Francis Corbet*, and the Trust declared by the said Doctor; the said Field, with some Land on this Side of the Road, making in all about three Acres, for which I pay yearly to the Dean and Chapter of St. *Patrick*'s * * *.

Whereas I have built a strong Wall round the said Piece of Ground, eight or nine Feet high, faced to the South Aspect with Brick, which cost me above Six Hundred Pounds *Sterling:* And likewise another Piece of Ground as aforesaid, of half an Acre, adjoining to the Burial Place called the *Cabbage-Garden*, now tenanted by *William White*, Gardener: My Will is, that the Ground inclosed by the great Wall, may be sold for the Remainder of the Lease, at the highest Price my Executors can get for it, in Belief and Hopes, that the said Price will exceed Three Hundred Pounds at the lowest Value: For which my Successor in the Deanry shall have the first Refusal: and it is my earnest Desire, that the succeeding Deans and Chapters may preserve the said *Vineyard* and Piece of Land adjoining, where the said *White* now liveth, so as to be always

---

[1] Vicar to the Dean of *Christ-Church*, and Master of both Choirs.

in the Hands of the succeeding Deans during their Office, by each Dean lessening One Fourth of the Purchase Money to each succeeding Dean, and for no more than the present Rent.

And I appoint the Honourable *Robert Lyndsay*, one of the Judges of the Court of Common-Pleas: *Henry Singleton*, Esq.; Prime-Sergeant to his Majesty: the Reverend Doctor *Patrick Delany*, Chancellor of St. Patrick's; the Reverend Doctor *Francis Wilson*, Prebendary of *Kilmactolway*; *Eaton Stannard*, Esq; Recorder of the City of *Dublin*; the Reverend Mr. *Robert Grattan*, Prebendary of St. *Audeon*'s; the Reverend Mr. *John Grattan*, Prebendary of *Clonmethan*; the Reverend Mr. *James Stopford*, Vicar of *Finglass*; the Reverend Mr. *James King*, Prebendary of *Tipper*; and *Alexander M'Aullay*, Esq; my Executors.

In Witness whereof, I have hereunto set my Hand and Seal, and published and declared this as my last Will and Testament, this third Day of May, 1740.

JONATHAN SWIFT.

> *Signed, sealed, and published by the above named* JONATHAN SWIFT, *in Presence of Us, who have subscribed our Names in his Presence,*

JO. WYNNE,

JO. ROCHFORT,

WILLIAM DUNKIN.

CODICIL TO THE WILL OF DR. SWIFT

In the name of God Amen. I *Jonathan Swift*, Doctor in Divinity, and Dean of the Cathedral Church of St. *Patrick*'s *Dublin*, being weak in Body but sound in Mind, do make this codicil Part of my last Will and Testament, and do appoint this Writing to have the same Force and Effect thereof.

Whereas the Right Honourable *Theophilus*, Lord *Newtown*, deceased, did, by his last Will and Testament, bequeath unto *Anne Brent* a legacy of Twenty Pounds *Sterling* a Year during her Life, in Consideration of the long and faithful Service of her the said Anne: And wheras the said *Anne*, since the Death of the said Lord *Newtown*, did intermarry with *Anthony Ridgeway*, of the City of *Dublin*, Cabinet-Maker; and that the said *Anthony Ridgeway* and *Anne* his Wife, for valuable Considerations, did Grant and Assign unto me, the said Dr. *Swift*, the said Annuity or Rent Charge of Twenty Pounds *sterling, per annum*, to hold to me, my Executors, and Administrators, during the Life of the said *Anne*; and the said *Anthony Ridgeway* being since dead; Now I the said Dr. *Swift*, do hereby devise and bequeath unto the Rev. Dr. *John Wynne*, Chanter of St. *Patrick*'s *Dublin*, the Rev. Mr. *James King*, Curate of St. *Bridget*'s, *Dublin*, and the Rev. Dr. *Francis Willson*, Prebendary of Kilmactolway, and the Survivor or Survivors of them, their Heirs, Executors, and Administrators, the said Annuity or yearly Rent Charge of Twenty Pounds *Sterling, per annum*; devised by the said Lord *Newtown* to the said *Anne*, to have, receive, and enjoy the same during the Life of the said *Anne*, to the Uses, Intents, and Purposes herein after specified; that is to say, it is my Will, that my said Trustees, and the Survivor or Survivors of them, his, and their Heirs, Executors and Administrators, shall, (so soon after as they shall have received the Annuity, or any Part thereof, as conveniently as they can,) Pay or cause to be paid unto the said *Anne Ridgeway*, the said Annuity of Twenty Pounds *Sterling, per annum*, during her Life. In Witness whereof, I, the said Dr. *Jonathan Swift*, have hereunto set my Hand and Seal, and published this Codicil, as Part of my last Will and Testament, this Fifth Day of May, 1740.

JONATHAN SWIFT.

Signed, sealed and published in Presence of us, who witnessed this Codicil, in presence of the said Testator.

JOHN LYON,
WILLIAM DUNKIN,
ROGER KENDRICK.

APPENDIXES

L A W S

FOR

The Dean's Servants.

Dᴇᴄᴇᴍʙᴇʀ 7th, 1733.

IF either of the two men-servants be drunk, he shall pay an English crown out of his wages for the said offence, by giving the Dean a receipt for so much wages received.

When the Dean is at home, no servant shall presume to be absent, without giving notice to the Dean, and asking leave, upon the forfeiture of sixpence for every half-hour that he is absent, to be stopt out of his or her board-wages.

When the Dean is abroad, no servant, except the woman, shall presume to leave the house for above one half-hour; after which, for every half-hour's absence, he shall forfeit sixpence: And, if the other servant goes out before the first returns, he shall pay five shillings out of his wages, as above.

Whatever servant shall be taken in a manifest lie, shall forfeit one shilling out of his or her board-wages.

When the Dean goes about the house or out-houses, or garden, or to Naboth's Vineyard, whatever things he finds out of order, by neglect of any servant under whose care it was, that servant shall forfeit sixpence, and see to get it mended as soon as possible, or suffer more forfeitures as the Dean's discretion.

If two servants be abroad together when the Dean is from home, and the fact be concealed from the Dean, the concealer shall forfeit two crowns out of his or her wages, as above.

If, in waiting at table, the two servants be out of the room together, without orders, the last who went out shall forfeit threepence out of his board-wages.

The woman may go out when the Dean is abroad for one hour, but no longer, under the same penalty with the men: But provided the two men-servants keep the house until she returns; otherwise, either of the servants, who goes out before her return, shall forfeit a crown out of his wages, as above.

Whatever other laws the Dean shall think fit to make, at any time to come, for the government of his servants, and forfeitures for neglect or disobedience, all the servants shall be bound to submit to.

Whatever other servant, except the woman, shall presume to be drunk, the other two servants shall inform the Dean thereof, under pain of forfeiting two crowns out of his or her wages, besides the forfeiture of a crown from the said servant who was drunk.

T H E

DUTY of SERVANTS at INNS.

BE mounted before your Master. When you see him mounted, ride out before him. When he baiteth at noon, enter the Inn Gate before him, and call the Ostler to hold your Master's Horse while he alighteth. Leave your Master to the Servants of the Inn; go you with the Horses into the Stable; chuse a Place farthest from the Stable-Door; see the Standing be dry; send immediately for fresh Straw; see all the old Hay out of the Rack, and get fresh put in; see your Horses Girths be loosed and stuffed; take not off the Bridle until they are cool, nor Saddles in an Hour; see their Hoofs be well picked; try if the Heads of the Nails be fast, and whether they be well clinched, if not, send presently for a Smith; always stand by while the Smith is employed. Give the Oats the last Thing. Water your Horses when you are within a Mile or more of the Inn. Never keep above forty Yards before or behind your Master, unless he commandeth you. Try the Oats by smelling and weighing them; see you have good Measure; stand by while your Horses are eating their Oats. When you enter your Evening-Inn, let your Horses Feet be stuffed with Cow Dung every Night.

Observe the same Rules, only be sure if any Thing be wanting for a Smith, let it be done over Night.

Know the Time your Master will set out in the Morning: Allow him a full Hour to get himself ready. Contrive both at Morn and Noon to eat, so that your Master need not stay for you. Do not let the Drawer carry the Bill to your Master, but examine it first carefully and honestly, and then bring it yourself, and be able to account for every Article. If the Servants have not been civil, tell your Master before their Faces, when he is going to give them Money.

Duty of the other Servant, where there are two.

Ride forty Yards behind your Master, but be mounted before him. Observe now and then whether his Horse's Shoes be right. When you come to an Inn at Noon, give your Horse to the Ostler; bestir yourself to get a convenient Room for your Master; bring all his Things into his Room, full in his Sight; enquire what is in the House, see it yourself, and tell your Master how you like it. Step yourself now and then into the Kitchen to hasten Dinner or Supper, and observe whether they be cleanly. Taste the Ale, and tell your Master whether it be good or bad. If he wanteth Wine, go you with the Drawer and chuse a Bottle well filled and stopped: If the Wine be in Hogsheads, desire to taste and smell it; if it be sour, or not clear, or ill-tasted, let your Master know it, that he may not be at the Charge of Wine not fit to be drank. See the Salt be dry and powdered, the Bread new and clean, the Knives sharp. At Night observe the same Rules: But first chuse him a warm Room, with a Lock and Key in order, then call immediately for the Sheets, see them well aired, and at a large Fire; feel the Blankets, Bed, Bolster, and Pillow, whether they be dry, and whether the Floor under the Bed be damp. Let the Chamber be that which hath been last lain in: enquire about it. If the Bed itself be damp, let it be brought before a large Fire, and air it on both Sides. That you may forget nothing in the Inn, have a fair Lift of all that you want to take out; and when you put them up, compare them with your Lift.

You are to step now and then into the Stable to see whether the Groom performeth his Duty.

For packing up your Things, have a list of Linen, *&c.* In packing take Care that no two hard Things be together, and that they be wrapped up in Paper or Towels. Have a good Provision of large coarse Paper, and other waste Paper. Remember to put every Thing in their proper Places in the Portmanteau. Stuff the Shoes and Slippers at the Toes with a small Lock of Hay; fold up the Cloaths, so as that they may not be rumpled. When your Master is in his Room at Night,

put all his Things in such a manner as he has them at Home.
Learn to have some Skill in Cookery, that at a Pinch you may
be able to make your Master easy.

The Groom. Carry with you a Stirrup-Leather, an Awl,
twelve Horse-Nails, and a Horse's Fore-Shoes, Pick and an
Hammer, for fear of an Accident; and some Ends, and Pack-
thread, a Bottle-skrew, Knife, and Penknife, Needles, Pins,
Thread, Silk, Worsted, *&c.* Some Plaisters and Scissars.

Item, The Servants to carry their own Things. Have a
Pocket-Book, keep all the Bills, date the Time and Place;
and indorse the Numbers.

Enquire in every Town if there be any Thing worth seeing.
Observe the Country Seats, and ask who they belong to;
and enter them, and the Counties where they are.

Search under your Master's Bed when he is gone up, lest
a Cat or something else may be under it.

When your Master's Bed is made, and his Things ready,
lock the Chamber Door, and keep the Key until he goeth to
Bed; then keep it in your Pocket until Morning.

Let the Servants of the Inn be sure to wake you above an
Hour before your Master is to go, that he may have an Hour
to prepare himself.

If the Ostler hath been knavish or negligent, do not let
him hold your Master's Horse. Observe the same Rule at a
Gentleman's House; if the Groom hath not taken Care of
your Horses, do not let him hold your Master's.

Enquire at every Inn where you stay, which is the best
Inn in the next Town you are to come to; yet do not rely on
that, but likewise, as you enter into any Town to stay, ask
the People which is the best Inn, and go to that which most
People commend.

See that your Master's Boots be dried and well liquored over
Night.

o

CERTIFICATE
TO
A DISCARDED SERVANT

WHEREAS the bearer served me the space of one year, during which time he was an *idler* and a *drunkard*; I then discharged him as such; but how far his having been five years at sea may have mended his manners, I leave to the penetration of those who may hereafter chuse to employ him.

J. SWIFT.

Deanry House,
Jan. 9, 1739.

The CASE of the *Woolen* Manufacturers of the City of *Dublin*, and Liberties thereunto adjoyning, truly stated.

To the Nobility, and Gentlemen, and other Well-wishers to the Happiness and Prosperity of this Kingdom.

Cari sunt Parentes, cari Liberi, Propinqui, Familiares; sed omnes omnium Caritates Patria una complexa est. Tul. Offic. Cap. xvii.

NOTHING is more apparent, at the first View, than that the Employment of the Hands of the Poor, in any Nation, in some useful Manufacture, is highly conducive to the Welfare and Happiness of that Nation: There is an interest attends it, which diffuses itself through the whole Community; because, by this Means, the remitting of several Sums of Money to other Countries, in order to be furnished with Conveniencies, is prevented; which helps to keep the Ballance of Trade as it should be.

Whereas, if the Imports of a Nation be more than its Exports, the Ballance of Trade must be consequently against it; which, in Time, will consume its Vitals, as it drains, by Degrees, its Substance from it.

Nothing is also more apparent, than that the greater the Encouragement is, which is given to the Consumption of any Manufacture, the greater Improvement will be made in that Manufacture; Poverty, and the Consequence of this, the Want of sufficient Materials, being grand Impediments in the Way of any Business.

This, your late Experience has fully proved to be true, since you were pleased to enter into that noble Agreement to countenance our Undertakings, and encourage the Industry of your own Poor.

Every thing was going on successfully with us, and we thought ourselves extremely happy in your Benevolence; but there is a Storm now rising, which, we are greatly afraid, will turn all that Happiness we proposed to our selves into Misery; our Sun will soon set in Darkness, unless we can perswade you to interpose in our Behalf, and hinder our impending Ruin.

No doubt, ye are surprized at this, and cannot imagine what can alarm us now: But, the Custom-House Entries will soon discover the Occasion of it.

There it will appear, that too many make their own particular Interest the Measure of all their Actions, and care not how many starve, and perish, so they can but fill their own Pockets, and compleat their mercenary Projects.

There it will appear, that a vile, base, private Spirit reigns in the Hearts of many Woollen-Drapers in this City; who, this Moment, are endeavouring to sacrifice that Branch of Trade to their Avarice and Ambition.

As we maintain a good Cause, the Cause of our Country, we are neither afraid, or ashamed to let you know their Names.

The Principal then of them, are these following, viz. Mr. *Hinde*, and Mess. *Bradshaw* and Company, in *Castle-street*; Mr. *Dobson*, Mr. *Card*, Mr. *Lombard*, and Mr. *Richard Eustace*, in *High-street*; as also, Mr. *Mc. Kenzie*, on *Essex-Bridge:* These, in Conjunction with some other Merchants in this City, we affirm, have imported into this Kingdom, within these four Months past, 15000 Yards of Woollen Commodities, and several Thousand Yards of rich foreign Silks, and other Manufactures, to the Value of 14000 *l. Sterl.*

Now, *my Lords and Gentlemen*, as your Estates are in this Kingdom, and as in Consequence of this, your Interest is interwoven with that of the Publick; we hope you will take

Notice of the pernicious Practices of those Enemies to the Commonwealth.

Certainly, should their Designs, so detrimental to our *Irish* Manufacture, succeed; that is, if those Goods are bought, and thereby these Drapers be encouraged to continue their Scheme; several Thousands of the inferior Sort of People, that are now supported, and maintained by the Woollen Trade at home, and that rely entirely upon your kind Disposition towards them, as breathing the same Air with you in poor *Ireland*, must inevitably come to great Want.

Their Cries can scarce be out of your Ears yet, since the last low Ebb of Trade.

Were they not then the most miserable Spectacles? The greatest Objects of Compassion and Charity? In short, it is impossible to have a just Idea of their Calamity, unless ye had been Eye-Witnesses of it.

Were we not then forced to apply for the *Concordatum* Money, to keep them from starving? And were there not publick Collections made throughout the whole City, for their Relief?

Now, will not the same Cause produce the same Effects again? Will not their Miseries increase, in Proportion to the Encouragement given to foreign Manufacturers, 'till at last they are reduced to the same deplorable Circumstances, and in the same melancholly Condition beg Relief at your Hands?

But this is not the only Evil that will be the Consequence.

We need not inform you, that the Heads of the Populace are extremely giddy; that they are ever prone to Mischief when idle; so that it was always accounted, if it was only for Peace Sake, an excellent Piece of Policy to keep them employed.

But what Disorders, and what Rapine would ensue, if they should not only be idle, but also want Bread? This would be a Spur to their depraved Inclinations; and would assuredly urge many of them on to injure their Neighbours, as often as Opportunity served.

But, perhaps, those Drapers, that would starve our Poor, or subject them to such Temptations, as Flesh and Blood would find difficult to resist; may say, as we hear they frequently do, by Way of Excuse, that they would not import a Yard of foreign Cloth, if the Clothiers here were not defective both in the Quality and Quantity of their Goods.

To this we answer, and say, We appeal to their own Consciences, whether we have not made Goods, for several Years past, equal to any that have come from Abroad.

To prove this farther, we are willing to produce them this present Time, if any Gentleman will be so curious as to make an Enquiry.

The Truth then, as to the Quality of them, fairly appearing, it will consequently follow, that it is in our Power to have any Quantity, if proper Encouragement be given, and the Natives and Inhabitants of *Ireland*, like so many worthy Patriots, join in the Consumption of it.

We can with Confidence assure those, that are Lovers of their Country, that no Pains or Expence has been spared by some industrious Men amongst us, to bring this Manufacture to the greatest Perfection in all its Branches.

But this is not the only Piece of Craft they have devis'd; for we have Reason to believe they have sold several foreign Cloths of a middle Price for our superfine; and so have abused many well-dispos'd Gentlemen, who honestly intended to have serv'd the Nation.

Nay, to shew their Deceit more plainly, and that nothing is too difficult for Minds prone to Mischief, to get over, we can even prove they have attempted to corrupt our Sealmaster, and endeavour'd to perswade him to seal their foreign Cloths with the Seal of *Ireland*.

So that we desire all those who sincerely wish well to the Land they live in, to take Notice, that the *Irish* Seal, which is the Harp, is fixed at the Head End of all our Pieces. This will continue till we agree upon some common Mark, to prevent all Counterfeits; which shall be carefully advertis'd.

This Caution, together with your Encouragement, we presume, will restore Trade; and the Price of Wool, which falls and sinks under such wicked, and destructive Practices as are mention'd in this Paper. By which Means your Rents will be better paid, and the Kingdom in general will flourish.

We shall beg Leave to mention one Thing more; which is, to let you know how these Men, with many other Shop-keepers in Town, serve us in point of Payment.

All our Money, which we should lay out for Wool in proper Seasons of the Year, is employ'd in the Payment of foreign Bills; so that we seldom get a Sum together that is of any Service: In short, they keep us standing at their Doors (like poor Petitioners) till meer Necessity will oblige us sometimes to take a Moydore or two, where fifty or a hundred are due; and that for nine, twelve, or eighteen Months together. A Practice shameful to the last Degree, and we hope will be resented by you in a proper Manner.

It is the Business of every worthy Patriot to support the publick Good.

He should ever lay this down as a fundamental Maxim, *viz*. That he thrives in the Prosperity, and suffers in the Loss and Damage of his Country.

The Streams therefore of his Affection and Love should always direct their Current thither, as to their ultimate End, and be all swallowed up in that Ocean.

Since it is plain, that no Kingdom, or State can subsist, unless the Members thereof are engaged with a commendable Zeal mutually to promote the Interest of their respective Establishments, it may be fairly inferr'd, that it is the indispensable Duty of every one of them, to apply the Use of those Means, without which, this noble End will be entirely frustrated.

We conclude all with our unfeigned, and hearty Thanks to you, for the Encouragement given hitherto to our *Irish* Woollen Drapery, and hope your kind Dispositions towards us will be continued, while we take Care to deserve them.

This will animate us to prosecute our Trade with Vigour, and put it in our Power to improve it daily.

This will keep our Poor continually employ'd, hinder them from becoming Robbers or Objects of Charity, and prevent a great deal of Money from being sent out of the Kingdom.

UPON GIVING

B A D G E S

TO THE

P O O R.

THE continual concourse of beggars, from all parts of the kingdom to this city, having made it impossible for the several parishes to maintain their own poor, according to the antient laws of the land; several Lord Mayors did apply themselves to the Lord Archbishop of Dublin, that his Grace would direct his clergy, and the church-wardens of the said city, to appoint badges of brass, copper, or pewter, to be worn by the poor of the several parishes. The badges to be marked with the initial letters of the name of each church, and numbered 1, 2, 3, &c. and to be well sewed and fastened on the right and left shoulder of the outward garment of each of the said poor, by which they might be distinguished. And that none of the said poor should go out of their own parish to beg alms; whereof the beadles were to take care.

His Grace, the Lord Archbishop, did accordingly give his directions to the clergy; which however, have proved wholly ineffectual, by the fraud, perverseness, or pride of the said poor, several of them openly protesting they will never submit to wear the said badges, and of those who received them, almost every one keep them in their pockets, or hang them on a string about their necks, or fasten them only with a pin, or wear them under their coats, not to be seen. By which means the whole design is eluded, so that a man may walk from one end of the town to the other, without seeing one beggar regularly badged, and in such great numbers, that they are a mighty nuisance to the public, most of them being foreigners.

It is therefore proposed, That his Grace the Lord Archbishop would please to call the clergy of the city together, and renew his directions and exhortations to them, to put this affair of badges effectually in practice, by such methods as his Grace and they shall agree upon. And I think it would be highly necessary, that some paper should be pasted up, in several proper parts of the city, signifying this order, and exhorting all people to give no alms, except to those poor who are regularly badged, and only while they are within the precincts of their own parishes. And, if something like this were delivered by the ministers, in the reading-desk, two or three Lord's-days successively, it would still be of further use to put this matter upon a right foot. And that all who offend against this regulation, be treated as vagabonds and sturdy beggars.

Deanry-house,
Sept. 26, 1726.

CONSIDERATIONS

ABOUT

MAINTAINING the POOR

WE have been amused, for at least thirty years past, with numberless schemes in writing and discourse, both in and out of parliament, for maintaining the poor, and setting them to work, especially in this city; most of which were idle, indigested, or visionary, and all of them ineffectual, as it hath plainly appeared by the consequences. Many of those projectors were so stupid, that they drew a parallel from Holland and England, to be settled in Ireland; that is to say, from two countries with full freedom and encouragement for trade, to a third where all kind of trade is cramped, and the most beneficial parts are entirely taken away. But the perpetual infelicity of false and foolish reasoning, as well as proceeding and acting upon it, seems to be fatal to this country.

For my own part, who have much conversed with those folks who call themselves Merchants, I do not remember to have met with a more ignorant and wrong-thinking race of people in the very first rudiments of trade; which, however, was not so much owing to their want of capacity, as to the crazy constitution of this kingdom, where pedlars are better qualified to thrive than the wisest merchants. I could fill a volume with only setting down a list of the public absurdities, by which this kingdom hath suffered within the compass of my own memory, such as could not be believed of any nation, among whom folly was not established as a law. I cannot forbear instancing a few of these, because it may be of some use to those who shall have it in their power to be more cautious for the future.

The first was the building of the barracks, whereof I have seen above one half, and have heard enough of the rest, to affirm that the public hath been cheated of at least two thirds of the money raised for that use, by the plain fraud of the undertakers.

Another was the management of the money raised for the Palatines; when, instead of employing that great sum in purchasing lands in some remote and cheap part of the kingdom, and there planting those people as a colony, the whole end was utterly defeated.

A third is the insurance-office against fire, by which several thousand pounds are yearly remitted to England (a trifle it seems we can easily spare) and will gradually encrease until it comes to a good national tax. For the society-marks upon our houses (under which might properly be written, *The Lord have Mercy upon us*) spread faster and farther than the * colony of frogs. I have, for above twenty years past, given warning several thousand times, to many substantial people, and to such who are acquainted with Lords and Squires, and the like great folks, (to any of whom I have not the honour to be known:) I mentioned my daily fears, lest our watchful friends in England might take this business out of our hands; and how easy it would be to prevent that evil, by erecting a society of persons who had good estates, such, for instance, as that noble knot of bankers under the style of Swift and Company. But now we are become tributary to England, not only for materials to light our own fires; but for engines to put them out; to which, if hearth-money be added (repealed in England as a grievance) we have the honour to pay three taxes for fire.

* This similitude, which is certainly the finest that could possibly have been used upon this occasion, seems to require a short explication. About the beginning of this current century, Doctor Gwythers, a Physician and Fellow of the University of Dublin, brought over with him a parcel of frogs from England to Ireland, in order to propagate the species in that kingdom, and threw them into the ditches of the University-park; but they all perished. Whereupon he sent to England for some bottles of the frog-spawn, which he threw into those ditches, by which means the species of frogs was propagated in that kingdom. However, their number was so small in the year 1720, that a frog was no where to be seen in Ireland, except in the neighbourhood of the University-park: but, within six or seven years after, they spread thirty, forty, and fifty miles over the country; and so at last, by degrees, over the whole nation.

A fourth was the knavery of those merchants, or linen-manufacturers, or both; when, upon occasion of the plague at Marseilles, we had a fair opportunity of getting into our hands the whole linen-trade with Spain; but the commodity was so bad, and held at so high a rate, that almost the whole cargo was returned, and the small remainder sold below the prime cost.

So many other particulars of the same nature crowd into my thoughts, that I am forced to stop, and the rather because they are not very proper for my subject, to which I shall now return.

Among all the schemes for maintaining the poor of the city, and setting them to work, the least weight hath been laid upon that single point which is of greatest importance; I mean that of keeping foreign beggars from swarming hither out of every part of the country; for, until this be brought to pass effectually, all our wise reasonings and proceedings upon them will be vain and ridiculous.

The prodigious number of beggars throughout this kingdom, in proportion to so small a number of people, is owing to many reasons: To the laziness of the natives; the want of work to employ them; the enormous rents paid by cottagers for their miserable cabbins and potatoe-plots; their early marriages, without the least prospect of establishment, the ruin of agriculture, whereby such vast numbers are hindered from providing their own bread, and have no money to purchase it; the mortal damp upon all kinds of trade, and many other circumstances too tedious or invidious to mention.

And to the same causes we owe the perpetual concourse of foreign beggars to this town, the country landlords giving all assistance, except money and victuals, to drive from their estates those miserable creatures they have undone.

It was a general complaint against the poor-house, under its former governors, that the number of poor in this city did not lessen by taking three hundred into the house, and all of them recommended under the minister and church-warden's hands of the several parishes; and this complaint must still continue, although the poor-house should be enlarged to maintain three thousand, or even double that number.

The revenues of the poor-house, as it is now established, amount to about two thousand pounds a year; whereof, two hundred allowed for officers, and one hundred for repairs, the remaining seventeen hundred, at four pounds a head, will support four hundred and twenty-five persons. This is a favourable allowance, considering that I subtract nothing for the diet of those officers, and for wear and tare of furniture; and, if every one of these collegiates should be set to work, it is agreed they will not be able to gain by their labour above one fourth part of their maintenance.

At the same time the oratorial part of these gentlemen seldom vouchsafe to mention fewer than fifteen hundred, or two thousand people, to be maintained in this hospital, without troubling their heads about the fund, * * *

Prefaces to Swift's Works, Dublin, 1735

THE
WORKS
OF
J.S, D.D, D.S.P.D.
IN
FOUR VOLUMES.
CONTAINING,

I. The Author's MISCELLANIES in PROSE.

II. His POETICAL WRITINGS.

III. The TRAVELS of Captain *Lemuel Gulliver.*

IV. His Papers relating to *Ireland*, confisting of
several Treatises; among which are, The
DRAPIER'S LETTERS to the People of *Ireland*
against receiving *Wood's* Half-pence: Also,
two Original DRAPIER'S LETTERS, never before publifhed.

In this Edition are great Alterations and Additions; and likewife many Pieçes in each Volume, never before publifhed

---

DUBLIN:
Printed by and for GEORGE FAULKNER, Printer
and Bookfeller, in ESSEX-STREET, oppofite to
the Bridge. M DCC XXXV.

THE FIRST VOLUME

Publisher's Preface.

*H*AVING *received great Encouragement from both Kingdoms;
and especially from this, to publish a compleat and correct
Edition in four Volumes, of the Works supposed to be
written by the Reverend Dr. S. D. S. P. D. we desire Leave to inform
the Readers how we have proceeded in this Affair. We do not find,
that the supposed Author did ever put his Name to above two
Compositions, which were both writ in Prose; the former is a Letter
to the Lord Treasurer* Oxford, *upon a Proposal for correcting and
ascertaining the* English *Language; the other is a Letter upon a
different Subject to the Lord Chancellor* Middleton, *which was
never printed before; but we found the Name subscribed at Length
in the original Manuscript. This Way of proceeding in the Author,
hath put us under the Necessity of complying with the general
Opinion, which hath fixed certain Writings both in Verse and Prose
upon him, whether truly or no we shall not presume to determine;
for, we are assured he never directly owned to his nearest Friends any
Writings which generally passed for his; the unavoidable Consequence
whereof was, that besides those Poems or Treatises, which the
judicious Part of the World agreed to have come from his Pen; many
others were vulgarly fixed on him, which a Writer much inferior (at
least if Printers and Booksellers were to be the Judges) might have
just Reason to complain of; and yet, we are equally assured by those
Gentlemen in this Kingdom, who seem to know the Author best, that
when People of more Curiosity than Taste or Manners, offered to
charge him with some Trifles which he had not writ, he would never
give them the least Satisfaction, by owning or denying it.*

*If we are truly informed, the supposed Author hath often pro-
tested, that he never did write three Copies of Verses with the least
Intention to have them printed, although he was easy enough to shew
them to his Friends, and at their Desire was not very scrupulous in
suffering them to take Copies; from whence most of those Poems were*

occasionally printed in both Kingdoms, either in single Papers, or in Miscellanies.

Several Applications have been made to the supposed Author for two Years past by most of his Friends, that he would give us Leave to print those Writings in Verse and Prose, which are universally imputed to him: The Arguments made use of were, that such a Collection as we proposed could not be printed in London; *because several Copies, and some whole Treatises were the Property of different Booksellers, who were not likely to agree in Partnership, nor had the same Advantage with us of consulting the supposed Author's Friends, who were pleased to correct many gross Errors, and strike out some very injudicious Interpolations; particularly in the Voyages of Captain* Gulliver: *Not to mention several Things in Prose as well as Verse, which we procured from some Gentlemen who were either connived at, or suffered to take Copies. We add, that if we did not undertake this Work, it would certainly be attempted by some Bookseller, who probably might not be so ready to submit to the Advice and Direction of the supposed Author's Friends. That we offended against no Law in acting as we did; because in this Kingdom, neither Authors, Booksellers or Printers, pretended any Property in Copies; which in* London *is fixed as certainly as any other legal Possession.*

But our Arguments were of little Effect; further, than that the supposed Author was prevailed on to suffer some Friends to review and correct the Sheets after they were printed; and sometimes he condescended, as we have heard, to give them his own Opinion.

In printing the four Volumes we have been advised to observe the following Order: The first Volume consists of those Miscellanies, which were published in London *about thirty Years ago; that is to say, the Prose Part of them; but in this Impression are several considerable Additions. The second Volume contains all the Poetical Writings, that we could collect, and which are generally ascribed to the same Author; wherein we entirely submitted to the Directions of his Friends. The third Volume makes up the four Parts of Captain* Gulliver's *Travels. The last Volume is a compleat Collection of all those Tracts relating to* Ireland, *which are universally allowed to have been written by the same Author; and may probably be useful upon many Occasions to this poor Kingdom in future Ages; and even* to England *itself, where most of them have been printed, and well received.*

This is all we have been allowed to prefix as a general Preface; but before each of the three ensuing Volumes, there may perhaps be a short Advertisement.

As the Works have been delayed some Months longer than was promised, it is to be hoped, that the Subscribers will not take it ill, because we were willing to give them all the Satisfaction in our Power, by collecting as many original Pieces as were possible to be got of the supposed Author's from his Friends in England, *which we found a great Difficulty in procuring. By this Delay the Works have swelled to many Pages more than was at first imagined, by which means we have been at much more Expence.*

THE SECOND VOLUME

Advertisement.

THE *first Collection of this Author's Writings were published near thirty Years ago, under the Title of Miscellanies in Verse and Prose. Several Years after, there appeared three Volumes of Miscellanies, with a Preface to the first, signed* J. Swift *and* A. Pope. *In these the Verses, with great Additions, were printed in a Volume by themselves. But in each Volume were mixed many Poems and Treatises, writ by the supposed Author's Friends, which we have laid aside; our Intention being only to publish the Works of one Writer. The following Poetical Volume is enlarged by above a third Part, which was never collected before, although some of them were occasionally printed in* London *in single Sheets. The rest were procured from the supposed Author's Friends, who at their earnest Request were permitted to take Copies.*

The following Poems chiefly consist either of Humour or Satyr, and very often of both together. What Merit they may have, we confess ourselves to be no Judges of in the least; but out of due Regard to a Writer, from whose Works we hope to receive some Benefit, we cannot conceal what we have heard from several Persons of great Judgment; that the Author never was known either in Verse or Prose to borrow any Thought, Simile, Epithet, or particular Manner of Style; but whatever he writ, whether good, bad, or indifferent, is an Original in itself.

Although we are very sensible, that in some of the following Poems, the Ladies may resent certain satyrical Touches against the mistaken Conduct in some of the fair Sex: And that, some warm Persons on the prevailing Side, may censure this Author, whoever he be, for not thinking in publick Matters exactly like themselves: Yet we have been assured by several judicious and learned Gentlemen, that what the Author hath here writ, on either of those two Subjects, had no other Aim than to reform the Errors of both Sexes. If the Publick be right in its Conjectures of the Author, nothing is better known in

London, *than that while he had Credit at the Court of Queen* Anne, *he employed so much of it in favour of* Whigs *in both Kingdoms, that the Ministry used to rally him as the Advocate of that Party, for several of whom he got Employments, and preserved others from losing what they had: Of which some Instances remain even in this Kingdom. Besides, he then writ and declared against the* Pretender, *with equal Zeal, though not with equal Fury, as any of our modern* Whigs; *of which Party he always professed himself to be as to Politicks, as the Reader will find in many Parts of his Works.*

Our Intentions were to print the Poems according to the Time they were writ in; but we could not do it so exactly as we desired, because we could never get the least Satisfaction in that or many other Circumstances from the supposed Author.

THE FOURTH VOLUME

Advertisement.

THE ensuing Volume, which compleats the Set, contains all such Writings imputed to the Author, as relate to Ireland; whereof the principal are called, The Drapier's Letters; and to these we have added two which were never printed before. They were procured from a Friend of the Author's in the original Manuscript, as we are assured, and have good Reason to believe; those who are better Judges will soon determine, whether they are genuine or no. It is the Opinion of several wise Men, that the following Letters, and the other Writings relating to our poor Country, may be very useful to Posterity, by warning them for the future to oppose the same, or the like evil Designs, however plausible they may at first appear to unthinking People; or however artfully they may be represented, (like this destructive Project of William Wood) by those who were to divide the Spoil with that Impostor; or lastly by prostitute Flatterers, who are sure to find their private Account in the Ruin of the Kingdom; which Ruin would have certainly followed, if the Author, whoever he were, had not published his Letters in the most proper Juncture, and fitted to all Sorts of Readers; whereby in two or three Months he turned the whole Nation, almost to a Man, against that iniquitous Scheme.

Perhaps the Reward which the Author met with may appear extraordinary to those who may come after us; and we hope it will never be forgot. Upon the Publication of his fourth Letter, a Proclamation was issued out by the Lord-Lieutenant and Council, promising 300 l. as a Reward to any Person who should discover the Author of that Letter: But he was then become too popular to be betrayed; and besides we are informed, it never lay in the Power of the Printer to discover him; for the Copies were always sent to the Press by some obscure Messenger, who never knew the Deliverer, but gave them in at a Window, as the Author himself observes in a Letter to Harding the Printer. His Amanuensis was the only Person *trusted; to whom about two Years after he bestowed an Employment of 40 l. a Year, as a Reward for his Fidelity.*

But lest the Particulars of this pernicious Project may be forgot, we think it proper to give a short Account how it took its Rise.

About the Year 1722, under the Government of Charles Duke of Grafton, one William Wood, a Hard-Ware Man from London, and a Bankrupt, by applying himself to some in Power, and alledging the great Want of Copper-Money in Ireland, procured by very indirect Means a Patent for coining 108,000 l. to pass as current Money in this Kingdom. It was soon discovered by the Author to be a vile Jobb from the Beginning to the End; and that the chief Procurers of his Patent were to be Sharers in the Profits. These Politicians here, who outwardly favoured the Project against their Consciences, (if they had any) called every Opposition to this Patent, by the Name of flying in the King's Face.

This is enough for the Information of future Readers, because the Author in the Course of his Letters, gives full Satisfaction upon all Particulars necessary to be known.

TO THE PROVOST AND SENIOR FELLOWS
OF TRINITY COLLEGE, DUBLIN

July 5, 1736.

Rev. and worthy Sirs,

AS I had the Honour of receiving some Part of my Education in your University, and the good Fortune to be of some Service to it, while I had a Share of Credit at Court, as well as since, when I had very little or none, I may hope to be excused for laying a Case before you, and offering my Opinion upon it.

MR. DUNKIN, whom you all know, sent me some Time ago, a Memorial intended to be laid before you, which, perhaps, he hath already done. His Request is, that you will be pleased to enlarge his Annuity at present, and that he may have the same Right in his Turn, to the first Church Preferment vacant, in your Gift, as if he had been made a Fellow, according to the Scheme in his Aunt's Will; because the Absurdity of the Condition in it, ought to be imputed to the old Woman's Ignorance, although her Intention be very manifest, and the Intention of the Testator in all Wills, is chiefly regarded by the Law. What, I would therefore humbly propose, is this, that you would increase his Pension to One hundred Pounds a Year, and make him a firm Promise of the first Church Living in your Disposal, to the Value of Two hundred Pounds a Year, or somewhat more. This I take to be a reasonable Medium between what he hath proposed in his Memorial, and what you allow him at present.

I AM almost a perfect Stranger to Mr. *Dunkin*, having never seen him but twice, and then in mixed Company, nor should I now know his Person if I met him in the Streets. But now I know he is a Man of Wit and Parts; which, if applied properly, to the Business of his Function, instead of Poetry, (wherein it must be owned he sometimes excells) might be of great Use and Service to him.

I HOPE you will please to remember, that since your Body hath received no inconsiderable Benefaction from the Aunt;

it will much increase your Reputation, rather to err on the generous Side, towards the Nephew.

THESE are my Thoughts after frequently reflecting on the Case under all its Circumstances, and so I leave it to your wiser Judgements.

I am, with true Respect and Esteem,
Reverend and worthy SIRS,
Your most obedient, and
Most humble Servant,

J. SWIFT.

Deanry-House,
July 5, 1736.

TO THE HONOURABLE THE SOCIETY OF THE GOVERNOR AND ASSISTANTS, LONDON, FOR THE NEW PLANTATION IN ULSTER, WITHIN THE REALM OF IRELAND, AT THE CHAMBER IN GUILDHALL, LONDON.

April 19, 1739

Worthy Gentlemen,

I HEARTILY recommend to your very worshipful Society, the reverend Mr. William Dunkin, for the living of Colrane, vacant by the death of Dr. Squire. Mr. Dunkin is a gentleman of great learning and wit, true religion, and excellent morals. It is only for these qualifications that I recommend him to your patronage; and I am confident that you will never repent the choice of such a man, who will be ready at any time to obey your commands. You have my best wishes, and all my endeavours for your prosperity: and I shall, during my life, continue to be, with the truest respect and highest esteem,

Worthy Sirs,

Your most obedient and most humble servant,

Jon. Swift.

TO THE RIGHT WORSHIPFUL THE MAYOR, ALDERMEN, SHERIFFS, AND COMMON-COUNCIL OF THE CITY OF CORKE

Deanry-House, Dublin, August 15, 1737.

Gentlemen,

I Received from you some Weeks ago, the Honour of my Freedom in a Silver Box, by the Hands of Mr. *Stannard*;[1] but, it was not delivered to me in as many Weeks more; because I supposed he was too full of more important Business. Since that Time, I have been wholly confined by Sickness, so that I was not able to return you my Acknowledgement; and it is with much Difficulty I do it now, my Head continuing in great Disorder. Mr. *Faulkner* will be the Bearer of my Letter, who sets out this Morning for *Corke*.

I could have wished as I am a private Man, that in the Instrument of my Freedom, you had pleased to assign your Reasons for making Choice of me. I know it is a usual Compliment to bestow the Freedom of a City on an Arch-Bishop or Lord Chancellor, and other Persons of great Titles, merely upon Account of their Stations or Power: But, a private Man, and a perfect Stranger, without Power or Grandeur, may justly expect to find the Motives assigned in the Instrument of his Freedom, on what Account he is thus distinguished. And, yet I cannot discover in the whole Parchment Scrip any one Reason offered. Next, as to the Silver Box,[2] there is not

[1] *Eaton Stannard*, Esq.; then Recorder of *Dublin*, and afterwards made his Majesty's Prime Serjeant at Law, in the Room of *Anthony Malone*, Esq.; since promoted to the Chancellorship of the Exchequer.

[2] In Consequence of this Letter, there was an Inscription, and the City Arms of *Corke*, engraved on the Box, and Reasons in the Parchment Scrip for presenting him with the Freedom of that City.

so much as my Name upon it, or any one Syllable to shew it was a Present from your City. Therefore, I have, by the Advice of Friends, agreeing with my own Opinion, sent back the Box, and Instrument of Freedom by Mr. *Faulkner*, to be returned to you; leaving to your Choice, whether to insert the Reasons for which you were pleased to give me my Freedom, or bestow the Box upon some more worthy Person, whom you may have an Intention to Honour, because it will equally fit every Body.

> I am, with true Esteem
> And Gratitude, Gentlemen,
> Your most obedient, and
> Obliged Servant,

> JON. SWIFT.

ADVERTISEMENTS ABOUT ENDOW-MENTS OF SWIFT'S HOSPITAL, &c.

A LETTER FROM THE REVEREND DR. SWIFT, D.S.P.D.

To Mr. Faulkner.

Sir,

I desire you will print the following paper, in what manner you think most proper. You see my design in it: I believe, no man had ever more difficulty, or less encouragement to bestow his whole fortune for a charitable use.

I am,

your humble servant,

J. SWIFT

Thursday, July 13,

1738

It is known enough, that the above named Doctor hath by his last Will and Testament, bequeathed his whole fortune (excepting some legacies) to build and endow an Hospital, in, or near this city, for the support of Lunaticks, Ideots, and those they call Incurables: But, the difficulty he lies under, is, that his whole fortune consists in mortgages on lands, and other the like securities. For, as to purchasing a real estate in lands, for want of active friends, he finds it impossible; so that, much against his will, if he should call in all his money lent, he knows not where to find a convenient estate in a tolerable part of the kingdom, which can be bought; and in the mean time, his whole fortune must lie dead in the hands of bankers: The great misfortune is, that there seems not so much publick virtue left among us, as to have any regard for a charitable design; because none but the aforesaid unfortunate objects of charity, will be the better for it; however, the said Doctor, by calling in the several sums he hath lent, can be able with some difficulty to purchase three hundred pounds per annum in lands, for the endowment of the said hospital, if those lands could be now purchased: Otherwise, he must leave it as he hath done in his will, to the care of his executors, who are very honest, wise, and considerable gentlemen, his friends; and yet, he hath known some of very fair, and deserved credit, prove very negligent trustees. The Doctor is now able to lend two thousand pounds, at five per cent. upon good security; of which the principal after his decease is to be disposed of by his executors, in buying land for the further endowment of the said hospital.

NOTICE IN THE *DUBLIN JOURNAL* JANUARY 6, 1738–9

THE Rev. Dr. Jonathan SWIFT, Dean of St. Patrick's, Dublin (having been for some Years past resolved to leave the Bulk of his Fortune to a charitable Use) did on Tuesday, the second of this Instant January, lend the sum of two thousand, one hundred and twenty pounds at five per cent. and intends that the Interest thereof shall go towards encreasing the said Charity. The Dean would rather have purchased an Estate in hand for the same Use, and hath often communicated his Intention to several Persons, but he could not find any to assist him, even with Advice: so great is the Dearth of Publick-spirited People in this poor unhappy Kingdom.

ADVERTISEMENT CONCERNING THE THEFT OF
LEAD FROM ST. PATRICK'S ROOF.

WHEREAS certain wicked and sacrilegious People did
in the dead Time of the Night, between the 17th and
18th of December last, steal a considerable Quantity
of Lead from the Roof of the Cathedral Church of St. Patrick's,
Dublin: we therefore, the Dean and Chapter of the said Church,
do hereby promise the Sum of Five Pounds to any Person
concerned in that impious Robbery, who shall first discover
his Accomplice or Accomplices, so that he or they be convicted
thereof, or to any other Person or Persons whatsoever, not
concerned therein, which Sum, upon Conviction of the
Criminals, shall be instantly paid by the Rev. Dr. Francis
Wilson, Proctor of our Oeconomy.

And we further promise to apply to their Excellencies the
Lords Justices for a Pardon for such Person or Persons, who
was or were concerned, or hath or have been Accomplice or
Accomplices in the aforesaid impious Robbery, who shall
make such Discovery and by his or their Testimony, convict
those sacrilegious Wretches.

JONATHAN SWIFT. Dean

Deanery House
Jan. 1st, 1738–9

APPOINTMENT OF WYNNE AS SUB-DEAN

WHEREAS WE JONATHAN SWIFT Doctor in Divinity Dean of the Cathedrall Church of Saint Patrick Dublin being oftentimes, as We now are, not able by reason of Sickness to be present and personally to preside in the Chapter of our said Cathedrall Church, and being desirous that nothing belonging to the Office of Dean of the said Church may be wanting in the mean time, or any way omitted, or neglected to the detriment of any person on Account of our Absence. WE therefore nominate and by these presents substitute our beloved in Christ, our Brother, the Reverend John Wynne Doctor in divinity, Chanter of our said Cathedral Church, to be Subdeane of our said Church during our Absence, and from time to time as often as We shall not be able to be present rightly and lawfully to exercise the Office of Subdeane thereof, And We Give and Grant to our said Subdean, as much as in us lyes and as far as the Ecclesiastical Laws of this Kingdom allow, all and all manner of lawfull power and Authority in our place and stead to Rule and Govern our aforesaid Cathedrall Church and all the Members thereof, and as often as it shall be necessary to convoke the Chapter, and preside therein in order that he may concurr therewith in all Matters whatever tending to the Good of our said Church, to restrain faults and irregularities, and to punish Offenders, to hold the Visitation on the usual Day, and if need be to adjourn the same from time to time, and to compell all persons obledged to it to appear therein, To yield assistance and obedience after the usual manner to the Right Reverend Father in God the Archbishop of Dublin in all things by Law appertaining to his Archiepiscopal Visitation or any other Government whatever of our aforesaid Church, And Lastly to exercise the very same power and jurisdiction in all matters, anyway belonging to our aforesaid Church or the Dean thereof Which We the Dean ourselves might or could do if we were present EXCEPTING allways and reserving to our selves in our proper person all and singular Collations and proposalls to the Chapter of Curates of Churches whatever together with all profitts Revenues Sallarys and Emoluments whatsoever to the Dean of our aforesaid Church by Law or Custom appertaining SAVING also to ourselves a power at pleasure of revoking and makeing voyd under our hand and Seal this our Substitution, and of Substituting any other lawfull Subdean whenever We shall think proper IN TESTIMONY whereof We have caused our Deanry Seal to be affixed to those presents the Thirtieth day of Aprill in the year of our Lord One Thousand Seven Hundred Thirty Nine.

WILL SHIELL
Registrar.

EXHORTATION TO THE CHAPTER OF ST. PATRICK'S, DUBLIN

To the Very Reverend Doctor John Wynne, Sub-Dean of the Cathedral Church of Saint Patrick, Dublin, and to the Reverend Dignitaries and Prebendaries of the same.

January 28, 1741–2

WHEREAS my infirmities of age and ill-health have prevented me to preside in the chapters held for the good order and government of my Cathedral Church of St. Patrick, Dublin, in person, I have by a legal commission, made and appointed the Very Reverend Doctor John Wynne Precentor of the said Cathedral, to be Sub-Dean in my stead and absence: I do hereby ratify and confirm all the powers delegated to the said Dr. Wynne in the said commission.

And I do hereby require and request the Very Reverend Sub-Dean, not to permit any of the Vicars-Choral, choristers, or organists, to attend or assist at any public musical performances, without my consent, or his consent, with the consent of the Chapter first obtained.

And whereas it hath been reported, that I gave a licence to certain vicars to assist at a club of fiddlers in Fishamble Street,

I do hereby declare that I remember no such licence to have
been ever signed or sealed by me; and that if ever such pretended licence should be produced, I do hereby annull and
vacate the said licence; intreating my said Sub-Dean and
Chapter to punish such vicars as shall ever appear there, as
songsters, fiddlers, pipers, trumpeters, drummers, drum-
majors, or in any sonal quality, according to the flagitious
aggravations of their respective disobedience, rebellion, per-
fidy, and ingratitude.

I require my said Sub-Dean to proceed to the extremity
of expulsion, if the said vicars should be found ungovernable,
impenitent, or self-sufficient, especially Taverner, Phipps, and
Church, who, as I am informed, have, in violation of my Sub-
Dean's and Chapter's order in December last, at the instance
of some obscure persons unknown, presumed to sing and fiddle
at the club above mentioned.

My resolution is to preserve the dignity of my station,
and the honour of my Chapter; and, gentlemen, it is incumbent
upon you to aid me, and to show who and what the Dean
and Chapter of St. Patrick's are.

Signed by me,

> Jonathan Swift
> Dean of St. Patrick's.

Witness present,
James King.
Francis Wilson.

Q

FRAGMENT OF EARLY DRAFT OF
A WILL
(Huntington MS. 14346)

A 100ll a year to be purchased in any Province
but Connaught, of Land not let in lease above 40
years. Lease not to be for above 21 years. the Tenant
bound by penl clauses to improve [?] &c No fine taken [?]

The Present Tenant, if requird [?] to be preferrd [?] G 8 pr
cent (but) but not Sinck. The Fellow to be chosen by
Provost and 7 Senrs. Provost to have the casting Voice
or to elct junr fellow to make up 9. (A) if this
refusd, the land to be left to Dr. Stephens hospitll

The fellow to be called Swift's Fellow To go to
Engld in a Winter [?] to stay

———

All this wrong on Dr Delany's
Scheam; For mine was to have (the)

(an) the Fellow chosen evry year, to have
the 100ll a year /

———

The Executors to meet once a month
about this affair

CODICIL TO SWIFT'S WILL
(Huntington MS. 14347)

JONATHAN SWIFT TO MARTHA (SWIFT) HARRISON WHITEWAY

Fol. 1a.

As soon as Mrs Whiteway hears of my Decease, she is to
come immediatly to the Deanry, and first take all the —
Keys of my Cabinets, and Seal them up in a Paper, in the —
presence of ⟨Roge⟩ Mrs Anne Ridgeway, Roger Kenrick [?] my Verger

A 100ll a year to be practised in any Province
but Connaught, of Land not let in Leases above 40
years. Leases not to be for above 21 years. the Tenant
bound by such clause to appear to the purchasers.
The [Present] Tenant. if [agreed] to be [purchased] 6 & 8 p
cent but let not [sink] the Fellow to be chosen by
Provost and 7 [Sen.] [Present] to have the casting Voice
or to [add] [just] [fellows] to make up 9. & if they
refuse, the Lead to be [left] to Dr [Stephens] & 9 [with]
The fellow to be called [Scisits] Fellow to go to
[Exd] in a Minute. to Pay _____

All this wrong as Dr [Delany's]
Scheam; Far [more] was to have the
[the] the Fellow chosen every year. to have
the 100 ll a year

The Executors to meet once a month
about this affair

[SH]g 78   97

and Henry Land, if any of them be then alive, and in the —
Neighbor^hood. Then, Mrs Whiteway is to send for as many
of my Executors as are in Town; and opening my Scrutore
deliver them my Will, and let ⟨Th⟩[?] one of the S^d Executors
Read my Will and Codicills: There should be three of my
Executors present at l^east; they are all in Number nine
Then, Mrs Whiteway, is to take all the ready money she
can find, if there be two hundred pounds, but no more;
which likewise she may lend to the S^d Executors, upon
their notes; In case I should happen to have not Cash
enough, or Banker's bills, to pay the Charges of transporting
my Body to Holy-head and ^for my Burial in the Church of
that Town, as directed in my Will: Then, she is to assist
my Executors in sending my Plate to some Banker, together
with ^my Valuable Curiosityes, which she knows where to
fine [sic], many of which are bequeathed: I desire likewise that
the Number of my Books be taken, which are bequeathed to John
Whiteway younger son to Mrs Martha Whiteway, and sent to the
S^d Martha to be kept for the use of her S^d Son. except some —
books bequeathed in my S^d Will, or Codicills

Fol. 1b.

I have written the Names of my Executors in the Page in the Page [sic]
on the right hand of this Paper.

Mrs Whiteway is to secure the Bound Paper-book in quarto
wherein the Debts due to me, and the Debts I ow [sic] entred to this
present Month of April 1737 —— seven, together with the whole
State of my Fortune in debts Mortages [sic] &c, and Plate, ⟨and⟩, and valuable
Curiosityes, Household-goods, Arrears of Tythes, and Interest &c. which
my Executors are to have a Copy of; And Mrs Whiteway knows
where to find all my Mortgages, Bonds &c, which she is to give
to my S^d Executors, taking their ⟨note⟩ Receit in order to receive the
Severall Interests or Principalls to purchase Land as declared in my

last Will, which when my S^d Executors have entred in form in
the proper Court, they are humbly desired to fullfill as soon as
they conveniently can.   Signed and Sealed April 22^d 1737—Seven
Witness present

[signed] Jonathan Swift ◯ [seal of

[signed] Ann Ridgway   Socrates's head]

[signed] Alexr Brouders [?]

Fol 2a.

Robt Lyndsay Justice in the Common-Pleas

Henry Singleton Prime Sergeant

Doctor Delany

Richard Helsham M.D

Eton Stannard Recorder

Robert Grattan of St Audoens

John Grattan of St Nick within

James Stopford of Finglas

James King of St Brides

Fol. 2b.

[Written at top for purposes of docketing, in Swift's hand:]

             3. Apr. 16   For Mrs Whiteway to read.

                1737   and keep, when finished —— Codicill

[Written lengthwise, as an address:]

          To

    Mrs Martha Whiteway

FAULKNER'S PREFACE TO HIS EDITION OF SWIFT'S WORKS, DUBLIN, 1763

TO THE READER

IT may be expected that the Editor of this, and the other Editions printed by him, should give some Account of the Author and himself, which he will endeavour to do in the most concise Manner.

In the Year 1726, when Lord *Bolingbroke* (often mentioned in these Works) returned from his Exile in *France*, the Author went to *England* to visit him and some other Friends, where they often met at his Lordship's House in *London*, at Mr. *Pope*'s at *Twittenham*, and at other Places, then much resorted to by the greatest Persons of the Age, for Genius, Wit and Learning, where the Dean was highly caressed by them all, and treated with the greatest Respect and Distinction.

In the Year 1724, Dr. *Swift* wrote the Drapier's Letters, and other Papers to the People of *Ireland*, against *Wood*'s Patent for coining Halfpence and Farthings for this Kingdom; which Writings had a wonderful Effect in uniting People of all Religions and Parties against that wicked Scheme of *Wood*; on which the Patent was withdrawn.

The Year following, 1725, many People were desirous of having the Papers written on this Occasion preserved and collected together, which was accordingly printed by the Editor, Mr. *John Harding*, the first Printer being dead.

The present Editor was in *London* in 1726, upon his own Business and private Affairs, when he used to visit the Author at his Royal Highness the Prince of *Wales*'s at *Richmond* Lodge, as well as at Mr. *Pope*'s at *Twittenham*, where the Dean introduced him, and recommended him to several of his Friends, many of whose Works, and separate Pieces, he afterwards printed, particularly Mr. *Pope*'s entire original Works, by his own Directions, now in the Editor's Hands, many of Lord *Bolingbroke*'s, Mr. *Gay*'s, and other Pieces. The Dean also recommended him to many of his other noble Friends, particularly the Earl of *Oxford*, Son of the Lord High Treasurer, who made the Editor many valuable and curious Presents, and often had him at his Table, where he was treated in a most easy, familiar Manner, as an intimate Friend.

In the Month of *August* this Year the Dean returned to *Ireland*. And, early in the Year 1727 he went to *England*, where he was more caressed than ever by the Royal Family and People of greatest Distinction, many of whom strongly solicited him to settle there, where they proposed to give him Church Livings equal to what he had in *Ireland*, which he refused for many Reasons, mentioned in his Letters to Mr. *Pope*, &c.

In 1726, the Miscellanies of Dr. *Swift* and Mr. *Pope* were published together in *London*, and afterwards in *Dublin* in three Volumes, together with a Preface thereto, and both Names were signed. This Collection, although very agreeable to many People, did not please all; which made several of the Dean's Friends apply to the Editor, to solicit the Author to give him his entire Works to print, free from the Mixture of others, only where they were necessary. Accordingly he made Application to the Dean, who did not seem willing to consent, as the Publisher might be a Loser by printing them; the Editor told him he would run all Hazards, being very positive, he should be a great Gainer by them; but the Dean still persisted; then the Editor said, he would print them by Subscription, and make a faithful Return of the Subscribers Names to him, when he could easily judge whether he would gain or lose by the Undertaking. Accordingly Proposals were published, and Subscriptions came in very fast, which were shewn to the Author, who consented to the Printing, on the following Conditions; That no Jobb should be made, but full Value given for the Money; That the Editor should attend him early every Morning, or when most convenient, to read to him, that the Sounds might strike the Ear, as well as the Sense the Understanding, and had always two Men Servants present for this Purpose; and when he had any Doubt, he would ask them the Meaning of what they heard; which, if they did not comprehend, he would alter and amend until they understood it perfectly well, and then would say, *This will do*; *for I write to the Vulgar, more than to the Learned*. Not satisfied with this Preparation for the Press, he corrected every Sheet of the first seven Volumes that were published in his Life Time, desiring the Editor to write Notes, being much younger than the Dean, acquainted with most of the Transactions of his Life, as well as with those of several of his Friends; the Author being very communicative to the Editor; who, if there should be any Errors in them, will be glad to be set right, and will, with Pleasure, print an Errata for that Purpose, to render this Edition as correct as possible; and, he most humbly thinks, he hath some Degree of Merit with the Publick, by the Publication of these Works, which would never have been collected together, had he not been favoured with the Author's Friendship and Intimacy, who never concealed any Part of his Affairs from him; but, as OTHELLO says, *Gave him the Story of his Life from Year to Year*; insomuch, that he owned to him his being Author of the *Tale* of a *Tub*.

Perhaps, it may be thought singular, that the Editor should be so vain as to publish some trifling Letters to him from the Author; but the Publick, it is hoped, will excuse this; because, being Printer and Publisher of a News-paper, it was in his Way to get the Dean early and better Intelligence of Estates, their Valuation, the Titles and Security of them, than many others could do; which, probably, had his Advice been taken in some Degree, the Income for St. *Patrick*'s Hospital for the Reception of Idiots and Lunaticks, founded by Dr. *Swift*, would have been double to what it is now, had the Purchase been made in the Dean's Life; but, for what Cause we cannot say, objected to by some People, who afterwards made a very dear Bargain for Lands at *Saggard* in the County of *Dublin*, attended with a Law Suit, and a very great Expence, before the Trustees of the Hospital got the entire Possession.

Other trifling Letters may also be thought not worth Publication; but, as it will convince the World of the Intimacy the Author was pleased to favour the Printer with, he hopeth he may escape Censure; these Letters being now first printed, to satisfy the Reader, that Mr. *Faulkner* was not only the Dean's

Publisher, but favoured with his Friendship, and consulted by him on many Occasions. To explain this, it is proper to inform the Curious, that Dr. *Hawkesworth*, a learned and ingenious Gentleman, who was imposed upon by some *London* Bookseller, wrote a Preface and a few very trifling Notes to an Edition of the foregoing Miscellanies, mingled with some Writings of Dr. *Arbuthnot*, Mr. *Gay*, and others, wherein the Letters between *Swift* and *Pope* are omitted, and published in Dr. *Warburton's* Edition of *Pope's* Works. Dr. *Hawkesworth* and some other Editor, were also imposed on in that Affair, by saying that *Faulkner* was not known to Dr. *Swift*; which Letters of the Dean to the Editor, relative to many Pieces of Writing, as also to many of his Friends, may convince these Commentators of the great Esteem he expresseth for him, and how grosly they have been mistaken.

The Editor having been many Years compiling these Works, and at very great Expence and Trouble, most humbly hopes for the Favour of all People of Taste and Candour, being well assured, that some Criticks, who have no Relish for low Wit or Humour, will object to them; but the Editor begs Leave to inform them, that some of the best Scholars and most learned Men in *Europe*, were against omitting one Piece, or even a single Sentence of *Swift's*, by saying, all his Weeds were Flowers in the best Gardens, and all the Trash, the Choppings of the richest brilliant Diamonds.

It is therefore most humbly hoped, that all the Lovers of Morality, good Sense, Wit and Humour, will favour this Edition, and set an Example to this Nation of their Encouragement to all Undertakers in the Literary Way, and particularly to the Editor of these Works, who hath with so much Labour now finished them, as, he hopes, to the entire Satisfaction of all his worthy Readers, and that they will be pleased to look with a generous Eye and good Heart upon his genuine Editions, which have been most justly obtained from the Author by great Cost and Trouble, the Editor having suffered severely in his private Property, as well as in his Health, by his being ordered into Custody by the House of Lords for printing the following in the *Dublin Journal*, Feb. 26, 1731-2.

The following Queries are an Extract from a Pamphlet,[1] in the Press, writ by the Rev. Dr. S. D. S. P. D. which being somewhat long, and the Time pressing, it was thought fit to publish these Queries, that contain some of those Arguments, made Use of in the said Pamphlet, &c.

Some Queries humbly offered.

'Whether the House of Commons may not think the Bishops have Power enough already?

'Whether a Gentleman would not rather have a creditable Parson than a Beggar to converse with?

'Whether this Scheme of multiplying beggarly Clergymen, may not, by their Numbers, have great Influence on Elections, being entirely under the Dependence of their Bishops?

'Whether a Clause against Parsons having Votes should not be inserted?

'Whether Gentlemen and Farmers would not be easier in their Tythes with a rich Minister, than a poor one? For a hungry Louse biteth sore, &c.

'If the Bill shall depend so long as to print the Pamphlet entire, or shall be thrown out, the said Pamphlet shall be published next Monday, for the Satisfaction of those who may desire to read the Arguments against them.'

Which Censure was not taken off until the Session following, by his presenting a Petition to the House of Lords, who were pleased to order him to be discharged on his paying the Fees, which amounted to a very large Sum; in the Payment of which he was very much favoured by Sir *Multon Lambert*, then Gentleman Usher of the Black Rod, as well as by some other Officers of that House.

The succeeding Session of Parliament be was taken into Custody of the House of Commons, for printing a Paper, entitled *A Proposal for the better Regulation of the Game of Quadrille*[2], confined closely in Prison three Days, when he was in a very bad State of Health, and his Life in much Danger;

---

[1] See Considerations, &c., Vol. VI, p. 137.   [2] See Vol. X, p. 359.

on which he petitioned the House for his Liberty, which he obtained on paying all the Fees. He was also at different Times in Custody of Messengers for printing against the Reduction of the Gold Coin and some other Affairs, but could never be prevailed on to discover the Authors, which endeared him so much to the Dean, that he gave him the Title of *his right trusty and faithful Friend*, and frequently offered to pay *Faulkner* the Expences he had been at on those Occasions, and to raise him Subscriptions, to reward him for his Fidelity and Sufferings, which *Faulkner* always refused; so that the Editor most humbly thinks, that, according to the Laws of Justice or Reason, he is most truly entitled to the Property of these Works; the Author having bestowed them to him, and corrected seven Volumes in his own Life-Time, as well as many small Tracts published at different Periods, which are inserted in their proper Places in this Edition, for the Benefit of the Subscribers.

In *England*, the Property in Copies of Books is as fully secured by Law and Custom, as any Lands, Houses, Tenements, or Funds, *&c.* to the very great Advantage of Learning and Authors, and to the Production of many fine printed Editions of Books and Prints. Mr. *Tonson* the Bookseller, and many of his Predecessors, have been long in Possession of the Works of *Shakespear*, *Beaumont* and *Fletcher*, *Milton*, *Dryden*, *Congreve*, and many other Authors Works, which never have been disputed with them.

The Parliament of *Great-Britain*, being truly sensible of the great Advantages of Learning, Wit and Humour to that Nation, have made many Acts of Parliament to secure the Property of Writing, not only to Authors and Booksellers, but even for Inventions of Painting and Engraving; insomuch, that an Act was made some Years ago, in Favour of the ingenious and celebrated Mr. *Hogarth*, to secure his Property in all Prints whatever, designed, painted, or engraved by him, which Act extendeth to all Planners and Engravers of any Designs; and, by which Means, the *English* are now the most celebrated of any in *Europe* for their witty and humorous Prints, and also for Designs in Architecture, Gardening, *&c.*

as also for their very fine Editions of Books in all Arts and Sciences, and in most Languages. This Encouragement to Authors and Learning hath induced many Gentlemen of Genius, Learning, and Fortune, to have Printing-Offices in their own Houses, or in others near adjoining, where they have printed the most elegant and correct Editions of ancient and modern Books, as well as others of their own Writing. Mr. *Viner*, who wrote the Abridgment of the Law in twenty-five Volumes in Folio, (and who left a Legacy to the University of *Oxford* to read Lectures on the Common Law) printed the above Abridgment at his own House near *Aldershot* in *Hampshire*; and the Hon. *Horace Walpole* printed, at his House at *Strawberry-Hill* near *Richmond* in *Surry*, his very agreeable and entertaining Book, entitled, *A Catalogue of the Royal and noble Authors of England*, written by himself: He also printed at the same Place, for his own Amusement, as well as for the Satisfaction of the Publick, some superb and very elegant Editions of the Classicks, which are very well esteemed by all the Curious.

But, alas! it is not so in *Ireland*, where many, without any Cause whatever, immediately pyrate on their innocent Brethren, who never once offended them in their Property, either by Word, Thought, or Deed, which is a Reason that few Books have been well printed here, nor will be for the future, the Demand here being very small. And, what is contrary to the Custom of other Countries, Law, Justice and Reason, some of these Pyrates will not even suffer Authors to sell or bestow their Works to fair Purchasers, or their best Friends; wherefore it is hoped our Legislature will take it into their serious Consideration to make Resolutions, or enact Laws, to secure the Property of Authors to themselves, their Friends, or Purchasers, otherwise the State of Learning must daily decline, which is now at a low Ebb in *Ireland*, although we have many learned Men in all Arts and Sciences, to whom it may not be convenient to go to *England* to dispose of their Works. Several excellent Performances have lately been published by some Fellows of our University, and many others would appear, if Property could be secured to them and to the fair Purchasers.

TEXTUAL NOTES

1. DIRECTIONS TO SERVANTS

The manuscripts have been already described; see *Introduction*, pp. viii f. As they are both incomplete, they could not be used as a copy-text, but the following collations give the readings in Swift's holograph MS, now in the Rothschild collection, in Cambridge, and the readings of a copy made by an amanuensis, now in the Forster collection, in the Victoria and Albert Museum.

Rothschild MS.: original readings S
corrections in Swift's hand Sc
Forster MS: original readings A
corrections Ac

The present text is taken from the first edition printed from a manuscript, still incomplete, but containing further material not in either of the above, by Faulkner in Dublin, with a Preface, dated Nov. 8, 1745 (45).

It was immediately reprinted in London by Dodsley in 1745 (L).

See above, p. 3, facsimiles of these title-pages.

It was reprinted in Dublin, *Works*, 1746, Vol. VIII, pp. 1–25, 1–77 (46), and again in *Works*, 1751, Vol. VIII, pp. 15–106 (51).

These two editions have also been included in the collations, because in a rather inexplicable fashion, a number of corrections are made in 1751, which are based on the corrected readings of the Forster MS. Wherever the copy is not followed, I have indicated the source of the reading adopted.

Note. The first edition of Faulkner follows the manuscript in using the forms of the third person indicative in 's', which are changed in his reprint of 1746 to the ending 'eth'; and this process is carried further in 1751. It has been thought unnecessary to cumber the apparatus by including these spelling variants; typographical changes and differences of capitalization are likewise ignored; and only the most important variants in punctuation are recorded.

Page	Line	PRESENT TEXT	VARIANTS
5	18–19	which . . . subject to	to which . . . subject 46
	21	although 51	altho' 45, 46
7	15–16	who therefore are . . . Faults they A, 51	who therefore are . . . Faults you 45
			you are therefore . . . Faults you 46
	25	saving A, 51	sparing 45, 46, L
	b.	you have A, 51	you will have 45, 46, L
8	3–4	the better confirmed	confirmed A; the more confirmed Ac
	10	or eight	eight 51
	13	Word. But A	Word: But 45 &c.
	21	for you to sell A	to you to sell 45 &c.
	22	find A, 51	get 45 &c.
		till	until 51
	23	next	on 51
	24	were forced	was forced 51

Page	Line	PRESENT TEXT	VARIANTS
9	1	for your A, 51	to your 45 &c.
	11	say, he	say that he A
	17	the shortest Ac	and shortest A, 45 &c.; shortest 51
	20	as you go out	at your going out Ac
10	5	know A	have known 45 &c.
	7	till	until 46, 51
	13–14	hold Small-Beer ... Jordan	and or in case of necessity ... Jordan, or hold Small Beer A
	25	Point	Part 46
	27	fewer than those of their Masters	fewer than the Masters A
	7 f.b.	observed	observable A
11	2	pinned up	pinned A *with marginal note:* (Better expressed in another place)
	7	may	might 51
	9	will be Ac	must be A &c.; may be 46
	17	shall	should Ac
	19	all Servants A	all the Servants 45 &c.
	7 f.b.	on a Visit	a Visit A; to Visit Ac
	6 f.b.	House, unless you have a Black-guard-boy)	(*at the end of the sentence in* A)
12	1	all is safe Ac, 51	always safe A; you are always safe 45 &c.
	5–6	is just ... is dying Ac	but just ... was dying 45 &c.
	17	Fault that he A, 51	Fault he 45 &c.
	21	Master or Lady	Master and Lady A
	23	less than half	half A
	26	charged A	charge 45 &c.
	27	why you	why they A
	29	was Malice	Malice A
	5 f.b.	I advise you ... comes	*Note added in* A: (This said in the other Parts); *passage omitted in* 51
13	3	are sent	be sent Ac
	4–5	Pocket (which is very usual) A, 51	Pocket 45 &c.
	7	becomes ... at	became ... on 51
	11–12	to you	with you A
	21	your best A, 51	the best 45 &c.
	22	of a S	on a 51
	23	till	until 46, 51
	9 f.b.	Rope	a Rope A, L
	b.	will have A, 51	shall have 45 &c.
14	6	in a	or in a A
	10	Dough, or	Dough, a Bundle of Shavings, or 46
	11	a Loaf A, 51	the Loaf, 45 &c.
	13	particular A, 51	peculiar 45 &c.

Page	Line	Present Text	Variants
	23	all Expedients	*Beneath this in* A: (More Expedients)
	25-26	Tongs are A, 51	Tongs be 45 &c.
	7 f.b.	Jordan, in case of need, he A, 51	Jordan, he 45 &c.
	2 f.b.	Floor Ac	Ground A, 45 &c.
15	4	your Candle End A, 51	the Candle End, 45 &c.
	5	until	till A
	16	to cross	cross 51
	18	Pantry A, 51	Pantry Door, 45 &c.
	27	Dining-Room	Dining Room Door 51

DIRECTIONS TO THE BUTLER

17	H.T.	Directions to Servants Sc	Directions to Poor Servants S
	6-7	long Observation, Sc	own Observation, and Experience S
	7	Butler Sc.	Brother Butler S
		Party S, Ac, 51	Person A, 45 &c.
	14	Drink and Glasses. S	Drinking Glasses: A, 45 &c.
	18	as the Hazard A	as Hazard S
		Give no Person Sc	Then give no man S
	19	till he has S	till he hath A; until he hath 45 &c.
	21	and thus your Master's Liquor be saved S	be saved (*added above the line* S)
			will be saved Ac, 51
	6 f.b.	Ale; First S	Ale, first A, 45 &c.
	5 f.b.	in it Ac.	in S, A
		know Sc, 51	see S, A
	3 f.b.	wipe the Mouth Sc.	wipe of the Slobber of S
		that you may not be mistaken ... the Palm of	(*added above the line* S)
18	3-4	or a dependent Cousin	or a depending cousin (*added* S)
		(*Marginal note to this paragraph:* 'said under Footman' S, A)	
	6	discover Sc	find out S
	9-10	rest; and ... Lady	rest. (*with marginal note:* 'Find a a reason' S, A)
	14	and Salvers	(*added above the line* S)
	15	if any one S, A, 51	when any one 45, 46, L
	17	Tankard top-full S, Ac	Tankard cupfull A;
			Tankard-cup top-full 45, 46, L
	18	the Sin of	(*added above the line* S)
	20	an honest Perquisite Sc, 51	a Perquisite full as honest S, A, 45 &c.
	22	to your self Sc, Ac, 51	for your self 45 &c.
	22-23	are not to ... value Sc, A, 51	are to ... will not care for S, Ac, 45 &c.
	24	although Sc.	tho' S; altho' A
	26-29	Take ... fill it.	(*This sentence comes before the previous paragraph* S, A)
	28	every Bottle Sc	the Bottle S

Page	Line	PRESENT TEXT	VARIANTS
	8–4f.b.	If you ... want you. (*This sentence is conflated from the two following in* S, A:	

1. When you are drawing Ale, and find it will not run, do not be at the Trouble of opening a Vent, but blow strongly into the Fosset, and you will find it immediately pour into your Mouth. (*Marginal note:* Qu? before S: same after S, A.)
2. If you are sent down in hast to draw Drink; take out the Vent to make it run (the A) faster; but do not stay to put it in for fear your Master should want you. (*Marginal note:* it is said after S; said after A.)

Page	Line	PRESENT TEXT	VARIANTS
	3f.b.	choice Bottles S, A	choicest Ale Ac
	b.	them S, A	the Bottles Ac
19	6	Small beer: You Sc	Small-beer, you S, A
	13	certain 45, 46, L	secure S, A; sure 51
	14	often forget Sc, 51	are apt to forget S, A, 45 &c.
	15	be sure you Ac	be sure S, A, 51

(*After this comes the passage quoted in the note above* (2) *in* S *and* A; *and then in* S *the following:*
If you are sent to the Cellar for Ale at night, Hold your Candle between your Fingers just over the Cup to save fouling a Candlestick. *This is crossed out and has a marginal note:* stet if it be but once)

Page	Line	PRESENT TEXT	VARIANTS
	19	of the Bottom A	at the Bottom S
	20	directly (*added above the line* S, A)	
	21	make the Liquor (*added above the line* S)	
	24	foul Table Sc, 51	dirty Tables S, A, 45 &c.
	25	Day; for, Sc	to save (1) fouling (2) the wearing out for S
	26	besides you save Sc, 51	and besides you save S, Ac and besides it saves A and besides it will save you 45, 46, L
	27	in Reward of which Sc, 51	and in Reward of such S, A &c.
	29	to be Night-caps Sc, 51	for Night-caps S, A &c.
	9–7f.b.	When you clean &c. (*This sentence inserted here as in* 45, 46, L. *It comes much later in* S, A, 51, *but is marked by Swift with a note* Sd *before.*)	
	5f.b.	than the Sc	than in the S, A, 45 &c.
	4f.b.	of other S, 51	of the other A, 45 &c.
	2f.b.	leaving your Sc, 51	leaving to your S, A, 45 &c.
	b.	apply them Ac, 45, 46, L	apply S, A, 51
20	3	although Sc, 51	though S; altho' A, 45 &c.
		be called S, Ac, 51	are called A &c.
		ever Sc	never S, A &c.

(*Here follows in* S *this passage, crossed out, with note in margin* stet, *is non ante aut post and* said before:
When you want a Candle, for your own use, to save the wearing out of Candlesticks, stick (*thus far also in* A) it either in Butter, Oatmeal, Salt, a Mug, a Bottle, an old Shoe, or cling

Page	Line	PRESENT TEXT	VARIANTS
		it against the Wall. (*Added later:* But of this more hereafter, or drop some of its own grease on a table, and there stick it.)	
	5	Top, then S, 51	Top, and then A, 45 &c.
	7	and handsomer S, A	and the handsomer 51
	11	Smuts S, 51	Smoak A; Smoke 45, 46, L

(*Here follows in* S *this passage, crossed out, with note in margin* said before:

Allways blow out the Candles with your (1) Mouth (2) breath, which will both wast them less, and leave them in better order for lighting the next day.

When you put C——)

| | 13 | the great Extravagance of late Years S, Ac, 51 | of late years the great Extravagancy A &c. |
| | 14 | Article Sc, Ac, 46, 51 | Articles S, A, 45, L |

(*Marginal note in* S *and* A: Something wanting here. *The two paragraphs which follow in the text occur much later in the MSS, but with marginal note can be before.*)

	19–20	are always to Sc	should always S
		should do Sc	(1) should (2) must S
	25	be not Sc	is not S
	9f.b.	and your self . . . used	and your self much Labor. (For the Sconces spoyld they cannot be used.) (*Added between the lines* S; *also in* A)
	5f.b.	in your House Sc	here S
	4f.b.	Neighbours, who Sc	neighbours, that S

(*After this sentence in* S: This should be under the Footmans article *deleted.*)

21	1	if you find Sc	you will find S
	3	best Glasses Sc	finest Glasses S
	6	at worst S, A, 51	at most 45, 46, L

(*Here follows in* S, *with a marginal note* this after:

Cut your bread for dinner with a knife that you have just used to cut Onyons, or garlick, which will give it a high tast. Cut it very thin to save your Masters bred, and three hours before dinner, for fear of forgetting it, and likewise to make it go further.)

	17	you think it better to shake Sc	you shake S
		among S, A	amongst 45 &c.
	20	Ale, Wine S, A, 51	Wine, Ale 45, 46, L
	24	many S, A	any 46
	8f.b.	if it be dark	*added above the line* S

(*Here follows this sentence, with marginal note* Footman *in* S, A:

When you are ordered to stir up the fire, clean away the ashes from between the barrs with the Fire brush. *See* p. 42, ll. 11–12.)

| | 5f.b. | is expected at Sc, etc. | comes to S |
| | | Evenings S, A | the Evenings 45 &c. |

(*Here follows in* S, A, *this sentence:*

The art of bottling being an affair of great importance in

R

Page	Line	PRESENT TEXT	VARIANTS
		your office, I hope you will allow me to enlarge my instructions upon so weighty an article.	
		Opposite this in S:	what follows must be writ first and compard with the fo (?)
		The rest of the page in S *marked in the left margin with a* Q^r *and a line to the bottom of the page; and above the passage is inserted:* All this must be compared with P. inserted after P. 14.) P. 14 *of* S *is lost, but the passage contained in* A, *pp.* 24–25.	
22	9	cannot complain.	*Here follows in* A: That your Bottles may not leak (*deleted*)
	14	Jill	Naggin A (*underlined and in margin* Q^r)
		by to A, L, 51	by you to 45, 46
	18	the Liquor A, 51	your Liquor 45, 46, L
	20	praise your S, A	praise you for your 45 &c.
	25	give to the S, A	give the 46, 51
	28	if a Pint be	when a pint is S, A
	2 f.b.	Cook. What signifies S, A	Cook; what signify 51; Cook; for what signifies 45, 46, L
	b.	But make ... wronged	(*Not in* S *or* A *here; taken from the additional page at the end in* A
23	2	wronged	defrauded A
		get drunk, A	be drunk S
	12	Tea-kettle, from the Pot Sc, A	Tea-pot from the Skellet S
	14	acid corroding S	acid and corroding A, 45 &c.
	18	until	till S, A
	20	smell the Snuffs S	Snuff A, 51; shall smell the Snuff 45, 46, L
		(*Here follows a passage with a marginal note:* for some other Servant *in* S, A: Rub the Floor the Windows the brass locks and clean your shoes with foul napkins because one washing will clean them, and save Rubbers.	
		And another, marked s^d *before:* When you clean your plate leave the whiting plainly to be seen in all the chincks, for fear your Lady should not believe you had cleaned it. (Printed in 45))	
	21	his Snuff-box S, A, 51	a Snuff-box 45, 46, L
24	1	for then S, A	for 45 &c.
	5	your moist Sc	the moist S
	7	in his View S, Ac, 51	in View A, 45, 46, L
	14	cost Sc	will cost S
	22	the Candle	your Candle S, A
	25	Point Sc	Bottom S
	27	from your Mouth 46, 51	with your Mouth S, A, 45
		(*Here follows a page consisting of passages used elsewhere,* S, A)	
	4 f.b.	harder S, Ac	hardest A, 45 &c.
25	2	Cistern, three or four times, until S, A, 51	Cistern, until 45, 46, L
	4–5	Methods to shew him some Sc	(*word deleted*) ways to give him S
	22	Servants S, A	Servant 46

Page	Line	PRESENT TEXT	VARIANTS
	25	them to Coffee-houses Sc	to Coffee-Houses, S, 45, 46, L; to Coffee-House-keepers A them to the Coffee-Houses 51
	26	cards at (*after this point some pages are missing in* S)	
	27	this Service A	the Service 45 &c.
	4 *f.b.*	Master's Family Ac.	Master's Pocket A
26	3	are *not to answer A	*Qʳ *in the margin* A
	10–18	If your Master . . . Blame from you.	(*This passage varies considerably from* A, *which is much shorter, but with a marginal note:* 'Something like this Page 21'.)

The two passages are as follows:

If your Master orders you to buy a large Number at once, never trouble him with Accounts of what are broken, while you have sufficient to furnish your Side-Board; then tell him they are all gone, and that a new Sett must be bought, for it is the Office of a good Servant to discompose his Master and Lady as seldom as he can.

P. 21. If you have a large Stock of Glasses, and you or any of your Fellow Servants happen to break any of them without your Master's knowledge, keep it a secret, till there are not enough left to serve the Table; then tell your Master that the Glasses are gone. This will be but one Vexation to him, which is much better than fretting once or twice a Week, and here the Cat and the Dog will be of great use to take the Blame from you.

	20–21	and at a general Washing A	and a general Washing 45 &c.
	26	till you A	until you 46, 51
27	1	two or three Quarts	a Bottle or two A (Qʳ in margin)
	3–6	When you . . . come in.	(*Marginal note in* A: Something like this before)
	4	in the A, 51	into the 45 &c.
	7	Dark (as clean Glasses &c.) A	Dark 45 &c.
	10	*Directions*	Instructions S, A

Inserted immediately below the title:
I am in doubt whether it should not be a Man-Cook S

	20	and paid Sc, A	and more generally payd S
	21	Prog Sc	Stock S
28	1	upon your going S, A	when you are going 45 &c.
	3	to both S, A	for both 45 &c.
	11	Cat or Dog S, A	Cat or a Dog 45 &c.
		accused for S, A	accused of 46
	15	Bottoms S	Bottom A, L
	21	If you live in a rich Family	*added above the line* S
	25	you be Sc	you are S, A, 45 &c.
	26	can: S	can; A, L, 51; can, 45, 46
	27	Honour; S	Honor, A; Honour, 45 &c.
	28	can afford Sc	is bound S
	9 *f.b.*	alway safely swear S	charge safely; swear A, 45 &c.

Page	Line	Present Text	Variants

*N.B.—A good example of misreading Swift's hand. The open 'a'
and 'lw' look very like 'cha'.*

	4 *f.b.*	very justly S, A, 51	justly 45, 46, L
29	1	it would be S, A, 51	it will be 45, 46, L
	7	for what Cook . . . just the same	and lest the pen-feathers should offend the gentry, I advise you to flay all small birds instead of pulling them S, A

*(The passage in the text is taken from a later page of S and A—
marginal note in S: Vid. P. 22—with the following variants:*

		of any Spirit	of Spirit S, A
		just the same Sc	never the worse S
	13	in Market S, A	in Marketing 46
	19	with the Muzzle	*added above the line in* S
		Tongs and Poker S	the Tongs and Poker A, &c.
	23	keep them Sc, 51	have them left S, A, &c.
	4 *f.b.*	handsomer S	handsome A
30	5	commend Sc	admire S
	8	being half raw	*added above the line in* S
		serve for S, A, 51	serve 45 &c.
	10	must S, A	may 46, &c.
	15	find it necessary to go to Sc, 51	go to S; find it necessary to market A, 45 &c.
	18	constantly to attend you S, A, 51	to attend you constantly 45 &c.
	20	a few Coals and all the Cinders Sc	Coals and Cinders S
	24	scum it well S, 51	stir it well A, 45, 46: stir it well in L

| | 7 *f.b.* | *(The first of the supplementary passages inserted here in* L. *See below, p. 33, ll. 5–9.)* | |

(Here follows in S *a passage of three sections marked with crosses
and a line in the margin—with above* (mistake) *and below:* The place
from the mark X mistaken (Footman).)

31	2	roast Meat S, A &c.	roasted Meat 46
	4–5	gone to the Necessary-house	*(added above the line* S)
		trussed your Pullets Sc	trussed your Fowl S, A &c.
			thrusted your Pullets 51
	6	till . . . the second Course; S, A	until . . . your second Course 45 &c.
			till . . . your L
	7	fouled S, A, 51	fouler 45, 46, L
	8–9	many Things . . . over	*(written above the line; after which deleted).*
	13	stand Sc	watch S
		with one Hand	*(added above the line* S)
		with the other	*(added above the line* S)
	15	some Sc, 51	any S, A, 45, 46, L
	17	hath Ac	has S, A, hath *written above* Sc
	26	may fairly lay S, A, 51	may lay 45, 46, L

Page	Line	Present Text	Variants
	28–29	mixed with fresh large Coals	(*added above the line* S)
	7 f.b.	Cinder-women S	Cinder-woman A, 45 &c.

(*Here follows in* S *this passage marked in the margin:* [Before] A thorow Cook should think it below her to understand roasting and boyling, therefore when there is no nice dish to be sent up, you ought to leave that vulgar business entirely to the Scullion.

	5 f.b.	a great Family Sc	the family S
32	4	hath Ac	has S, A
	11	as well on . . . without the Sweetbread S, A, 51	as well at . . . without it 45, 46, L

(*Here follows in* S *and* A *the passage which was already used on* p. 11. *Marginal note in* A: This before page 28.)

	14	on your S, A	upon your 45, &c.
	15	were forced S, 51	was forced A, 45 &c.
		too much boiled and roasted Sc, &c.	overdone S

(*Second supplementary passage inserted here in* L. *See below*, l. 28.)

| | 21 | for Sc, 51 | and S, A &c. |
| | 28–31 | black; make room for the Saucepan by wriggling it on the Coals &c.: This . . . Housekeeping: And in S | make room . . . Coals &c. *added at the foot of the page* S *and marked* X. *It has been wrongly inserted at the end of the sentence in* A, 45 &c. |

(*In* 51, *this passage is changed further by inserting the two paragraphs (not in* S *or* A) *first printed at the end of the book as a '*Postscript' *in* 45, *with the note:* The following paragraphs belong to the Cook, but were left out by mistake. *More appropriate places were found to insert them in* L; *they were simply placed at the end in* 46 *and that has been done here. See below*, p. 33, ll. 5 ff.)

	6 f.b.	have the Bole Sc	let the bole S, A; let half the Bole 45, 51; Bowl 46
	5 f.b.	This Spoon owes Sc	This Spoon has done S
	3 f.b.	Water-gruel Sc	milk S

DIRECTIONS TO THE FOOTMAN

Note above the top line in S: Vide mistake p. 20.

33	5 f.b.	and to understand Men and Manners	(*added above the line in* S)
	b.	many of your Tribe Sc	some of your Tribe S
		have good Commands Sc	have Commands S
34	4	and my Lady's Waiting-woman	(*added above the line in* S)
	5	Skipkennel	Skipkennels A
	7	your Order Sc	your Office S
	8	accepting an Employment Sc	taking an employmᵗ S
	13–14	your Brethren Sc, 51	them A, 45 &c.
	15	regarded S, A	be regarded 51
	19–20	prevent which Ac	prevent this A

Page	Line	Present Text	Variants
	24	Chambers S	Chamber A, 45 &c.
		and then S, A, 51	then 45, 46, L
	25–26	keep him ... with Scraps	*(added above the line in* S)
	28	Brother Servant S, 51	Brother-Servants A, 45 &c.
	8*f.b.*	Plate at Meals	Plate, when you wait on your Master, and his Company, at Meals 51
		some	some Butlers 51
35	3ff.	Others again ... Mouth	Keep a Plate under your arm, or within your waistcoat, that you may have both your hands ready upon any occasion; but when you (have occasion *del.*) are forced to cough, take out the plate and hold it before your mouth to shew your good breeding.
			(The whole doctrine of plates mentioned P. quod vide S, A; *marginal note:* P. refer to it S.)
	29	the largest Dishes, and set them on	a heavy Dish of Soupe from the table S, A
	30–32	to shew the Ladies ... may fall	to shew your Strength; but always do it between two Ladys, that if it happen to spill, the Liquor may fall A
35, 6*f.b.*–41,19		By this Practice ... lose any	*(Not in the MSS)*
36	1	at certain	in certain 51
	14	when you come	as you come 51
	20	your Hand	your Hands 51
37	2*f.b.*	Case by using 51	Fate of 45 &c.
38	22–23	poor or covetous	covetous or poor 46
39	6	at jarr	at jar L; a-jarr 51
	10	the Burthen	your Burthen 51
	14	take a Pot	drink a Pot of Ale 51
40	4	would be	would 51
	6	the Message	your Message 51
	14	your Master's	their Master's 51
	21	his Service	his Honor 51
	26	the Blackguard Boy	your Blackguard boy 51
	9*f.b.*	Hand	Hands 51
41	11	dirt yourself	dirty yourself 51
	20	when you wait at Meals	*(added above the line in* S)
	22	most Ladies Sc	the Ladyes S
		of young Men's Toes	*(added above the line in* S)
	23	the Vapours	their Vapors S, A; Vapours Ac
	8*f.b.*	your Master's Linnen, and a natural and improved Confidence	Your Master's linnen ... and improved *added above the line in* S; an improved Confidence added to a natural Ac

Page	Line	PRESENT TEXT	VARIANTS
42	1	keep on one Side S	keep you on the other side A; keep you on one side Ac
	4	if either of them Sc, A	if your Master or Lady S
	5–6	use but your Thumb and one Finger Sc, A	use but one Finger S
	9	your Master . . . his Coals Ac	your Mistress . . . his coles S; your Mistress . . . her Coals 51
	18	scurvily S, Ac	saucily A
	26	with *Tom* behind S, A	with her Footman Tom behind Ac
	27	Coachman mistook S, A	Coachman purposely mistook Ac
	5*f.b.*	and when he was . . . Service	(*added above the line in* S)
	2*f.b.*	at Court	(*added above the line with a marginal note:* Craigs)
43	4–5	and from wearing a Livery . . . carry S	and from *wearing . . . carry* A
	8	are ready to Sc, A	are waiting and ready to S
	9	if they chance A	if you chance L
	12	Mop 46 &c.	Map 45
	15–16	their Bed-chamber A, 51	the Bed-chamber 45, &c.
	18	of all the Servants A	of the Servants Ac
	19	Innovations A	Innovation 51
	21	Be not proud in Prosperity etc.	(*This paragraph missing in the MSS*)
44	24	I shall give Ac, 51	I give you 45 &c.
	8*f.b.*	At your Tryal deny Ac	Deny 45 &c.
45	3	crimson or black	crimson A
	5	Eyes Ac, 51	Hands A, 45 &c.

COACHMAN

	12	*N.B.*—S contains none of the remaining pieces. A has the following in a different order from the printed texts, *viz.*: Dairy-Maid, Children's Maid, Nurse, Laundress, House-Keeper, House-Steward and Land-Steward, Porter, Coachman. Note in A: A great Allyance between him and the Groom, that many things may serve for both.
	2*f.b.*	him, and is A	him; and he is 51

GROOM

Page	Line	PRESENT TEXT	VARIANTS
47	12	loves 51	and loves 45 &c.
	16	the Roads	that the Roads 51
	24	the Landlord 51	your Landlord 45 &c.
	2*f.b.*	his Withers	the Withers 51
48	26	that Hay 51	the Hay 45 &c.
	6*f.b.*	sure to employ one 51	sure employ some 45 &c.
	3*f.b.*	this also 45, 51	that also 46, L
49	5	fail to make	fail to try 51
	10	Hedges and Ditches &c.	Hedge and Ditch 51
50	1	them up close with &c.	them with 51

Page	Line	Present Text	Variants
	2	preserve &c.	prevent 51
51	12	the Ale-house	an Ale-house 51

HOUSE-STEWARD AND LAND-STEWARD

| | 4 *f.b.* | with Repairs | for Repairs A |

CHAMBER-MAID

52	3 *f.b.*	and, if you serve . . . among the Neighbourhood	*omitted in* 46
53	9 *f.b.*	Pound	Pounds 51
54	10	in its Flight	to its Flight 51
	18	to contrive a Story that will better hang together	*omitted in* 51

THE WAITING-MAID

57	14	her Daughters	the Daughters 51
58	3	or a Fool . . . but, if the former	*omitted in* L
	4	in less Awe	less in Awe L, 51
	16	that she is rich enough to make any Man happy	*omitted in* 51

THE HOUSE-MAID

61	11	Garret L, 51	Garrets 45, 46
	12	Back-sides	Back-side 51
	13	their own	your own L
	28	Doors L	Door 51
	9 *f.b.*	the Bed-chamber	her Bed-chamber L, 51
62	5	put the	thrust the 51
	10	frighten away	affright L
	16	Windows	Window 51
	b.	see	be convinced of 51

CHILDREN'S MAID

| 63 | 8 *f.b.* | to your Ac | for your 45 &c. |

NURSE

| 64 | 3 | let the Child fall | let fall the Child A |

LAUNDRESS

| | 7 *f.b.* | Always wash your own Linen first | *omitted in* A, 45, L, 51 |

HOUSE-KEEPER

| 65 | 6 | to your Office A &c. | into your Office 51 |

TUTORESS, OR GOVERNESS

| | *b.* | tender-hearted &c. | tender-hearted. |
| | — | *FINIS* | The END. 51 |

2. SOME CONSIDERATIONS IN THE CHOICE OF A RECORDER

Half-sheet. Two columns printed on one side only. No place or printer. Printed in the Year MDCCXXXIII.

The text has been printed from a copy in the National Library, Dublin.

Reprinted in Dublin by Faulkner, *Works*, 1746, viii. 308–10
                                        1751, viii. 374–6.

and in London in *Miscellanies*, printed for C. Hitch etc. 1746, xi. 203–6, and by Hawkesworth, *Works*, 1755, 4to, vi. (pt. ii) 207–8.

3. PREFATORY LETTER TO *POEMS ON SEVERAL OCCASIONS* BY MRS. BARBER

London: Printed for C. Rivington, at the *Bible* and *Crown* in St. *Paul*'s *Church-yard*. M.DCC.XXXIV.

The text is printed from this edition, pp. iii–viii.

4. ADVICE TO THE FREEMEN OF THE CITY OF DUBLIN

Broadside, printed on both sides, 2 pages.

Printed in the YEAR 1733.

The text has been printed from a copy in the Haliday Collection, Royal Irish Academy, Dublin.

Reprinted with the following note:

The following Piece was published in the Year 1733; and, as it may be useful upon a like Occasion, we think proper to insert it here.

in Dublin by Faulkner, *Works*, 1746, viii, 196–205
                                   1751, viii, 377–386

and in London, in *Miscellanies* (C. Hitch etc.) 1746, xi. 187–189
                 and by Hawkesworth, *Works*, 1755, 4to. vi (pt. ii) 200–206.

Page	Line	PRESENT TEXT	VARIANTS
81	9f.b. never be possibly 33, 55		never possibly be 46, 51
82	7f.b. Love of 33, 55		Love for 46, 51
83	5f.b. up all at 33, 55		all up at 46, 51

5. OBSERVATIONS OCCASION'D BY READING A PAPER, ENTITLED
The Case of the Woollen Manufacturers etc.

Written probably in December, 1733, but no printing known at that time. The text is taken from *Miscellaneous Pieces in Prose and Verse*. By the Rev. Dr. Jonathan Swift. Not inserted in Mr. Sheridan's edition of the Dean's Works. London: Printed for C. Dilly, in the Poultry MDCCLXXXIX, 8vo. pp. 127–131.

It may well have been printed from Swift's MS like the only other tract in the volume of which no earlier publication has seen found, viz. *On the Bill for the Clergy's Residing on their Livings*. See vol. xii of this edition, pp. 181–6

S

6. SOME REASONS AGAINST THE BILL FOR SETTLING THE TYTHE OF HEMP BY A MODUS

First printed by G. Faulkner, Dublin, 1734. See facsimile of title-page, facing page 94.

It was reprinted in Dublin, *Works*, 1746, viii, 101–121
Works, 1751, viii, 127–146.
and in London by Hawkesworth, vi (pt. i), 247–258.

The present text is taken from the first edition. The variants in the reprints are of no significance, though it may be noted that Faulkner's 1751 edition is more heavily punctuated throughout, and on p. 136, l. 7 *f.b.*, the compositor skipped a line, omitting the words 'to their great Impoverishment, and sometimes'.

7. LETTER ON THE FISHERY, March 23, 1734

First printed by the recipient, Francis Grant, a Scottish merchant living in London, in the middle of his own tract, published in Dec., 1749, entitled A LETTER TO A MEMBER OF PARLIAMENT, Concerning the *Free British Fisheries*; with Draughts of a HERRING-BUSS and NETS, and the Harbour and Town of *Peterhead*. London: Printed for R. Spavan, in *Ivy-Lane, Pater-Noster Row*, 1750. The present text is taken from this edition.

Reprinted in *A Supplement to the Works of Dr. Swift*. London: Printed for F. Cogan, at the Middle Temple Gate, Fleet-Street, 1752, pp. 70–74.

In 1762 it appeared in the *Gentleman's Magazine*, and was reprinted in Dublin by Faulkner, in *Works*, x, 431–6, with a note in which the recipient is mistakenly said to be Admiral Vernon. This confusion may have been due to the fact that Admiral Vernon had also published a pamphlet in 1749, entitled CONSIDERATIONS UPON THE *WHITE HERRING* AND *COD* FISHERIES etc.

In 1765, it was included by Deane Swift in *Works*, viii (pt. ii) 266–269 under the title *A Letter to Francis Grant Esq; on the Herring-fishery*, with the following note:

Francis Grant Esq; of London, Merchant, younger son of Sir Francis Grant of Cullen, Baronet, having an high opinion of the herring and other fisheries in the British seas, writ and published a pamphlet in the year 1733, on that subject; principally with a view to excite the encouragement of the public, to such of the mercantile people as might engage in a project so extremely beneficial. The pamphlet was much esteemed; but the ministry of England, in those days, fearing to offend the Dutch, were not inclined to favour it. Whereupon, Mr. Grant writ a letter to the Reverend Jonathan Swift, Dean of St. Patrick's, Dublin, who was then very eminent in Ireland, to try if the patriot party there would espouse the design, and reap benefit to their country from what was thus rejected in England: To which letter the Dean writ the following Answer, which greatly shews the man, as well as the general opinion he had of those times.

Page	Line	PRESENT TEXT	VARIANTS
111	7 *f.b.*	opposing us	oppressing us F
112	15	six and seven	six or seven F

8. THE REV. DEAN SWIFT'S REASONS AGAINST LOWERING THE GOLD AND SILVER COIN

The present text is taken from a copy in the Haliday Collection in the Royal Irish Academy of the original edition of REASONS Why we should not Lower the COINS Now current in this Kingdom etc. To which is added, *The Rev*. Dean SWIFT'*s* OPINION, Delivered by him, in an Assembly of above One hundred and Fifty eminent Merchants who met at the Guild Hall, on *Saturday*, the 24th of *April*, 1736, in order to draw up their Petition, and Present it to his Grace the Lord-Lieutenant against lowering said Coin.

Dublin: Printed and sold by *E. Waters* in *Dame-street*. (1736)

It was overlooked by Swift's editors until referred to by Sir Henry Craik in his Life of Swift, and then reprinted by Temple Scott (vii, 351 f.).

9. CONCERNING THAT UNIVERSAL HATRED WHICH PREVAILS AGAINST THE CLERGY

An unfinished paper, dated May 24, 1736, which was first printed by Deane Swift in the London edition of *Works*, 4to, vii. (pt. ii), 246–9, and reprinted in Dublin by Faulkner, *Works*, 1765, xiii, 259–63.

The present text is taken from the London edition, which was reproduced without variants by Faulkner.

10. A PROPOSAL FOR GIVING BADGES TO BEGGARS

The proposal is dated April 22, 1737, and was first printed in Dublin by Faulkner in 1737, and in the same year by Cooper in London. See facsimiles of t.ps. above, pp. 129.

Reprinted by Faulkner in *Works*, 1738, vi, 213–232, and included in *Political Tracts. By the Author of Gulliver's Travels*. London, Printed for C. Davis in Pater-Noster-Row. MDCCXXXVIII. ii, 157 f.

Reprinted in London by Hawkesworth, *Works*, 1755, 4to, vi (pt. i), 42–52. The present text is taken from the first edition.

11. A LETTER TO THE PRINTER OF *Thoughts on the Tillage of Ireland*

The letter was dated Dec. 13, 1737, and the present text is printed from a copy of *Some Thoughts on the Tillage of Ireland; Humbly Dedicated to the Parliament*. To which is prefixed, A Letter to the Printer, from the Reverend Doctor SWIFT, Dean of St. *Patrick*'s, recommending the following Treatise. Dublin: Printed by and for George Faulkner. MDCC,XXXVIII.

The tract was written by Alexander McAulay, and was reprinted in London for T. Cooper, at the Globe in Pater-Noster-Row. 1737.

N.B.—The Yale copy contains a note, mistakenly attributing the authorship to Arthur Dobbs.

12. DR. SWIFT'S WILL

Written on vellum in his own hand, dated May 3, 1740, with a codicil written on paper, dated May 5. Destroyed by fire.

First printed in part by Faulkner on a half-sheet, usually found bound in at the beginning of his re-issue of *Works*, Vol. VIII, 1745, with the title: *The*

Last Will and Testament of the Revd. Dr. Jonathan Swift, As far as it concerns the Publick to know it. This consisted of the sections reprinted here, pp. 149–153, l. 11, and p. 157, l. 4 to the end. But there was an immediate demand for the full text, including the private bequests. This appeared in a sheet, paged i–xiv, containing the full text as reprinted here.

Reprinted in London (see t.p. reproduced on p. 147), with the addition of footnotes, printed above, pp. 153, 154, 156, and with the following note to p. 149, l. 22, explaining the emendation VINDICEM:

'In the *Irish* edition it is VINDICATOREM. But not so, I imagine, from the Dean's hand.'

I have not accepted the emendation, as Swift seems to have written VINDICATOREM, and that is what has been cut on the tablet in St. Patrick's cathedral.

Other Dublin reprints followed, and some spurious wills. The codicil, dated May 5, 1740, was first printed at the end of the text of *A true Copy of the late Rev. Dr. Jonathan Swift's Will Taken from, and compar'd with, the Original.* 8 pp., no printer's name or date, but probably Dublin, 1746.

APPENDIXES

A. (i) LAWS FOR THE DEAN'S SERVANTS

Dated Dec. 7, 1733. First printed by Deane Swift in *Works*, 1765, 4to, viii, 241–2, from which the present text is taken.

Reprinted by Faulkner in Dublin, *Works*, 1765, xii, 367–9.

(ii) THE DUTY OF SERVANTS AT INNS

Undated. First printed in Dublin by Faulkner in *Works*, viii, 343, from which the present text is taken.

(iii) CERTIFICATE TO A DISCARDED SERVANT

Dated Jan. 9th, 1739. First printed by Mrs. Pilkington in the third volume of her *Memoirs*, 1754, p. 78, where she relates that on her recommendation, the servant went with this certificate to Pope, who took him into his service, in which he remained until Pope's death. It was reprinted by Nichols in his *Supplement to Dr. Swift's Works*, 1779, p. 422.

B. THE CASE OF THE WOOLLEN MANUFACTURERS OF DUBLIN

Printed from a copy of the Dublin edition of 1733 in the National Library, Dublin.

C. (i) UPON GIVING BADGES TO THE POOR, Sept. 26, 1726
(ii) CONSIDERATIONS ABOUT MAINTAINING THE POOR

First printed by Deane Swift in *Works*, 1765, 4to, viii (pt. i), 220–225, from which the present text is taken. Reprinted in Dublin by Faulkner in *Works*, 1765, xii, 331–340.

D. PREFACES TO SWIFT'S WORKS, 1735

Reprinted from Faulkner's Dublin edition, Vols. I, II, IV. For Prefaces to Vol. III, see vol. xi of this edition. There can be little doubt that Swift provided

Faulkner with the new prefatory material for his edition of *Gulliver's Travels*, both the short *Advertisement* and *A Letter from Capt. Gulliver to his Cousin Sympson*.

E. PETITIONS ON BEHALF OF WILLIAM DUNKIN

(i) *Letter to the Provost and Fellows of Trinity College, Dublin*, July 5, 1736.
First printed by Faulkner in Dublin, *Works*, 1763, xi, 175, and reprinted in the London 4to edition, 1764, vii (pt. i), 229.
(ii) *Letter to the Society of the New Plantation in Ulster*, April 19, 1739.
First printed by Nichols, *Works*, xiv, 135.

F. LETTER TO THE MAYOR, ALDERMEN ETC. OF CORK

Dated August 15, 1737. First printed by Faulkner in 1763, *Works*, xi, 163, and reprinted in London, *Works*, 4to, 1764, vii (pt. i), 222.

G. ADVERTISEMENTS ABOUT ENDOWMENTS OF HOSPITAL

Printed from Faulkner's *Dublin Journal*, July 15, 1738, and Jan. 6, 1738-9.

H. (i) APPOINTMENT OF WYNNE AS SUB-DEAN

Printed from the MS in the Pierpont Morgan Library, New York.

(ii) LETTER CONCERNING THE VICARS CHORAL

Printed from the MS in the National Library of Ireland in Dublin.

I. EARLY DRAFT OF A WILL AND A CODICIL, April 16, 1737

Printed from MSS 14346 and 14347 in the Huntington Library, Cal. See 'Swift's First Will' etc. in HLQ, xxi, no. 4, Sept. 1958, p. 295, by George P. Mayhew, who provided me with the photograph and transcripts.

K. FAULKNER'S PREFACE TO SWIFT'S WORKS, 1763

This sample of Faulkner's own unaided composition may be compared with the Publisher's Prefaces to the 1735 volumes, issued under the supervision of Swift.

INDEX

Agar, Charles, 1st Earl of Normanton, and Archbishop of Dublin, xi

Ale, how to serve, 17–19

All Saints, Feast of, 150

Anne, Queen of England, Swift's credit at the court of, 185; silver medal of, 156; medal of with Prince George, 156; Swift's seals belonging to, 154

Arbuthnot, Dr. John, 204

Barbadoes, 8

Barber, John, Lord Mayor of London, xxv

Barber, Jonathan, woollen draper of Dublin, xxviii

Barber, Mary, wife of Jonathan, *Poems*, xxviii, 73 f.; bequest to, 156

Barracks, building of, 175

Beadles, salary and choice of, 137

Beaumont and Fletcher, booksellers' copyright in, 206

Beggars, proposal to give badges to, xxviii, 127 f., 172–3, *see* Dublin

Bettesworth, Sergeant Richard, xxix

Bolingbroke, Viscount, *see* St. John

Boucher, Richard, the Duke of Buckingham's steward, xx, 42–3

Bowyer, William, letter from Faulkner to, quoted, x

Bradshaw & Co., Castle Street, Dublin, woollen draper, 168

Brodrich, Alan, afterwards Viscount Middleton, Chancellor of Ireland, 181

Brouders, Alexander, witness to Swift's codicil, 1737, 200

Burton, Samuel, Alderman, M.P. for Dublin, xxiv, 79

Butler, directions to, 17–27

Caesar, Julius, seal of, 154

Candles, management of, 19–20, 23–4, 27

Card, High Street, Dublin, woollen draper, 168

Cards, perquisites for the butler, 25

Carteret, John, 2nd Lord, afterwards Earl of Granville, letter to Swift, xxiv; Proclamation against Swift, 112

Case of the Woollen Manufacturers of Dublin, The, xxvi, 89–92, 167 f.

Chamber-Maid, directions to, 52–6

Charles I, King of England, medal of, 156; picture of by Van Dyck, 155

Chester, cargoes of beggars from, 136

Chesterfield, Philip, 4th Earl of, Swift's *Works* dedicated to, xliii

Children's Maid, directions to, 63

China in exchange for old clothes, 56–7

Christ-Church, Dublin, Dean of, 151

Church, a Vicar Choral of St. Patrick's, 197

Cicero, *De Officiis*, cap. xvii, quoted 167

Clarendon, Edward Hyde, 1st Earl of, his *History of the Great Rebellion*, 156

Coachman, directions to, 45–6

Coffee, preparation of, 39

Colrane, living of, 189

Comedies, Restoration, reading for girls, to soften their nature, 65

Concordatum money, for public relief in Dublin, 169

Congreve, William, booksellers' copyright in, 206

Connaught, province of, 134; no land to be purchased in this province, 150, 198

Cook, directions to, 27–33; instructions for marketing, 28–9

Corbet, Rev. Dr. Francis, rents the Vineyard, 156

Cork, city of, freedom to Swift, xxxix, 190

Counley, John, leases to, 154

Dairy-Maid, 63

Delany, Dr. Patrick, bequest to, 156; executor, 157, 200; his scheme for a Fellowship at T.C.D., 198

Denmark, 83

Dingley, Rebecca, bequest to, 150

227